Reimagining and Reshaping Events:

Theoretical and practical perspectives

Jeff Wrathall and Effie Steriopoulos

(G) **Goodfellow Publishers Ltd**

(G) Published by Goodfellow Publishers Limited,
26 Home Close, Wolvercote, Oxford OX2 8PS
http://www.goodfellowpublishers.com

British Library Cataloguing in Publication Data: a catalogue record for this title is available from the British Library.

Library of Congress Catalog Card Number: on file.

ISBN: 978-1-911635-88-8

DOI: 10.23912/9781911635871-4918

Design and typesetting by P.K. McBride, www.macbride.org.uk

Cover design by Cylinder

Printed by Printforce, Biggleswade

Distributed by UK Marston Book Services, www.marston.co.uk

Contents

Preface

For centuries a broad array of planned events and festivals have defined cultures, communities, nations and other collectives. For individuals, planned events may represent important milestones, are often memorable and sometimes transformational. This book examines the management of those events in terms of:

- ▓ The key concepts essential to an understanding of planned events and how they can be designed and managed in a manner that generates anticipated outcomes and legacies.

- ▓ Case studies that provide the context for those concepts, that enrich our understanding of planned events, and highlight essential elements associated with the management of planned events.

- ▓ Controversies that arise as a result of the nature of planned events, the people that design and manage them, the multitude of event stakeholders that influence their outcomes, and the impact that they have on people and communities around the world.

- ▓ Industry expert profiles, reflections and perspectives on future trends in the events industry

The book is divided into 11 chapters which commence with learning objectives, include definitions and explanations of key concepts, elaborate on the associated controversies and end with relevant case studies. It is targeted at higher education students of business related degrees that offer streams or majors in event management / marketing.

Partly due to the COVID-19 crisis of 2020 and 2021, the events industry is undergoing fundamental change. It seems likely that the 'new normal' will be characterised by a quite different, transformed, events landscape. In addition to the COVID-19 crisis, other forces that are transforming the events industry include technological advances that had commenced well before COVID-19, and more informed approaches to event sustainability.

About the authors

Dr Effie Steriopoulos

Effie is an event management lecturer at William Angliss Institute, Melbourne, Australia. She coordinates and teaches: the event industry, marketing and communications, business development in events, social media and brand strategy, and event evaluation and innovation. Her PhD is situated in the marketing discipline and explores how transformative experiences act as a catalyst for consumers and create brand loyalty. Her research approach is based on phenomenological practice and a qualitative design incorporating thematic analytical approaches. Effie's research interests are transformative experiences, experiential and emotional marketing with a consumer behaviour focus.

Effie also sees events as ways to engage with students, offer them authentic educational experiences and create opportunities for individual transformation. She has published papers in 'experiences' relating to tourism and events, overseas study tours and iconic brands. She keeps abreast of event industry developments running annual seminars for students, alumni, and industry. She is also interested in exploring how events can be used as tools for place and destination marketing, while promoting brands and social inclusivity.

Effie is on the executive board for the Council of Australasian Tourism and Hospitality Education (CAUTHE), a CAUTHE Chapter Director and co-chair of the Event Special Interest Group (SIG).

She lived in Greece for 17 years, worked as a tour guide offering immersive tourism experiences, and decided to move back to Melbourne in 1996. She also speaks Greek and basic German. https://www.linkedin.com/in/effiesteriopoulos/

Dr Jeff Wrathall

Dr Jeff Wrathall is a Senior Lecturer in the Faculty of Higher Education and Course Leader of the Bachelor of Event Management at William Angliss Institute, Melbourne, Australia. He has also worked as a Senior Lecturer at Monash University, Gippsland Campus for approximately 18 years. At Monash University, Jeff initiated the development of a range of international business events for senior executives from China and other parts of Asia.

Jeff holds a PhD in Education which explored alternative designs for the content and delivery of MBA programs offered by Western universities in China and was based on an examination of Chinese culture and Chinese learning styles. This reflects Jeff's current research interests in cultural differences and the implications in terms of the design and management of international events.

Jeff has also worked as the Director of Australia-China Executive Training (ACET) where he was involved with the design and management of a range of business events including training events and conferences conducted in China and Australia for Chinese executives. These events were aimed at the provision of leadership training and the provision of management knowledge, skills, and expertise required to operate effectively in a globally competitive and dynamic environment. ACET was also involved with a range of consulting programs, activities, and events throughout China, as well as the development and maintenance of a broad network of event industry professionals, locally and internationally

In addition, Jeff has worked for one year as a Visiting Associate Professor at Wuhan Iron and Steel University in Wuhan, China. During that time, Jeff was involved with the delivery of MBA subjects to managers in the Chinese iron and steel industry, as well as consulting activities with a diverse range of client organisations in China's public and private sectors. He has also co-authored a previous textbook in Event Management.

Acknowledgements

The authors would like to express their thanks to William Angliss Institute for their support during the writing of this book.

Our sincere thanks go to Sally North, Editorial Director, for her tremendous support during such a difficult period.

The authors would further like to acknowledge the contribution and expertise of several event professionals, and to thank them for the photographs and illustrations which they have supplied:

Allison Anderson

Annmaree Angelico

Almila Bailey-Ertürk

Sharon Calleja

Leo Gester

Conan Gomes

Grant Gray

Meegan Jones

Peter Jones

Nicholas Kalogeropoulos

Garth Lategan

Joe McGrath

Bennett Merriman

Jenny Mitten

Georgie Stayches

Kate Stewart

1 An industry transformed and reimagined: Events after COVID-19

Learning objectives

On completion of this chapter, you will be able to:

➤ Identify the various types of planned events and the associated career paths

➤ Describe the short and longer-term impact of the COVID-19 crisis

➤ Recognise the impact of the emerging transformation economy and explain the subsequent shift in emphasis from memorable events to transformative events

➤ Recognise the impact of stakeholder responses to the COVID-19 crisis

➤ Evaluate the combined longer-term impact of the COVID-19 crisis and the changing focus of planned events to transformative experiences

➤ Reflect on potential strategies for operating successfully in a transformed events industry.

As a result of the COVID-19 crisis of 2020 and beyond, as well as other forces associated with the emerging transformation economy (Neuhofer, Celuh & To, 2020), the events landscape is currently in the midst of incredible levels of change and adjustment. However, before considering the transformations that are now reshaping and refocusing the events industry, it would be useful to gain a basic appreciation of the enormous scope of planned events.

> **Definition:** events are temporary occurrences and gatherings of people, at a given place and time. They represent unique settings and have a beginning and an end. Source: Getz, 2013.

The scope of planned events

It is partly because of the incredible scope of events that Event Studies is such a fascinating area of inquiry. The usual way in which event size or significance is categorised is as follows:

Mega events

The largest and most well-known events are the so-called **mega events.** Examples of mega events are:

- Sporting events such as the Olympics, the FIFA World Cup and Grand Slam Tennis Championships;
- International music festivals such as Glastonbury, Summerfest and Coachella; and
- World exhibitions.

Regarded by many as 'must see' events, mega events are widely discussed in the national and international media, and generally have a huge economic, social and cultural impact. Their legacies are often significant and long lasting.

What long-term legacies might an international music festival have?

Hallmark event

The term **hallmark event**, although not strictly associated with size, refers to events that Getz and Page (2016: 57) describe as *"those that possess such significance, in terms of tradition, attractiveness, quality or publicity, that the event provides the host venue, community or destination with a competitive advantage."* Staged repeatedly in the same location, these events eventually come to symbolise that location or destination. Hence, when people discuss the event, they automatically think of the location and perhaps, vice versa. Examples of hallmark events are:

- the Wimbledon Tennis Championships;
- the Sydney Gay and Lesbian Mardi Gras;
- the Edinburgh Fringe Festival; and
- the Melbourne Cup Carnival.

What might be the likely effects of changing the location of a hallmark event?

Case study 1.1. Hallmark event: Melbourne Cup (Australia)

The Melbourne Cup is run by the Victoria Racing Club (VRC) in Australia and is the highlight of the Melbourne Spring Carnival, which runs annually in November. As this event is characterised by its location (Melbourne) it is regarded a hallmark event. It is also a mega event due to the national and international media coverage. The event is run at Flemington, 5kms from Melbourne Central District, on the first Tuesday in November and is timed to commence shortly after the end of the national sporting event, AFL grand final, and shortly before the start of the cricket season. The day is declared a public holiday and draws crowds well in excess of 100,000. Melbourne Cup Carnival remains the highest economic generator of any sporting event in Australia.

Major events

Events that are categorised as **major events** generally lack the scale or international recognition of mega events and may lack the significance of hallmark events. However, they are often large national events that gain considerable coverage in the national media and provide significant economic benefits.

Can you think of examples of major events for each of the following locations:
- *the UK?*
- *the US?*
- *Australia?*
- *Asia?*

What is it that makes them major rather than mega?

Minor events

Events that are categorised as **minor events,** generally staged in local communities targeting local audiences, and found in most localities, are often supported, sponsored or run by local government. Examples include:

- Regional arts festivals;
- Local sporting competitions;
- Local cultural and community events;
- Local demonstrations.

Did you know? Organising public demonstrations require key event skills and collaborative activities. To ensure demonstrations remain peaceful, event managers must adhere to local government policies and procedures.

? *Give an example of a major event and a minor community event. What are the likely key differences during planning and event execution?*

Careers in the events industry

Unlike in more established industries, career paths in the events industry are not always clear or obvious. At the same time however, the events industry has been expanding rapidly over recent decades. It has become a highly competitive, global industry in which the search for talent is relentless and employment opportunities, particularly for passionate and committed individuals, continue to grow.

As a result, event career opportunities now exist in the public sector, the not-for-profit sector and the private sector, in both event specific organisations and a broad range of other organisations. Public sector jobs are becoming available at all levels of government where the scope of events and festivals, often with a strategic focus, is huge. Event careers exist in a range of different employment areas, consistent with the event management knowledge domains in the EMBOK (Event Management Body of Knowledge) model developed by Silvers (2007):

■ **Administration**, in which the focus is on the efficient and effective allocation, direction, and control of all of the resources generally required to complete an event project. Key employment areas include financial management, human resource management, information, procurement, stakeholder analysis and management, systems, and time management.

■ **Design**, in which the primary focus is on achieving, or at least facilitating, the experience amongst attendees that event organisers envisage. Hence, it involves the creative or artistic interpretation and operationalization of the purpose, goals, and objectives of the event project. Key employment areas include catering, content development, entertainment, the environment, production, programming and theming.

■ **Marketing**, in which the focus is on shaping perceptions about the event project, facilitating business development, and cultivating political and economic support. Key employment areas include market plan

1

development, materials, merchandise, promotion, public relations, sales management and sponsorship.

■ **Operations**, in which the focus is on the effective integration and coordination of the people, products and services that are required for successful completion of the event project. Key employment areas include the management of event attendees, communications, infrastructure, event logistics, the management of event participants, site management and technical production.

■ **Risk**, which deals with compliance issues, protective obligations and other legal issues associated with the event project. Key employment areas include compliance, decision management, emergency management, health and safety, the management of legal issues, and the management of issues associated with insurance and security.

As well as the job opportunities that exist in all of these domains, volunteerism has become an essential part of the events industry and is often utilised as a stepping-stone to full-time employment. Particularly for graduates, internships represent another possible point of entry into full-time employment in the events industry.

In what ways could volunteering assist in gaining full-time employment in the events industry?

Industry transformation

In 2020, just over a century after the last major flu pandemic, the COVID-19 crisis emerged with unparalleled force to reshape the way in which people throughout the world live, think and earn a livelihood. For decades, globalisation had promoted industrial growth and development, forged strategic alliances and business collaboration, and encouraged travel, communication, and interconnectivity. Global health concerns quickly reversed those trends and ignited fears of an impending economic crisis and industrial collapse. Virtually all industries were heavily impacted but none more so than tourism, hospitality, and events.

Explain how restrictions on travel impact on the events industry. What are the likely responses?

A range of short and longer-term responses to COVID-19 have significantly impacted on the events industry and more generally, on the way in which people work, interact and conduct business operations. These include:

- Community lockdowns
- Travel and mobility restrictions
- Social distancing measures
- Stay at home advice
- Self - or mandatory quarantine
- Encouragement of, or mandatory, wearing of masks
- Curbs on inside and outside gatherings

These and other more fundamental influences have changed the events industry forever. In the same way that the September 11 attacks of 2001 changed the role, significance and importance of risk and security management, and the way in which those functions are planned and implemented, the COVID-19 crisis has changed forever a range of functions associated with health, safety, and emergency management. And indeed, the real impact may go well beyond these functions and may represent a fundamental transformation in the nature and shape of the events industry.

However, while the impact of COVID-19 on the events industry, as well as responses of key event stakeholders to the crisis, can be regarded as transformational, presenting major opportunities for industry change and renewal, forces associated with the emerging transformation economy had begun to reshape and refocus the events industry well before COVID-19 (Neuhofer, Celuh & To, 2020):

- With the emergence of the experience economy (Figure 1.1) (Pine & Gilmore, 2011), the focus of planned events had already moved from celebrations, commemorations, and a range of other event purposes to providing event attendees with a memorable event experience.
- Following on from the experience economy however, the emergence of the so-called *transformation* economy led to a focus that had moved beyond extraordinary experiences towards experiences that could be regarded as transformative or even life changing.
- These transformative experiences are described by Neuhoufer et al. (2020, p. 2883) as peak experiences *"that allow individuals to flourish and transform"*, with the potential for self-fulfilment and self-actualisation.

This has important implications for event design with an emerging emphasis on not only creating triggers for transformation but also a framework in which long-term personal change can occur (Getz & Page, 2016). It also opens up the possibility that as well as being shaped and influenced by positive and negative life-events, values and attitudes can be shaped by planned events (Neuhofer et al., 2020). Based on positive psychology, a sub-field of psychology that has emerged over the last few decades and emphasises the development of an engaging, purposeful, and worthwhile life, the design of transformative events generally involves a triggering episode that engages the individual in a meaning-making process that aids and promotes long-term, personal transformation.

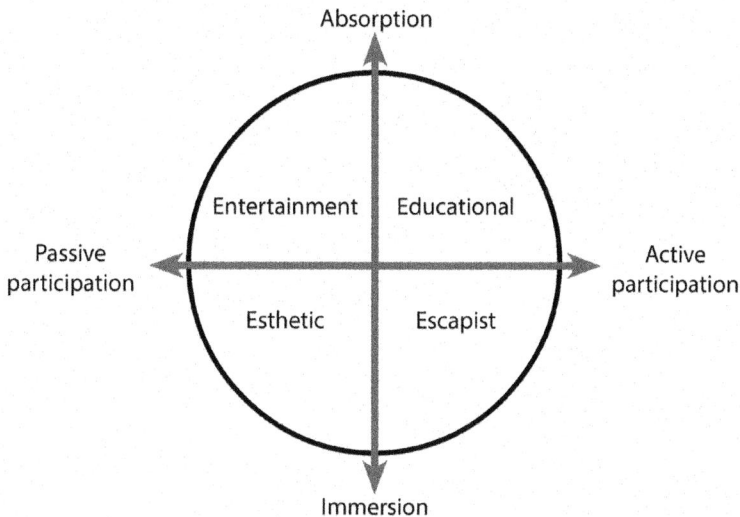

Figure 1.1: Pine and Gilmore Experience Economy model (2011)

Did you know? What hasn't changed is human nature and the need to celebrate special occasions, to commemorate special moments in history, to be entertained, to be informed, and to enjoy the company of others.

Hence, two sets of forces have come together, one involving a health crisis and the other, a perceived opportunity that taps into the needs and desires of a new cohort of event attendees, to create the foundations for a new, reimagined events industry. Successfully navigating the new events landscape will be challenging but potentially rewarding.

Can you think of an event that you have attended that you would regard as being personally transformative? Describe the impact of the event and what you think were the key elements of the event that made it transformative.

Impacts and changes

The short-term, negative impact of the first set of forces on planned events was crippling and while the industry moves back to a 'new normal' it has become obvious to most event practitioners that it will be a very different normal from what they dealt with in the past. With the added impetus of new technology and the emerging emphasis on transformative events, the events industry is in the process of being reconceived, reimagined, and reset.

Research note: Steriopoulos and Wrathall (2021) interviewed event experts during the pandemic asking for their views on how the industry is reshaping. The results revealed four key priorities for event practitioners when considering all phases of events:

a) Understand your audience, client needs and particularly the event objectives

b) Collaborate with diverse stakeholders for the enrichment of ideas

c) Aim for lifelong learning especially in the adoption of various technologies

d) Remain flexible and adaptable to cope with complex event situations.

Particularly for those event practitioners that see the impact of COVID-19 as not just a disaster but an opportunity for industry renewal, the current focus is on exploring future possibilities. Although much of what appears to be a fundamental shift may simply represent an acceleration of existing, underlying trends, there is no doubt that the events industry is undergoing fundamental change.

The need to plan events for human connectivity

In response to the human need to socially connect, planned events have, since the dawn of time, been designed, produced, and managed in communities, cities, countries and destinations around the world. These events have, throughout history, permeated and enriched virtually every aspect of human life. What also hasn't changed is an awareness at all levels of government of the increasing significance, importance, and value of planned events. Events and festivals are now regarded as valuable tools from a public policy perspective, particularly when considering strategies for economic growth, social capital and cultural enrichment in cities, regions, and destinations.

In what ways could government bodies effectively use planned events as vehicles for economic growth and the advancement of social and cultural objectives?

1

Key considerations in events

Other things that haven't changed but have perhaps been magnified, are the skills, attitudes, talents, and attributes that are required of event practitioners. Navigating the events industry has always required high levels of resilience, creativity, agility, and adaptability. These attributes are accentuated in meeting the demands and challenges of the future and, in fact, it's the capacity to embrace disruption and change, sometimes referred to as *anti-fragility*, that may be the most important characteristic of successful event professionals in the future.

Our inability to celebrate, commemorate, and engage in other planned events, in a traditional manner, has severely tested the patience and resilience of millions of people around the globe during the COVID-19 crisis. It has been in response to these pressures that the events industry has transformed itself, finding creative and innovative ways to offer people alternatives to the normal event experiences that they crave. Acceleration in the development of the technology, skills and talents required to produce effective, high quality virtual and hybrid events has fundamentally changed the shape of the events industry. Virtual and hybrid event strategies have not only filled a gap but provided a platform for future progress, expansion, and industry development. Hence, while much has changed, events of every type continue to be planned, designed, and managed.

Celebrations and private events

Celebrations and private events include weddings, birthdays, family get-togethers, graduations, rites of passage, religious and cultural events, as well as a broad range of other private, social, and cultural events. Health requirements involving social distancing have taken a heavy toll during the COVID-19 crisis, leading to event cancellations or, at best, postponements, or changes to formats. Weddings, for example, have changed dramatically in almost every respect. In the UK, Australia, the US, and around the world, wedding planners, caterers and florists have been forced to become far more creative and proactive about how to deal with pandemic rules and regulations and the associated health concerns. This has generally involved the conduct of micro weddings with fewer guests, guests wearing masks, the allocation of tables to members of the same family, and in some cases, multiple, smaller dance floors. It has also led to the development of hybrid event strategies with many guests participating through Zoom or other online tools.

Case study 1.2: A rustic private wedding

A rustic private wedding was chosen at a winery in the regional area of Yarra Valley (Victoria, Australia). An intimate and casual theme was adopted which created memorable moments for all guests. For the key elements that contribute towards creating the mood of the event, refer to below link:https://www.easyweddings.com.au/real-weddings/mr-mrs-smith-choose-yarra-valley-for-fresh-rustic-wedding/.

Image 1.1: Mr and Mrs Smith at Zonzo Estate, Yarra Valley (Victoria, Australia). Photo by Jason Arundell. Supplied by Jessica Derham.

However, while much has changed, weddings and other celebrations and private events are as relevant today as they ever were. Many of these celebrations hold deep personal significance for the people involved and often become part of the fabric of their lives, the milestones upon which they reflect and which give meaning to special occasions, achievements, and anniversaries. As pandemic regulations relax, these events return. However, lingering health concerns, as well as new, improved, and more cost-effective approaches and techniques, leave a more permanent, longer-term imprint.

? *Which event design elements do you think can help create personal meanings for people in private events?*

1

Commemorative events

Commemorations reflect a concern that we should not forget significant events from the past. Commemorative events have often been developed to remember and reflect upon military campaigns, battles and victories, rebellions, uprisings, and revolutions, as well as a range of other historical moments. Examples of commemorative events include:

- Armistice Day which commemorates the end of the First World War
- D-Day which commemorates the invasion of German-held, beaches of Normandy, France by Allied troops during the Second World War
- Bastille Day which commemorates the storming of the Bastille, a turning point of the French Revolution, and
- ANZAC Day which commemorates the landing of Australian and New Zealand troops in Gallipoli during the First World War (Case study 1.3)

From a national and cultural perspective, these events provide solidarity, as well as reverence and respect for the contributions and sacrifice of previous generations. However, in 2020, several commemorative events were cancelled, postponed, or significantly altered. In Australia for example, dawn services and public events associated with ANZAC day were cancelled for the first time in over 100 years. On Armistice Day in the UK, a majority of British people observed the traditional two minutes of silence at home, some standing on doorsteps to remember those who lost their lives in the First World War. In France, public gatherings and the organisation of festivals were forbidden during much of the year, disrupting the usual D-Day events at Normandy.

Case study 1.3: ANZAC day commemorative event

ANZAC is an abbreviated term for Australia and New Zealand Army Corps. The term symbolises the contribution of Australia and New Zealand army towards the efforts of World War I. The governments from Australia, New Zealand and Turkey combine human and financial resources to deliver an annual service in Gallipoli which attracts thousands of people. The forecast of overcrowding in 2015 led governments to impose a restriction in attendees of up to 10,000.

To view the 2015 ANZAC centenary event visit https://youtu.be/BPF9Hjpgp-w

Which commemorative events do you regard as the most important in terms of providing solidarity and a sense of community?

Despite event cancelations in 2020, the spirit, reflections, and memories associated with these events remained ensuring their continuation in future years, not necessarily in the same format as in the past but certainly with the same sentiments. For Armistice Day in the UK for example, a virtual race was planned for 11 November to 11 December 2021. Soldiers stationed around the world, as well as supporters, were able compete in 5km, 10 km or half-marathon options at outdoor locations throughout the UK. In Sydney, Australia, a dawn service was planned to commence at 4.15am with an ANZAC Day march commencing at 9am.

Festivals

People around the globe have always demonstrated a strong desire to be entertained, to relax and to retreat from the monotony of day-to-day routines and the vicissitudes of life. This desire is a normal part of human nature and has given rise to a broad range of music, comedy, and entertainment festivals. Often, these events have allowed people to give expression to particular interests, passions or preferred lifestyles.

For example, the Rainbow Serpent festival held each year in Victoria, Australia, provides a unique example of a music festival inspired by indigenous history and with a clear focus on alternative lifestyles. It has, over recent years, captured the interest and imagination of a particularly diverse range of event attendees.

Comedy festivals are also popular around the world, particularly in the UK. In Kilkenny, Ireland the Cat Laughs Comedy Festival is a favourite for many comedians throughout the UK and has developed a tradition in which Irish Comedians compete for the Cat Cup in a football match against comedians from the rest of the world. As with many other festivals, it was postponed in 2020.

What do you see as key social benefits of entertainment and comedy festivals?

Case study 1.4: Burning Man Festival

A unique and quite different festival is the Burning Man Festival which takes place each year in the Black Rock Desert in northern Nevada, in the United States. It commences on the Monday before the American Labour Day holiday and continues over the week until Labour Day. Burning Man takes its name from the ritual burning of a large wooden effigy on the Saturday evening. A temporary city with streets, villages, and camps, erected in the middle of the desert to accommodate an increasing number of event attendees is, consistent with a "leave no trace" policy, completely obliterated at the end of each festival. Emphasising radical self-expression, radical self-reliance, and community, the event has expanded rapidly over recent decades but was not staged in 2020 due to COVID-19. It was decided to take the Burning Man festival virtual in 2021. For more visit https://kindling.burningman.org/virtual-burn/

Sporting events

For thousands of years, people have also come together to compete in or enjoy the spectacle and drama of sporting events. Unlike most other events, sporting event outcomes are uncertain. In fact, it's the uncertainty and the harsh reality that there are winners and losers that makes sporting events so unique and so compelling. They are often associated with gambling which, amongst other things, serves to increase levels of intensity, anxiety, and anticipation, and provide spectators with an outlet for their emotions and fervour.

Due to COVID-19, many sporting events were cancelled in 2020, several were postponed, and some went ahead without spectators, a significant change given the nature of sporting events. Many of the world's largest and most popular mega-events are sporting events and they cover virtually all popular sports and include:

- The Olympic Games, a multi-sport event, is the world's foremost sporting competition featuring athletes from more than 200 nations. It is held biennially with Summer and Winter Olympics alternating. The 2020 Olympics was to be held in Tokyo, Japan but was postponed due to COVID-19.

- Other multi-sport events include the Commonwealth Games and the Asian Games, both held every 4 years.

- The FIFA World Cup, often simply referred to as the World Cup, is also held every 4 years. It is an international soccer competition contested by senior men's national teams of members of the sport's global governing body – the Federation Internationale de Football Association (FIFA).

- Another major soccer competition run held annually, is the UEFA Champions League, originally referred to as the European Cup.
- In rugby, the World Cup is organised by the International Rugby Board and held every four years and featuring twenty nations competing over a month.
- The Super Bowl is the annual American football championship for the National Football League (NFL) which culminates a season beginning in late summer of the previous year.
- In tennis, four majors are played but the oldest and most prestigious is Wimbledon, the only major still played on grass. Cancelled in 2020, it took place in mid-2021.
- In cricket, the ICC Cricket World Cup is the foremost international championship featuring men's One Day International (ODI) cricket and T 20 Cricket.
- In cycling, the Tour de France, first organised in 1903, is an annual multiple stage bicycle race primarily held in France, while occasionally passing through nearby countries.
- In motor car racing, Formula One or Grand Prix takes place on several race tracks around the world over a three day period.

? *What do you regard as the most important difference between sporting events and other events?*

Case study 1.5: Mother's Day Classic

Mother's Day Classic is an event which attracts thousands from all around Australia. The aim of the sporting event is to keep fit and stay healthy while celebrating Mother's Day and raising funds for breast cancer. Following restrictions, in 2021 the event transformed into various smaller settings around Melbourne with the additional option of participants being able to use their creativity and design their own route of walking. This led to smaller crowds at sites while the community was able to show local support. For more visit https://www.mothersdayclassic.com.au/local

Corporate and business events

Corporate events are a more recent phenomenon involving a broad range of corporate objectives and activities. However, business events including meetings, conventions, conferences, and exhibitions have a reasonably long history. These events have allowed people to meet and network, to be informed and educated, to socialise with others, and to develop contacts. With some events, the emphasis is more on socialising than on business – simply an opportunity to eat, drink and be merry.

As with other event types, the staging of corporate and business events was significantly curtailed due to COVID-19. Furthermore, changes to the format of these events have been significant and represent a longer-term industry transformation.

The importance of the human element

All of the occasions and events discussed so far have involved the efforts of people to plan and design, to bring together appropriate resources, and to implement. They have all required at least some degree of detailed and systematic planning, organisation, and co-ordination. Their successful implementation has always been contingent on, amongst other things, the skill, knowledge, and judgement of the people involved in their creation and execution. These things are unlikely to change and in fact, can be expected to become far more important in the future.

However, the scope, scale, and complexity of planned events has changed enormously over the last few decades, leading to the development and growth of what we now call the events industry. Event managers deal with an incredibly diverse range of events on a day-to-day basis and the challenges that they now face have never been greater. The way in which the events industry has grown, changed and adapted, the manner in which the conduct and management of planned events has been transformed, as well as the people that have led those transformations, provides an extraordinary and engaging narrative of human endeavour and ingenuity.

At the same time, not all events have been designed and planned with the noblest of intentions and this only adds to the controversy and debate that is often associated with the study of planned events. Furthermore, several events that have been developed with noble intentions have still resulted in appalling misjudgements and major disasters. Many of these problems could have been avoided or at least, ameliorated with better and more systematic event design, methodical planning, and careful implementation, as well as strong ethical standards.

Can you think of any recent events that have not achieved positive outcomes due poor design or mismanagement? What could have been done better?

Hence, there is a clear and urgent need for the management of planned events to be accorded due respect as a useful and necessary area of study and academic inquiry. This imperative is even more significant in times of change and uncertainty. It coincides with a growing recognition that event management has emerged as a profession in its own right, as well as a broader acceptance of the utilisation of planned events as an effective mechanism for facilitating the achievement of strategic goals in both the private and public sector.

Summary

Planned events have a long and rich history and have been an essential part of human existence for several centuries. They include celebrations and private events, commemorative events, music, comedy, and entertainment festivals, sporting events, and business and corporate events. While many of these events were cancelled, postponed, or significantly altered during 2020 and 2021, they continue to be developed in a variety of face-to-face, virtual, and hybrids categories. A diverse range of stakeholders continue to influence the events industry and the way in which events are planned, designed, and managed. Over the last few decades the scope, scale, and complexity of planned events has increased significantly, leading to the development of an events industry, the need for knowledgeable and highly skilled event professionals, and hence, the need for structured and systematic, event management education.

In 2020, the COVID-19 crisis changed the events industry forever. What hasn't changed is human nature and the need for celebration, commemoration, and entertainment, as well as other event experiences. In addition, the demands of event attendees, as well as broader socio-economic influences, have led to a focus on transformative events. Furthermore, all levels of government are aware of the increasing importance of planned events in terms of economic growth, social capital and cultural enrichment in cities, regions, and destinations. From a practitioner's perspective, successfully navigating the events industry and dealing with emerging demands and challenges now requires even greater levels of resilience, creativity, agility, and adaptability. While the short-term impact has been crippling, the industry is now in the process of being reimagined. Despite serious challenges, there are incredible opportunities for industry renewal with a focus on opportunities for transformation and growth.

Industry profile: Sharon Calleja, event sales manager

Sharon Calleja is an event sales manager responsible for ensuring that the execution of her events is seamless and successful. The success of events is determined by the effective management of all four stages:

- Design
- Planning
- Execution
- Evaluation/Follow up

Image 1.2: Sharon Calleja

Key skills and attributes that Sharon regards as essential in her event management role are:

Organisational skills: Event managers must be well organised. There are many moving parts to the planning and execution of an event. The ability to keep organised is important to ensure you are not missing any key elements.

- **Communication skills**: Event managers need to be great communicators. In fact, communication is key to effective event planning.
  - ☐ First with your client, to understand their vision and requirements is important;
  - ☐ Second, with your key stakeholders;
  - ☐ Third, with your team in order to ensure everyone is aware of what is required by them on the day.

- **Emotional intelligence**: Event managers need to be empathetic, charismatic and personable. The client's expectation is that you are present, emotionally, in their event. If it is a happy celebration, they expect their planner to be joyful, and if you are a part of an emotional event such as a funeral, they expect an empathetic approach. This is all apparent through our body language, speech and approach.

- **Approachable**: There is nothing worse than your staff members being too scared to approach you to inform you that they are unclear of expectations or that something is going terribly wrong. You want to be the first person they call if they require problem-solving or assistance!

Events managed by Sharon include an endless number of weddings! In addition, quite a few corporate Christmas parties and conferences, private events including birthdays, christenings, culturally themed events such as bar mitzvahs, and funerals/memorial services. Challenges faced by Sharon in managing these events include:

- An expectation that event managers work 24 hours a day, 7 days a week: Set your client's expectations of contact being only within working hours. If you do not make this clear, expect phone calls at any time of the day or night.

- **Balancing the planning of multiple events at different stages**: In a single working day you will need to wear multiple different thinking caps, and chat with many different types of people. It gets challenging from time-to-time switching your language and body language for different types of clients.

- **Clients wanting more for less**: it is typically an expectation that venues must provide every item necessary in order to execute the perfect event. Ensure that your clients are aware right from the very beginning of what any 'upgrade items' cost. They may wish to add items along the way. That's fine but it comes with an additional cost if they want to execute their dream!

- **Restrictions**: Due to the pandemic, there may be a number of 'unclear' restrictions. Further restrictions may vary per venue and outdoor site. No amount of research can clarify the answers to whether or not you are able to execute a particular element within a special event.

In terms of problem solving, there are a few things to remember. First, you must stay calm and not panic. Work out the best way to solve the problem, and who you need to assist you. Clearly communicate your message to those that need to be involved and ensure that everyone plays their part. If the client does not need to be aware that there is a problem, ensure it remains that way.

Key considerations to ensure a smooth delivery of events include:

- Ensuring that you have a clear idea of the client's event vision.
- Ensuring that you have a plan for execution.
- Clearly explaining this plan to all team members
- Ensuring that expectations are clear for the whole team to follow
- Making sure the plan gives due consideration to supplier timings for bumping in and out.
- **Play it safe**: current restrictions due to COVID are forever developing. Set your client's expectations on the worst case scenario to only blow them away with positive news at the execution stage.

In terms of change or new ideas, the following questions need to be answered:

- What are the key selling points which may make your venue/service unique?
- What is trendy on social media platforms and how can you differentiate this service from the way others are executing it?
- How can you create an impression or add a WOW factor to your service, without using expensive resources?

- Think outside the box to add to an event, to substitute elements which now must be obsolete due to restrictions. For example, during the time allocated to dancing, which was not allowed during COVID, play a trivia game from the table!

Different event types require a different focus. For example, when managing private events key considerations include:

- How do you make sure you enhance your client's special event occasion? It is essential to understand their vision, and then plan out an execution which is seamless for the client.

- What are some key touch points that raise the profile of your private events? Your personal relationship with the client is a key element. Private clients put their trust in you as a person to manage their event. Hence, they love to know more about you! Invite them in for a chat over coffee and make it informal and relaxed.

- How can you implement at least one point of differentiation from your last event and this coming event? You must remember that not all events are the same and clients want theirs to stand out.

There are some key issues that you face when planning private events:

- Private clients need an abundance of attention. Most have the mindset that they are the only client you are looking after. In fact, you need to treat every private client as if they are the only client you are currently looking after – regardless of the fact that you have a whole portfolio on your hands!

- Private clients typically work or study full time. Therefore, plan their event in their own time, typically after hours. This will mean that their expectation of contact time is out of hours. Ensure that you set realistic expectations of when a client can anticipate hearing from you.

- Private events at home currently hold a larger number of restrictions: stick to the rules and educate your client to understand consequences for your business and themselves if the law is broken.

Keeping abreast of the diversity of private event planning can also represent a significant challenge and requires:

- Developing a clear mutual understanding of expectations with your client, and sticking to those expectations.

- Matching your creative ideas to the different types of clients.

- Developing a plan of execution, sticking to it, and keeping yourself organised!

The management of corporate events has a range of other challenges. For example, raising your corporate client's image and brand reputation requires you to consider:

- Whether or not your own service brand/venue is the most suitable for a particular corporate client.

- The way in which you can incorporate their brand into your service.
- How big is your client's budget and how far can you go?
- Whether or not you can use social media platforms to enhance your client's brand.
- Communication needs to be straight to the point and most corporate events are organised by executive or personal assistants who have a lot of other work on their plate. Typically, events are the least exciting part of their job, therefore they do expect that an event manager will do end-to-end planning for them.

A key challenge is to motivate staff to assist with the common client goal. This involves:

- Conducting team meetings to inform staff of the importance of the client's goal.
- Understanding and communicating client's expectations in terms of staff appearance and language on the day of the event.
- Ensuring the most appropriate pool of staff is rostered for an event.

Discussion and research questions

1. What major events were you unable to attend due to the COVID-19 crisis? Did you or will you attend those events at a later date? Describe the feelings and the atmosphere.

2. Explain the impact of having no spectators at a major sporting event.

3. What would you regard as the key differences between the challenges faced by the organisers of a major outdoor festival and the organisers of a corporate event held at an indoor venue?

4. What do you expect to be key areas of innovation for future music festivals and events?

5. What key skills do you think are emerging as key requirements for the planning of future events?

6. Reflect on your personal and professional development throughout your course.

7. Brainstorm examples of WOW factors in corporate events and personal touch points in private events (weddings, christenings, anniversaries).

8. Why is it important to adopt a lifelong learning philosophy in events?

9. Provide examples of technologies used in online events during the pandemic.

10. Reflect on your individual skills and attributes and draw three columns:

   a) In first column, brainstorm and note down your personal strengths and personality attributes.

b) Refer to the industry voice by Sharon Calleja and in second column note down any areas (or skills) you need to build on

c) In pairs discuss the skill gaps and decide how you can best address them. Note down your responses in third column

References and further reading

Allen, J., Harris, R., Jago, L., Tantrai, A., Johnson, P., & D'Arcy, E. (2019). *Festival and Special Event Management*. John Wiley & Sons.

Aven, T. (2015). The concept of antifragility and its implications for the practice of risk analysis. *Risk analysis*, 35(3), 476-483.

Getz, D (2013), *Event Tourism*, New York: Cognizant.

Getz, D. & Page, S.J. (2016). *Event Studies: theory, research and policy for planned events*, 3rd edn, Milton Park: Routledge.

Neuhofer, B., Celuh, K., &To (2020). Experience design and the dimensions of transformative festival experiences. *International Journal of Contemporary Hospitality Management*, 32(9), 2881-2901.

Pine, B.J., & Gilmore (2011). *The Experience Economy*, Boston: Harvard Business Press.

Silvers, J.R. (2007). *Introduction to EMBOK: The Event Management Body of Knowledge*.

Steriopoulos, E., & Wrathall, J., (2021) 'Reset and refocus: the changing landscape of events', *Proceedings from the Council for Australasian Tourism and Hospitality Education (CAUTHE) Conference, Transformations in Uncertain Times: Future perfect in tourism, hospitality and events*, p. 431-433, February 9-11, https://search.informit.org/doi/10.3316/informit.687183998628868

Websites

www.easyweddings.com.au/real-weddings/mr-mrs-smith-choose-yarra-valley-for-fresh-rustic-wedding/

www.bbc.com/news/world-europe-32459375.

burningman.org/

kindling.burningman.org/virtual-burn/

www.flemington.com.au/melbournecupcarnival

www.mothersdayclassic.com.au/local

Videos

youtu.be/BPF9Hjpgp-w

2 Business development in events

Learning objectives

On completion of this chapter, you will be able to:

➤ Recognise the challenges associated with sustainable business development in the events industry

➤ Explain the nature of entrepreneurship in the events industry, as well as the associated skills, particularly in terms of creativity and innovation

➤ Develop an events industry business model and recognise the difference between business models and business plans

➤ Differentiate between event feasibility and business viability

➤ Recognise the strategic impact of planned events

➤ Describe the bidding process, as well as the associated problems

➤ Recognise the need for business development to be environmentally, socially, and economically sustainable

The challenges associated with establishing an events enterprise, or growing and sustaining an existing enterprise, share several of the features that characterise business development more generally. As with other industries, the development of a realistic and understandable business model is crucial when setting up event businesses. At the same time, most successful organisations in the events industry owe their initial existence, as well as their ongoing survival and growth, to the efforts, expertise, and tenacity of entrepreneurs.

Entrepreneurship in the events industry

The common stereotype of an entrepreneur is a fairly negative one and, in fact, there are many common misconceptions about what entrepreneurship is really all about. One common stereotype of entrepreneurs is that they are money hungry, risk takers that exploit opportunities (and other people) for personal gain. The reality, however, is that the key factors that generally drive and motivate entrepreneurs go much further than simply making money.

In fact, out of a huge array of entrepreneurial motivators, one of the most essential is curiosity or knowledge seeking. In general, entrepreneurs are intellectually curious. They love to learn and are constantly on the lookout for new insights, new perspectives, better way of doing things, and unique ways of finding 'an edge'. In this regard, curiosity may be regarded as entrepreneurial alertness, or the ability to notice opportunities that have previously been overlooked. That propensity to formulate an image of the future may be the essential trait that characterises entrepreneurial behaviour.

There are a huge number of definitions of entrepreneurship. Most of these definitions emphasise the following:

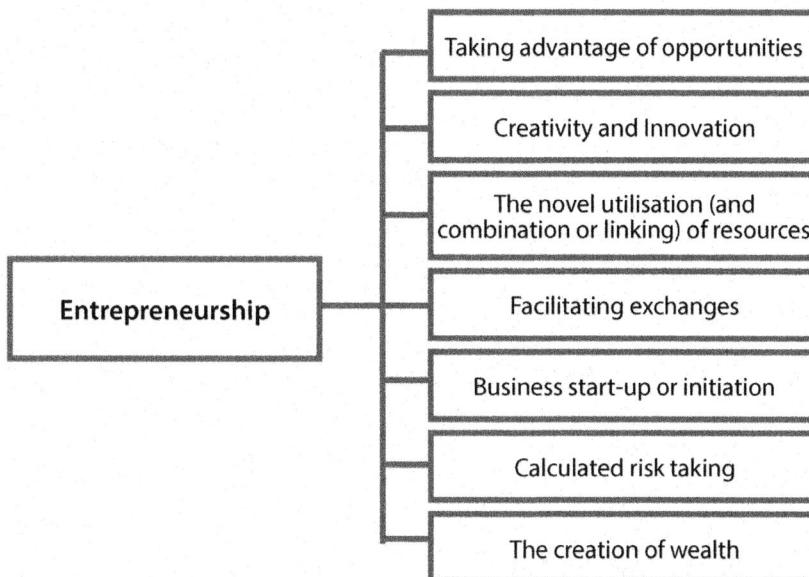

Figure 2.1: Various definitions of entrepreneurship

Consider this: Entrepreneurs are often distinguished by their creativity. So, what is creativity? Creativity can be defined by the ability to come up with new ideas, and identify new ways of thinking, in order to deal with a problem or an opportunity. Ideas may be exchanged among team members; they carry significant value and influence businesses positively.

Essential to most definitions of entrepreneurship and most descriptions of entrepreneurs is the concept of creativity, or the use of imagination and the generation of original ideas, generally involving divergent thinking. On the other hand, innovation is the application of creative ideas to something of value, and generally involves convergent thinking. These two concepts, creativity and innovation are at the core of entrepreneurship. Together they require the capacity to embrace both divergent and convergent thinking, a unique and illusive quality that often seems to distinguish entrepreneurs from non-entrepreneurs. As indicated earlier, a prerequisite to creativity and innovation is curiosity and a propensity to sense an opportunity where others just see chaos, contradiction, and confusion.

How would you distinguish entrepreneurial skills from management skills?

Another key characteristic of successful entrepreneurs is their capacity to network effectively and develop *social capital*. The notion of social capital is central to an understanding of the real value of networks and has been defined as *"the resources available in and through personal and business networks"*. Hence, social capital may be regarded as:

- First, the collective value of all personal and business networks, that is, the people we know

- Second, the reciprocity that arises from these networks, that is, the things we do for each other, and

- Third, the business knowledge that is gained through these networks.

What are some of the approaches that an entrepreneur in the events industry could utilise to develop and maintain social capital?

The entrepreneurial process

The entrepreneurial process can be viewed in several ways and has been described in different ways by several different theorists. However, regardless of the approach taken, an essential element of the entrepreneurial process in any industry is the development of a sound business model to describe a business idea. In the events industry however, the development of an event concept generally precedes development of a business model.

The event concept brings together the creative spark that inspires the event prior to the more practical considerations considered as part of the business model. It needs to be both inspirational and realistic with a view towards shaping expectations. Positive expectations can have a significant impact in terms of shaping event outcomes and influencing event success.

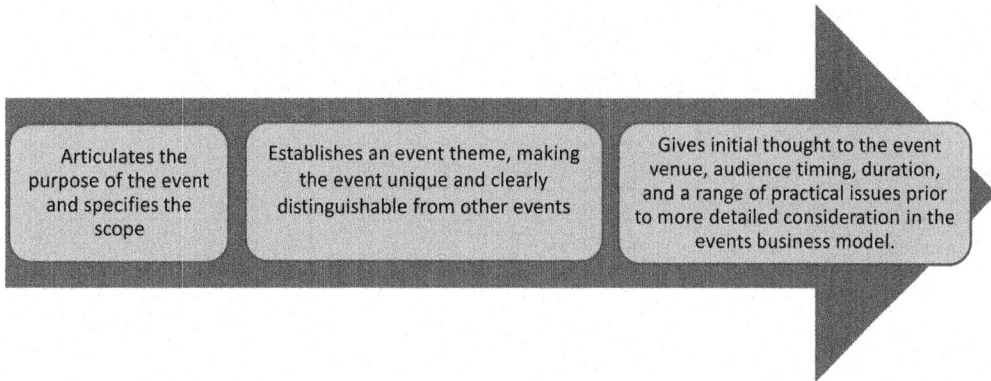

Articulates the purpose of the event and specifies the scope

Establishes an event theme, making the event unique and clearly distinguishable from other events

Gives initial thought to the event venue, audience timing, duration, and a range of practical issues prior to more detailed consideration in the events business model.

Figure 2.2: Process of entrepreneurship

Developing an events business model

The business model is a concept developed primarily by practitioners rather than theorists. Business models can be applied to virtually any industry, including the events industry, with a focus on the way in which value is created and hence, on the means and methods that the enterprise employs to earn revenue, survive and grow. Key aims of a business model are to provide an understanding of:

- The kind of value that can be created for customers with a certain project
- How that value can be captured
- What the corresponding value architecture or business design looks like.

The composition and nature of business models vary depending on the type of industry and whether in fact, we are dealing with a tangible product or a service. Events are services or more precisely, service experiences and hence, business models in the events industry are quite different from those that focus on a tangible product.

Did you know? Events form part of the service industries. Event managers offer key services and experiences therefore the element of service cannot be ignored. Refer to the case study by Airbnb which illustrates their business model and why it is successful. https://bstrategyhub.com/airbnb-business-model-how-does-airbnb-make-money

In fact, the 'event experience' is the essence of planned events and that experience is designed, or at least facilitated, by the event designer. While planned events come in many types and sizes, they all influence the individual or collective experiences of attendees. The event experience of those attendees may be influenced by a range of factors as seen in Figure 2.3.

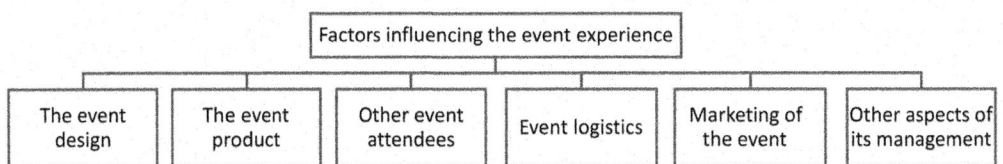

```
                Factors influencing the event experience
   ┌─────────┬──────────┬──────────┬──────────┬──────────┬──────────┐
The event   The event   Other event   Event logistics   Marketing of   Other aspects of
design      product     attendees                       the event      its management
```

Figure 2.3: Factors influencing the event experience

? *In what ways might other attendees impact the event experience of an individual?*

When developing a business model for survival and growth in the events industry, below key questions need to be considered (Figure 2.4):

SWOT	What are the Strengths, Weaknesses, Opportunities and Threats of your business?
Revenue	How will we generate revenue?
Audience	How will we attract people to the event?
Cost effectiveness	How will we create value in a cost effective manner?
Unique Selling Proposition	What unique features provide a competitive advantage?

Figure 2.4:. Key considerations for the survival of business models

Consider this: An event business could adopt the use of technology, such as apps, to support engagement at charity events, while also producing important profile data for the charity. The use of apps could set the business apart from others who simply run events the traditional way without any new ideas.

SWOT Analysis

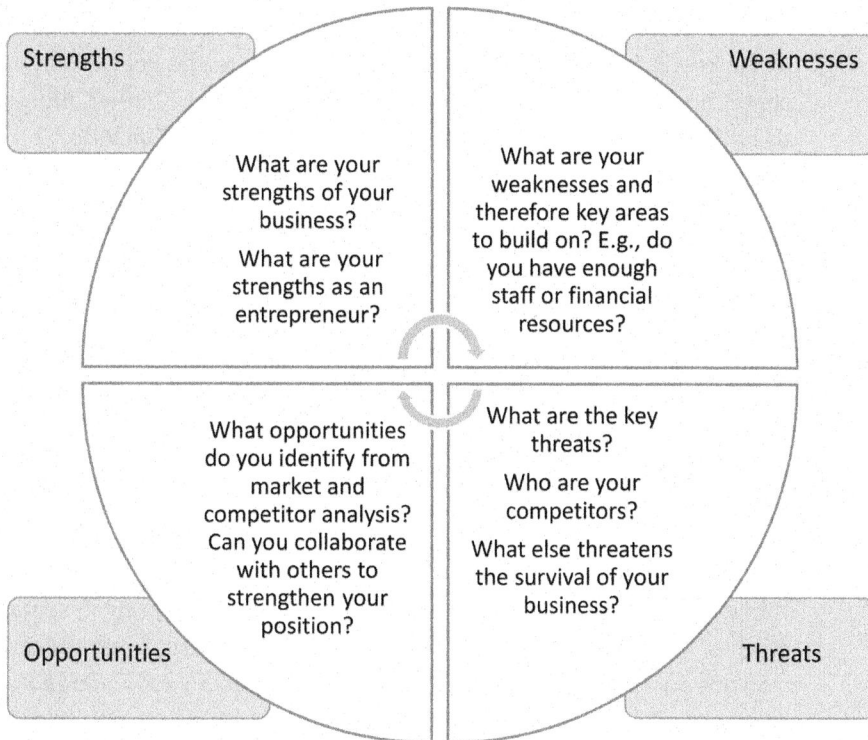

Strengths	Weaknesses
What are your strengths of your business? What are your strengths as an entrepreneur?	What are your weaknesses and therefore key areas to build on? E.g., do you have enough staff or financial resources?
What opportunities do you identify from market and competitor analysis? Can you collaborate with others to strengthen your position?	What are the key threats? Who are your competitors? What else threatens the survival of your business?
Opportunities	Threats

Figure 2.5: SWOT analysis

When developing your business model, the first step involves in depth research about the marketplace, competition, and various technological advancements. When conducting a SWOT analysis, entrepreneurs utilise matrices to help them understand market and environmental impacts in relation to their business. A SWOT can have internal factors (for example staff, volunteers) and externally factors (eg global pandemic, currency fluctuation etc). Refer to matrix in Figure 2.5.

Following the research effort, proceed with a strategy to address issues in the SWOT. For example, once you know who your competitors are, how can you differentiate from your competition to develop your competitive edge?

Further insight: https://www.business.qld.gov.au/starting-business/planning/market-customer-research/swot-analysis/conducting

How will we generate revenue?

This question goes well beyond making a pricing decision about entry to the event. Selling tickets at the gate or prior to the gate is one way of generating revenue, but not the only way. A number of other alternatives should be considered. Amongst other things these may include:

- Development of sponsorship agreements
- Establishing an association or social network and charging for membership
- Selling merchandise and other extras or perhaps developing VIP packages
- Franchising of all or part of the event
- Combining with marketing initiatives
- A combination of all or some of the above

How will we attract people to attend the event?

While this is the most basic and obvious question of all it sometimes receives scant attention. And while traditional forms of promotion are still relevant and often effective, the use of social media has emerged as the most effective and useful way to gain exposure and attract attendees.

Social networks that may be utilised include:

- Facebook
- Instagram
- Twitter
- LinkedIn
- YouTube

Where would you usually expect to find out about an upcoming event?

How will we create value for event attendees in a cost-effective manner?

The answer to this question is central to what a business model is all about. It needs to clearly articulate how attendees benefit from attending, what they receive, and how those benefits are captured and provided to attendees. In recent years the most significant changes in event offerings have related to the way in which this question is addressed. Furthermore, an appropriate response to this question requires an understanding of the event experience that attendees are likely to anticipate. It may sit some-where along the following continuum:

- A superficial short-term experience – entertainment, fun activity, killing a bit of time
- A more meaningful, short-term experience – interesting and engaging information, spectacle or activity
- A meaningful and memorable experience with a long term impact – novel and memorable experience or activity, perhaps authentic
- A transformational experience – associated with personal growth, self-awareness, self-fulfillment and perhaps, a sense of purpose

At different times and in different situations, event attendees may crave the type of event that falls anywhere on that continuum between a super-ficial entertainment experience and a deeply meaningful, transformational experience. Providing the event experience that attendees crave in a cost-effective manner is the essence of a sound business model.

Charities are good examples of growing business ideas. Many charities develop event concepts to engage participants and raise funds while providing engaging experiences. Small businesses and large corporations attach themselves to charities to demonstrate a sense of social corporate responsibility. Each country has many charities to concentrate its efforts and raise funds to solve issues. In Australia alone there are 56,000 regis-tered charities. The potential to develop event business ideas in order to support causes is greater now more than ever. (https://www.acnc.gov.au/).

Can you think of an event that you have attended that provided a transformational experience while supporting a good cause?

Case study 2.1: The CEO (Chief Executive Officer) sleepout

The CEO sleepout is an event idea that was developed to tackle the issue of home-lessness. CEOs take part at sleeping outdoors during one of the coldest nights in winter to show their support and donate to the charity. The idea began in 2006 and grew bigger in multiple locations around Australia. During the pandemic in 2020, CEOs were still able to support the cause by sleeping in their cars or their back yards.

To read more, visit https://www.ceosleepout.org.au/about-ceo-sleepout.

What unique features provide a competitive advantage?

Possibly the greatest challenge faced by event professionals involves finding ways in which to stage events that are memorable and, in some way, unique.

For example:

- A music festival may be unique because of its capacity to attract the best performers or a certain type of performer.
- A business event may be unique because of the reputation it has gained over the years, or simply the choice of location or facilities.
- A cultural event may be unique because of its capacity to tap into a culture in a particularly authentic or distinctive manner.
- A sporting event may be unique because of the significance that has been attached to the outcome.

It is that capacity to continuously offer something that is different, distinctive, and unique, and in a way that can't be easily duplicated or copied, that provides an on-going competitive advantage.

Hence, the development and articulation of a sound business model involves careful consideration of all the above four questions. In addressing those four questions, consideration may also need to be given to a broad range of issues, such as:

- The type of event being staged
- The target customer or event attendees
- Other key stakeholders
- Customer needs that must be addressed
- Other benefits provided by events
- The timing and duration of events
- The event venue
- Compliance issues that need to be addressed
- Activities to be included in the events
- What differentiates the events from other similar events?
- How will events be marketed?
- How will you generate a profit?

Consider this: What is your Unique Selling Proposition (USP)? How will you differentiate from your competition?

Event feasibility

The terms 'feasibility' and 'viability' are often used interchangeably. However, they have quite different meanings, particularly when utilised in an event business context. On the one hand, feasibility often refers to a single project or event and is primarily concerned with the related opportunities and threats, the required resources, and the associated likelihood of success. Viability, on the other hand, is concerned with the sustainability of business operations from a financial, social and environmental perspective. It is concerned with both medium-term and long-term business survival, as well as future business growth.

Hence, key differences between feasibility and viability relate to the scope of analysis and the time horizon. While feasibility may relate to one aspect of the business, viability generally refers to the whole business, and while feasibility is concerned with the short term, viability is concerned with the longer term. Event feasibility is not concerned with the staging of similar events in the future. These considerations are likely to be examined at a later stage. For example, the 2024 Paris Olympics and other future Olympics were not relevant to the decision to postpone the Tokyo Olympics in 2020. Although it was decided that a 2020 Tokyo Olympics was not feasible, the long-term viability of the Olympics was never in question. Once feasibility is established, it can be assumed that the event will, in fact, go ahead.

Both event feasibility and business viability are important areas of analysis in the business development process but in terms of event feasibility, the three over-riding requirements are that event needs to be staged:

■ On time
■ To budget, and
■ To specified standards.

Which of the above three requirements do you regard as the most important in an events context?

Elements of event feasibility

Events often seem like a good idea until a careful analysis of various aspects of feasibility reveal unacceptable problems, concerns or risks that were not previously taken into account. Possible considerations, or elements of event feasibility, may include:

Market feasibility

Whether or not people actually turn up at the event is obviously one of the most basic aspects of feasibility. Hence, an analysis of feasibility should include a profile of attendees that are expected at the event. When profiling attendees, characteristics that need to be considered may include the points in Figure 2.6.

By segmenting the market in a manner that reflects the key characteristics of the type of customer likely to attend a particular event, it is possible to more effectively target market segments that will yield optimum results. Based on a sound understanding of their customer profile, event managers can then develop a value proposition that lines up as closely as possible with customer needs in the market segments that are being targeted. Once the anticipated response to that value proposition indicates an adequate number of customers will attend the event, market feasibility has been established.

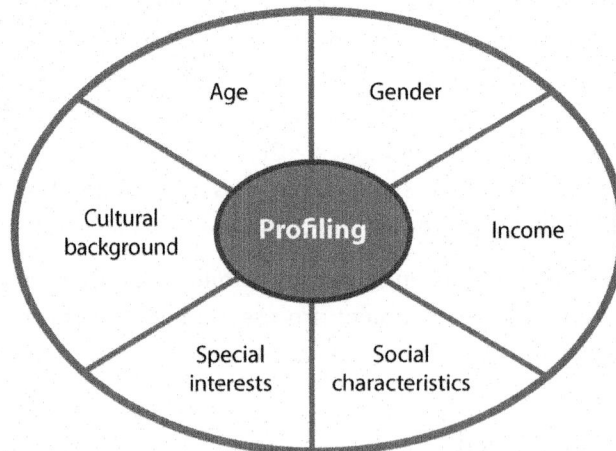

Figure 2.6: Profiling the market

What would you expect the customer profile at the Burning Man Festival to be?

Financial feasibility

Whether or not an event pays for itself is another basic consideration that follows naturally from market considerations. Regardless of whether the event is run by a private or public sector organisation, financial feasibility in some form, is an essential consideration.

Financial feasibility extends beyond an assessment of whether or not a profit will be generated. Particularly in the events industry, cash flows are a vital consideration. While a yearly budget may indicate that revenue will easily cover costs, a significant portion of those costs may relate to large expenses that occur early in the cycle. On the other hand, the generation of revenue may be heavily restricted until after the event has been staged. How temporary shortfalls are to be addressed must be given adequate attention. Key principles involved in avoiding cash flow problems are relatively straightforward but not always easy to achieve. The most basic strategy for addressing potential cash flow problems involves:

- Generating revenue as early as possible, and
- Delaying expenses for as long as possible.

Time feasibility

The staging of events allows for very little flexibility in terms of timing. In general, events can't be delayed without incurring significant financial and reputational costs. Adequate time is required to develop plans, implement promotional programs, arrange venues, and so on.

Managerial and staffing feasibility

As with all forms of organised human endeavour, success is unlikely in the absence of capable and motivated people, and this reality is particularly evident in the events industry. Partly because of the intangible nature of events, success depends critically on the talent, expertise and commitment of available human resources. Hence, critical elements that need to be considered are the availability of:

- Managerial knowledge and expertise relevant to the types of events.
- Motivated and talented employees that will drive the design, planning, implementation and staging of events.
- Enthusiastic, energetic and capable volunteers that will effectively carry out appropriate volunteer duties and also provide that extra spark that takes the event beyond mediocre and beyond satisfactory.

Venue feasibility

A relatively mundane but important consideration involves assessment and selection of an appropriate venue with appropriate sound and lighting, appropriate technology, and sufficient seating capacity. The venue needs to be of a standard that's acceptable for all stakeholders and with appropriate safety features including properly designed exits and entrances. In terms of safety issues, emergency management and the prevention of disasters, the venue is possibly the most important consideration.

Operational and physical feasibility

Another mundane but important consideration relates to the provision of appropriate equipment, facilities, and amenities. Lighting and sound equipment, if required, must be up to an appropriate standard. Furthermore, every aspect of the staging of an event must be possible in a manner that does not compromise the safety of employees, volunteers, attendees, the general public or any other stakeholders.

Environmental feasibility

Of critical importance now, and perhaps emerging as one of the most important considerations, is environmental sustainability and associated concerns. In this regard, it is important to recognise the fact that the staging of an event almost always has environmental impacts. These environmental impacts need to be minimised or offset, particularly in terms of the elements shown in Figure 2.7.

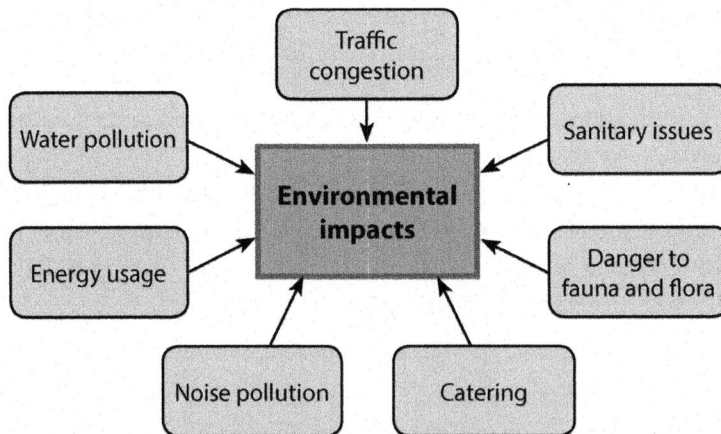

Figure 2.7:. Elements influencing environmental impacts

Political feasibility

Political support, not just from all levels of government but also from the host community, is a vital consideration. The extent of this support enhances the possibility of positive event outcomes. On the other hand, political opposition to the event generally brings with it a range of risks and costs that need to be considered and if possible, avoided.

With regard to the host community, what measures do you think an event organiser could take when planning for an outdoor music festival?

Legal compliance

Unless an event complies with state and federal legislation, as well as a range of local regulations, it is unlikely to proceed. Hence, all aspects of legal compliance need to be recognised and addressed. These include:

- Safety requirements (including Occupational Health & Safety)
- Insurance
- Contracts
- Licensing
- Permits
- Negligence mitigation requirements.

Risk summary

Successful event outcomes, as well as decisions about whether or not to stage an event depend on judgements about the associated risks:

- Market risks – will they actually turn up?
- Financial risks – will it make a profit, and can it be funded?
- Will everything be ready on time?
- Are appropriately motivated and talented human resources available?
- Is an appropriate venue available?
- Is the appropriate equipment and facilities available and can the event be staged in a safe and effective manner?
- Does the design, planning and management of the event demonstrate environmental responsibility?
- Is there political support for the event?
- Have all aspects of legal compliance been addressed?

Did you know? Safe Work Australia has detailed instructions to assist businesses in identifying Covid risks. As the core business varies, each organisation develops its own customised Covid safe plan following key steps. For more visit https://www.safework-australia.gov.au/covid-19-information-workplaces/industry-information/general-industry-information/risk-assessment.

Business viability and success

As discussed earlier, business viability is concerned with the sustainability of business operations, medium to long term business survival, and future business growth. It can be divided into similar categories to those that are relevant when considering feasibility, that is, market viability, financial viability, physical viability, supply viability, management viability, political viability, but also business model viability. When discussing business viability however, it is useful to consider some broader, more general determinants of business success. In this regard, there are several characteristics and qualities that differentiate viable and successful businesses from mediocre or failing businesses.

Successful businesses have generally moved beyond the development and articulation of a sound business model to the setting of realistic but challenging goals and operationalization of the business model. Goal setting is often a key element of business success and, as well as operationalizing the business model, may be a useful mechanism for monitoring performance and an important motivator for on-going effort and performance throughout an enterprise. Medium and longer-term goals should be developed but will generally need to be updated over time.

As indicated earlier, a key aspect of marketing success involves the development of an intimate, in-depth knowledge of customer needs, characteristics, and interests. This generally necessitates high levels of on-going engagement and communication with customers. In an events context, as in most business situations, success generally goes hand-in-hand with a deeply ingrained understanding of the importance of customers for business survival and a willingness to go the extra few yards to achieve real customer satisfaction. Successful event practitioners and event enterprises also tend to be characterised by agility, flexibility, and a passion for excellence. Moreover, a commitment to excellence, regardless of the industry or context, is an essential determinant of real success.

Business development job, role example

➤ Build relationships and identify business opportunities
➤ Conduct sales related activities
➤ Achieve sales targets
➤ Undertake sales trips and conduct sales meetings
➤ Identify targeting opportunities for different profile groups
➤ Identify partnership opportunities to generate new business
➤ Organise site inspections and develop client databases
➤ Represent the company on networking events
➤ Generate prospective sale leads and aim to convert leads into generating sales
➤ Collaborate with stakeholders to develop presentations and organise sales pitches.

The strategic impact of planned events

A significant industry trend over recent decades has been the utilisation of planned events as an effective mechanism for facilitating the achievement of strategic goals in both the public and private sectors. In the public sector, planned events have, for a long time, been used to support a range of economic, social and cultural strategies, particularly at a local government level.

In the private sector, planned events have emerged as a creative way of stimulating brand awareness and enhancing customer retention for a range of products and services in several industries. Sometimes referred to as experiential or engagement marketing, a major focus of many event companies around the world involves responding to requests for corporate or sales events that invite consumers to participate in brand experiences for the purpose of creating brand knowledge and loyalty. This approach is based on the view that people have started to ignore traditional approaches to marketing and advertising, and hence there is a growing need to connect with prospects and customers in a more active and meaningful way.

Experiential or engagement marketing primarily aims at encouraging active participation amongst customers in the marketing functions of an enterprise. This may be achieved through the conduct of a range of events designed and planned in a manner that provides mutual benefits to customers and the enterprise. This trend is likely to continue and accelerate rapidly in future years.

The bidding process

In order to gain business, that is, the right to stage an event, event organisations respond to tenders and often take part in a bidding process. This generally involves:

- Developing a bid proposal and submitting it to the selecting authority by the required date; plus usually
- Attending a meeting with the selecting authority to make a formal presentation (bid) and answer any questions.

While the structure and content of the bid proposal may vary depending upon what is actually asked for by the selecting authority, the development of a bid proposal is generally the result of a common bid process. The main purpose of the bid process is to:

■ Clearly demonstrate that the organisation bidding for an event has the capacity, resources and expertise to stage the event.

■ Provide evidence that indicates why the organisation should be selected over rival bidders.

Reasons for selecting a particular bidder may include:

■ Superior facilities compared with rival bidders

■ Greater access to finance than rival bids

■ Track record and a greater level of public support

■ High levels of project management and event management expertise

Did you know? One reason international cities bid for mega events is to promote their destinations for tourism purposes. See the bidding cities for the 2020 Olympic Games. Candidate cities: Istanbul, Tokyo and Madrid. https://youtu.be/HI3ErDjr4BY

Bid proposal content

The volume of work and the amount of detail that goes into a bid proposal is generally determined by the size, complexity, and importance of the event. However, proposals generally share a number of common themes and the bid process generally involves:

1. Recruiting an organising committee to oversight development of the bid proposal.

2. Determining possible dates.

3. Researching alternative venues to determine which is the most suitable.

4. Reviewing available resources.

5. Developing a budget.

6. Based on the above, developing the bid proposal.

The bid proposal must provide relevant information about the event management team, their expertise, event experience and qualifications, and the training that will be provided to volunteers as well as staff. A track record of success, as well as extensive managerial, project management or co-ordination experience, may also assist in attempts to win the bid.

Venue selection needs to be justified in a manner that clearly illustrates why the venue would be attractive to all event goers (performers, officials, spectators) and how it will cater for their needs. Hence, the bid proposal must outline all facilities available at the venue, including toilets, public transport availability, car-parking, the type of surface, lighting, seating, air-conditioning, electronic equipment, and so on. For outdoor events, information about the level of maintenance on turf, seating and shading for spectators, fencing, drainage, floodlighting, and change rooms should be provided. If the venue has staged similar events in the past, it should also be highlighted.

While information about the program should be provided, the level of detail may vary depending on the event. A sporting event proposal may suggest a competition program in terms of the number of days, and the start and finish times for each day or each event. Exactly when the venue is available may be an important issue. The program may include ceremonial events with visiting VIPs who may make speeches and present awards.

The bidder should draft a budget of probable income and expenditure. It should be realistic but attractive, which may be a difficult balance. While the budget shouldn't be expected to indicate that a loss is a probable outcome, exaggerating financial benefits can lead to longer-term problems, particularly in terms of credibility. The successful bidder may be able to apply for funding from various bodies and if so, details should be provided. There may be also an expectation that additional revenue will be generated through activities such as merchandise sales, food outlets, bars, raffles, and so on, and this should be reflected in the budget within the proposal.

Case study 2.2: Brisbane to bid for the 2032 Olympic Games

The state government of Queensland (Australia) confirmed their intention to bid for the 2032 Olympic Games. Part of the benefits of hosting the games includes international media exposure which places Brisbane on the forefront as a global sporting event destination. The decision by the International Olympic Committee (IOC), which city will host the games, comes as early as seven years before they actually take place. More info: https://www.hostcity.com/news/event-bidding/queensland-government-confirms-it-backs-2032-olympic-games-bid

The pitch

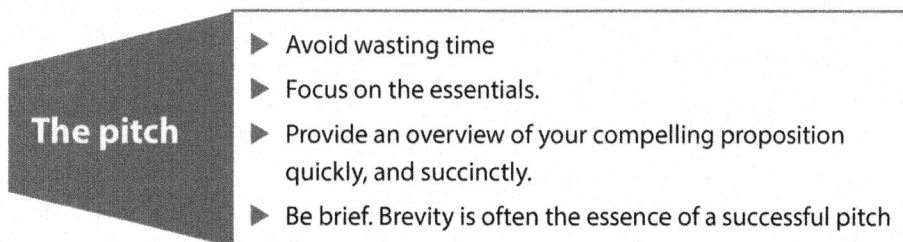

The pitch
▶ Avoid wasting time
▶ Focus on the essentials.
▶ Provide an overview of your compelling proposition quickly, and succinctly.
▶ Be brief. Brevity is often the essence of a successful pitch

Figure 2.8: The pitch essentials

A successful pitch generally depends less on what is said than on how it is said and given the fact that attention spans are getting shorter, it's important to consider the points in Figure 2.8.

In terms of powerpoint presentations, most people use too many slides, and this can become tiring and reduce audience attention. Too much text on each slide is also distracting so, where appropriate, use images. Data is used as a key part of the presentation and it needs to be interesting and compelling. Bids are produced as a team, therefore decide carefully who will represent the team to deliver a successful and engaging presentation.

While a range of problems may be associated with the bidding process, a sound understanding of how to create a successful bid proposal and pitch remain important areas of expertise for event practitioners, particularly for larger events.

Case study 2.3: Bidding for the Lexus Melbourne Cup Tour

Part of the Victoria Racing Club's vision is to position the Melbourne Cup as a globally recognised international event and to be recognised as a leader in racing and entertainment. The event holds important significance to the Victorian state economy which translates as a contribution of around $450 million. Alongside the economic and social impact of the international event, the Victoria Racing Club has adopted a sustainability strategy which tackles key issues such as material re-usage across all supply chains, while it has implemented its own desalination plant creating a net positive impact on water recycling. The event also comes with its own challenges and issues. A key legal and social issue associated with the staging of the Melbourne Cup relates to the consumption of alcohol. This is an important issue as it may affect the motivational factors for attending the sporting event (Lagos & Wrathall, 2014).

Each year the Victoria Racing Club invites submissions by local communities and destinations to host the Lexus Melbourne Cup Trophy visit. This involves destinations collaborating with local stakeholders and collaborators such as the media, aged-care homes, schools and hospitals to work on a bid and pitch to be able and host a visit of the trophy (worth $275,000 and 18-carat gold) in their local communities. The pitch involves creating an event experience where local communities come together and share their excitement by utilising various media channels and create local social impact and community support. In addition, the Victoria Racing Club donates thousands to remote communities. For example, in 2020 the community of Kangaroo Island, which was heavily impacted by the bushfires, received a donation of AUD 50,000, after winning the Lexus Melbourne Club Tour National Sweep. These are efforts by the Victoria Racing Club to engage with remote communities while developing partnerships at national and international levels.

For more on the Lexus Melbourne Cup Tour visit https://www.melbournecupcarnival.com.au/about/lexus-melbourne-cup-tour.

Listen to the interview with Joe McGrath on how the Melbourne Cup tour developed as a business idea https://youtu.be/KudDuDTCOZw.

See also the Industry profile of Joe McGrath on page 42.

2

Summary

Most successful enterprises in the events industry owe their initial existence to the efforts, expertise, and tenacity of entrepreneurs. Key characteristics of successful entrepreneurs include: creativity and intellectual curiosity; the capacity to network effectively and develop social capital; a propensity for calculated risk taking; and the capacity to embrace both divergent and convergent thinking.

The entrepreneurial process commences with the development of a sound business model to describe a business idea and provide an understanding of the means and methods that can be employed to earn revenue, survive, and grow. The business model needs to answer four basic questions:

1. How will revenue be generated?
2. How will people be attracted to attend the event?
3. How will value be created for attendees in a cost-effective manner?
4. What unique features provide a competitive advantage?

It's important to understand the distinction between event feasibility and business viability. Both are important but whereas event feasibility deals short-term issues regarding an event, business viability deals with the long-term survival of the enterprise as a whole. For event feasibility, three over-riding requirements are that event needs to be staged: on time, to budget, and to specified standards.

Once these requirements are satisfied, more detailed planning and implementation of the event can proceed. Event feasibility must consider a broad range of factors including market forces, financial issues, duration and timing, management and event expertise, the availability of appropriate venues, equipment, amenities and facilities, the environmental impact, levels of political support, legal compliance, and associated levels of risk.

When discussing viability, it is useful to consider some broad determinants of business success including the development of an intimate, in-depth knowledge of customer needs, an ingrained understanding of the importance of customers, and a willingness to do what is required to achieve customer satisfaction. Other characteristics of successful event practitioners and enterprises are agility, flexibility, and a passion for excellence.

Over recent decades, the use of planned events as an effective mechanism for facilitating the achievement of strategic goals has, in the public sector, led to them being used to support a range of economic, social and cultural strategies; in the private sector, events have been associated with engagement marketing as a mechanism for building brand awareness and loyalty.

Industry profile: Joe McGrath, International racing expert

Joe is an experienced International Relations Manager with a history of working in the sports industry. Joe was integral in the development of the Lexus Melbourne Cup Tour, a special community event that takes place every year and profiles the coveted Loving Cup trophy to many communities across the globe.

Image 2.1: Joe McGrath, Racing Engagements and Cup Tour Manager and Victoria Racing Club Ambassador At Large, Melbourne, Australia

The concept has evolved over time with the Cup integral to the development of key relationships across community, media, tourism, business and the racing industry. The concept originated in 2003 and approaches its 19th consecutive year in 2021. Communities as far reaching as Santa Teresa on the edge of the Simpson Desert in central Australia to Port Headland in the North West and Gove in the North East, have all benefited by a Cup Tour visit. It has been on these occasions that the Cup has united communities, promoted social inclusion and, in some cases, raised much needed charitable dollars for a worthy cause. It has allowed communities to hear the Cup stories and learn about what is truly a cultural icon.

Part of Joe's role has been to work with the media whilst on the road with the Cup, promoting the Melbourne Cup Carnival overall in the process. Joe's role has relied on marketing management, event management, account management and business development skills. The role also requires formal presentation skills. It has been of benefit of Joe that he grew up in a well known Victorian Racing family and has experienced everything from horse breeding; horse ownership; racehorse training; racing administration; bookmaking and several aspects of working with the media. Part of his role is to develop international racing partnerships for the Victoria Racing Club and has required the liaison with many strategic alliance race clubs across the globe. From York in the UK, to Auckland in NZ, relationships of this nature are important to the VRC in maintaining its position and relevance on an International Platform. Racing is a global sport which relies on the interchange of horses across many jurisdictions. Despite the pandemic over the past twelve months the pursuit of global competition has not waned.

How has COVID impacted on your role to develop business opportunities?

During COVID, the Lexus Melbourne Cup Tour learned to pivot and was delivered online. This involved adapting several tour elements beaming in virtually to 27 communities across the land.

What opportunities have arisen as a result of COVID?

As a result of the pandemic, we have needed to learn new ways by which to connect with communities. Virtual Presentations will continue to take place moving forward, and concepts such as the MYER Fashions on your Front Lawn and Lexus Melbourne Cup Tour will continue to rely on virtual technology in the future. Whilst there will always be an appetite to take the Cup on the road in a physical form, virtual presentation will continue to be an option which the VRC will explore and experiment with.

What future initiatives/ideas and projects can you foresee?

Throughout the pandemic, businesses across the globe learned new ways to do things and it was only under such tight restrictions that we needed to innovate for survival. Virtual technology has been a revelation to how we go about things and will continue to be utilised moving forward. I do see there will be an opportunity to showcase talent in other parts of the world to remote locations. On course, there will certainly be pressure to set up and adhere to acceptable protocols that will help promote social distancing under a COVID safe umbrella. There will be a quest to get crowds back on course, but we will be heavily guided by the government authorities.

Racing is an exciting sport to be involved with and there are many interesting people who are involved. Joe has always felt it a privilege and a pleasure being involved in this industry and looks forward to continuing well into the future.

Discussion questions

1. Differentiate the key features that distinguish business development in the events industry from those of other industries.

2. Identify and discuss the key characteristics and skills required by entrepreneurs in the events industry.

3. Explain the purpose of business models and the key differences between business models and business plans.

4. What is your understanding of unique selling propositions and of competitive advantage? Give examples.

Workshop activities (in pairs or small groups)

1. Choose a charity and create a business model specifically designed to raise revenue based on various types of events

2. Choose a major event and conduct a SWOT analysis highlighting key influences that signify opportunities to include additional events throughout the year

3. In groups of 3-4: Choose a small to medium size business. Conduct a brainstorming session to discuss financial viability by adding corporate and fundraising events.

4. Individual or in pairs: Create a new business model clearly highlighting key elements that demonstrate feasibility and unique advantages compared to other competitors

5. Review the candidate videos by the bidding cities for the 2020 Olympic Games (https://youtu.be/HI3ErDjr4BY). Identify the key elements that these tourism destinations highlight in their bidding efforts.

6. Review the intention to bid by the state government of Queensland (https://www.hostcity.com/news/event-bidding/queensland-government-confirms-it-backs-2032-olympic-games-bid). Discuss the advantages and disadvantages of hosting the games. Interpret the economic and social benefits that may place the city of Brisbane as a global sporting event destination

References and further reading

Arikan, A.M., Arikan, I., & Koparan, I. (2020). Creation opportunities: Entrepreneurial curiosity, generative cognition and Knightian uncertainty. *Academy of Management Review*, 45(4), 987-1002. https://doi.org/10.5465/amr.2018.0252

Byun, J., Leopkey, B., & Ellis, D. (2019). Understanding joint bids for international large-scale sport events as strategic alliances. *Sport, Business and Management*, 9(1), 39-57. https://doi.org/10.1108/SBM-09-2018-0074

Beliaeva, T., Ferasso, M., Kraus, S. and Damke, E.J. (2020), Dynamics of digital entrepreneurship and the innovation ecosystem: A multilevel perspective, *International Journal of Entrepreneurial Behavior & Research*, 26(2), 266-284. https://doi.org/10.1108/IJEBR-06-2019-0397

Karl, K.A. (2001). Achieving success through social capital: Tapping the hidden resources in your personal and business networks. *Academy of Management Perspectives*, 15(3), 146.

Kuratko, D.F. (2016). *Entrepreneurship: Theory, process and practice*. Cengage Learning.

Lagos, E, Wrathall J, and Alebaki, M, (2014) The Melbourne Cup: A case study in the motivations and expectations associated with attending major sporting events, *Proceedings from the 24th CAUTHE conference Tourism and Hospitality in the Contemporary World: Trends, Changes and Complexity*, p.963, Brisbane, February 10-13 Retrieved from https://search.informit.org/doi/10.3316/informit.408034621217929 (31 May 2021)

Richards, G., & Marques, L. (2016). Bidding for success? Impacts of the European capital of culture bid. *Scandinavian Journal of Hospitality and Tourism*, 16(2), 180-195. https://doi.org/10.1080/15022250.2015.1118407

Salama, M. (Ed.). (2021). *Event Project Management: Principles, technology and innovation*. Goodfellow Publishers Ltd.

Schrauder, S., Knock, A., Baccarella, C.V., & Voight, K. (2017). Takin' care of business models: The impact of business model evaluation on front-end success. *The Journal of Product Innovation Management*, 35(3), 410-426. https://doi.org/10.1111/jpim.12411

Websites

www.acnc.gov.au/for-public/understanding-charities/charities-and-fundraising

www.flemington.com.au/news/2019-04-18/2018-melbourne-cup-carnival-delivers-record-economic-benefit

www.heraldsun.com.au/news/victoria/melbourne-cup-2021-towns-encouraged-to-apply-for-trophy-hosting-duties/news-story/467c3b71f3e609c6c217723ec61a090c

www.hostcity.com/news/event-bidding/queensland-government-confirms-it-backs-2032-olympic-games-bid

www.melbournecupcarnival.com.au/about/lexus-melbourne-cup-tour/

Videos

youtu.be/KudDuDTCOZw (2021 Joe McGrath Lexus Melbourne Cup Tour)

youtu.be/HI3ErDjr4BY (2020 Olympics - Istanbul, Tokyo and Madrid Promotional Candidate videos)

3 Event and experience design

Learning objectives

On completion of this chapter, you will be able to:

➤ Recognise the benefits and potential impact of systematic event design

➤ Explain the nature and significance of the event experience and recognise the associated challenges in terms of event design

➤ Provide an understanding of how to conceptualise an event and recognise the importance of a sound event concept

➤ Explain how an event concept is supported and reinforced by theming and other aspects of event design

➤ Provide an understanding of the key event design principles

➤ Explain the role of setting, staging and logistics

➤ Describe the link between event design and event outcomes.

Event design is an important aspect of planned events, and events have the power to transform individuals. An emerging focus in event design is the focus on meanings and event experiences (Getz & Page, 2016). Event design, a core 'domain' or function of event management offers the potential to achieve, or at least facilitate these transformations. The emergence of the so-called transformation economy has been at least partly responsible for a movement in the focus of planned events beyond extraordinary experiences towards experiences that could be regarded as transformative or even life-changing. Described as peak experiences, these transformational events have important implications for event design.

? *What other societal changes can you think of that support or are consistent with the emerging focus on transformational events?*

The event experience

Event experiences are the essence of planned events. The potential impact of those experiences can be significant, particularly in the power of:

- Exhibitions and conventions to **spark the imagination**
- Music and entertainment festivals to **engage the senses**
- Conferences and other business events to **stimulate the intellect**
- Commemorative events to **invoke emotions**
- Sporting events to **stir passions and loyalties**
- Cultural and religious events to transform people and to **enliven the spirit.**

The key challenge for an event designer is to create or at least facilitate one or more event experiences in a way that matches or exceeds the expectations of event attendees. In this regard, the event designer may seek to provide a rich experience with which attendees can relax and enjoy or create an environment that provides the ingredients and the circumstances in which attendees can actively participate and become co-creators of that experience in a more active and meaningful way. Regardless of the approach, event design can be a crucial ingredient in the overall success of an event.

What type of experience is someone likely to be seeking when they attend a community cultural festival? What event elements or activities should be provided to enhance that experience and make it more memorable?

Frameworks to guide the design of event experiences
Transforming events framework

In a recent study, Steriopoulos and Wrathall (2021) conducted in-depth interviews with event experts on how the industry is transforming post COVID-19. Based on the findings, the researchers developed a framework highlighting key priorities that influence change in industry. The key concepts that resulted from the study are:

- the need for humans to socially connect and protect the environment;
- the design of meaningful event experiences;
- the capacity to adapt to complex event situations while remaining committed to ongoing learning; and
- the need for professionals to look after their personal and professional wellbeing.

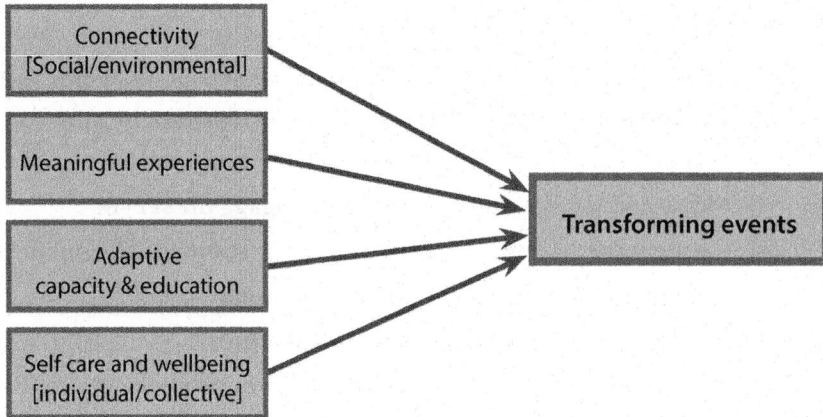

Figure 3.1: A conceptual framework on transforming events (Steriopoulos & Wrathall, 2021)

The PERMA Model

Crucial to the process of creating an event experience that is consistent with attendee expectations is the capacity of event designers to empathize with event attendees. Hence, an event designer needs to be able to understand what attendees want and what they don't want, what motivates them and what frustrates them. Accordingly, there is a new focus in event design which arises partly from positive psychology, emphasising well-being and the development of an engaging, purposeful, and worthwhile life. Specifically, one type of event that focuses on emotional engagement is the commemorative.

Seligman (2011) introduced the PERMA acronym to identify five elements of well-being. These are:

- *Positive emotions* such as excitement, satisfaction, and pride, that are frequently connected with positive outcomes including healthy relationships and longevity.

- *Engagement* or involvement in activities in a manner that builds on an individual's interests and allows the individual to become completely absorbed and deeply involved.

- *Relationships*, including work-related, familial, romantic, or platonic.

- *Meaning*, or the capacity to put everything, including work and relationships, into context.

- *Accomplishments* or the on-going pursuit of success and the associated feelings of pride and mastery.

Did you know? Commemorative events are an example where the PERMA model may be applicable; e.g. Canberra organises annual events to recognise the contribution of all those who served in World War One (WWI). These events can be emotional for families of the descendants who participate to pay respects to their ancestors. Source: https://anzacportal.dva.gov.au/commemoration/commemoration-days/anzac-day

PERMA provides a potential framework or starting point for the design of transformational events. Events designed in this manner have the potential for long-term transformation at a range of levels. Of course, not all events have a transformational impact, and in fact, not all transformational events are the result of conscious, well-devised and well-thought-out design.

3

Case study 3.1: Transformational power of Woodstock

Events had transformational power as early as the 1960s. The 1969 Woodstock Music Festival, for example, was clearly transformational and in fact, it's probably no exaggeration to say that it was an event that defined a generation and transformed the way in which we all think about music festivals forever. Yet Woodstock certainly wasn't the result of systematic or well-thought-out design. To start with, the sheer scale of the event took organisers by surprise. They expected the concert to draw about 200,000 people, nothing like the half million or so that actually turned up. As a result, Woodstock became a 'free concert' for hundreds of thousands of rock fans and, at least partly for that reason, was a financial disaster, relying on the proceeds of the 1970 Woodstock film to pay off around $1.4 million dollars of debt. The lack of sophisticated planning and design was a key reason for the inability of organisers to make the event the financial success that they had envisaged. Furthermore, it is highly likely that conscious efforts aimed at creative and skilful event design would have enhanced outcomes and avoided the associated problems.

As the value of event design as a contributor to event success becomes more accepted, and as we look to the future of the industry following the unprecedented impact of the coronavirus crisis, it seems more likely than ever that the success of planned events will depend upon *detail* and sophisticated *event design*. For more on the history and the significance of Woodstock festival watch the video on https://youtu.be/StFhvAlv3Js

Consider this: Can you think of any other event that was transformational and memorable yet lacked systematic design? What recommendations can you make in relation to design improvements?

A framework on human connectivity

Even prior to the pandemic Sheldon (2020) called for transformative experiences that connect humans. This connectivity is illustrated in the author's theoretical model which showcases four key concepts:

1. Deep human connectivity.
2. Engaged contribution.
3. Deep environmental connectivity and
4. Self-inquiry.

The need to prioritise humans and the design of personalised experiences is more important now than ever, given it will be a long time before events will be able to return to mass delivery and production. The COVID restrictions call for the design of smaller event experiences with Sheldon (2020) encouraging community events that also encourage participants to contribute towards environmental issues and positive outcomes.

Community events: Sheldon's (2020) priorities on human connectivity may be applicable on community events where people also come together for social outcomes. Designing community events would attract activities that allow people to work together and contribute to the environment. Examples include: Working bees, plant a tree or sustainable community festivals. These activities help rejuvenate communities while contributing towards bushfire recovery and related sustainability outcomes.

Case study 3.2: Experience design summit Year Zero 2021

In an experience design summit in June 2021 @ Spaceship Earth, the conference convenors launched a tool which helps practitioners design memorable experiences and human transformation based on four key design principles:

1 Aspiring

2 Playing

3 Co-Creating

4 Grounding.

The experience design compass is designed to unlock humans' potential and help transform thinking in order to design transformational events. The key principles assist event planners in creating immersive online experiences while rejuvenating personal and professional goals. For more visit www.exdsummit.com

Extending Pine and Gilmore's experience model

The experience economy model, also known as the 'experience realm' and introduced by Pine and Gilmore (2011), provides a framework that makes alternative approaches to event design a little clearer. For years this model was applied on various studies and experiences. Event experiences are categorised first, according to the level of guest participation (either *active* or *passive*) and second, according to the connection between the event attendee and the environment (either *absorptive* or *immersive*). In the current situation transformation is on the forefront of discussions (Neuhofer et al. 2020), and consideration needs to be taken of the elements that contribute to designing transformative experiences. With the contribution of the above models, especially following the influence of the pandemic, the experience economy model may be extended to include elements such as: human, environmental connectivity and authenticity. Figure 3.2 is an illustration considering the additional elements by the above frameworks.

Passive participation exists when attendees do not directly influence the event, whereas *active* participation occurs when attendees personally affect or influence the event.

The environmental relationship seeks to distinguish between the situation when the experience 'goes into' the customer (*absorption*), and when the customer 'goes into' the experience (*immersion*).

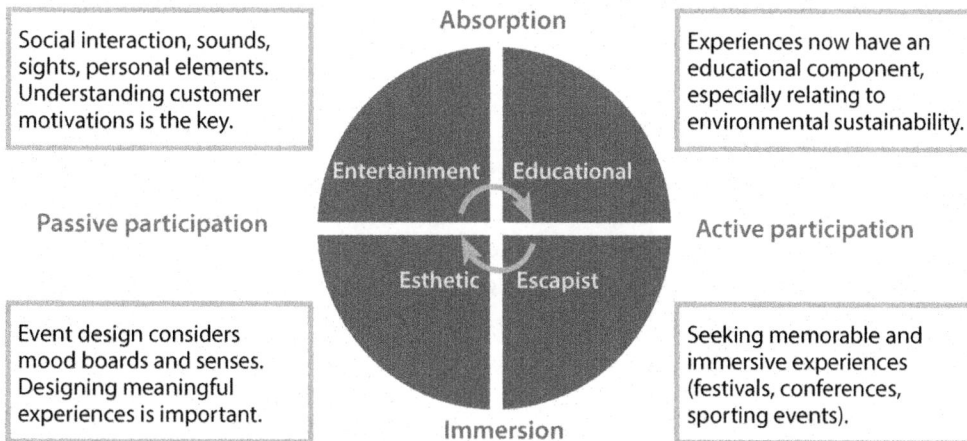

Figure 3.2: Extending the experience realm (Adapted from: Pine & Gilmore, 2011)

The extension of the quadrants produced by these two dimensions and identified by Pine and Gilmore (2011) are explained as follows:

- **Entertainment** which involves passive participation and absorption of the experience. Audiences view these on various media. In a post

COVID era these experiences may be personalised. It is important to understand the audience needs and motivational factors.

- **Educational** which involves active participation, still with absorption of the experience. Knowledge is important and a care for the environment is showcased via this experience design. Attending a small community event for example.

- **Escapist** which also involves active participation but with immersion in the experience. Attending pilgrimage events to commemorate the soldiers of WWI in the authentic place where the battles took place. Example includes Australians attending the commemorative and pilgrimage events in Gallipoli (Turkey).

- **Esthetic** which involves passive participation and immersion in the experience. Here, immersion in the event has little or no impact on it, leaving the environment but not the attendee essentially untouched. New elements include a focus on designing meaningful experiences.

Events can be generally designed with one or more of the experience realm categories being emphasised. The extended framework brings transformational elements together and provides event designers with a systematic framework with which to create or at least facilitate the event experience that is desired.

Can you think of any successful events that could be described as escapist events? What were the key event outcomes? What were the key design elements that made the event successful?

Conceptualising the event

Development of an event concept represents a key milestone in the planning of any event. It brings together what could be described as the creative spark that inspires creation of the event and the more mundane, practical considerations that need to be taken into account. The successful combination of both sets of considerations will go a long way towards determining event outcomes and the overall success or failure of the event.

A key benefit associated with developing and articulating a sound event concept is that it can influence expectations, and, in this regard, positive expectations can have a profound impact in shaping and determining a range of event outcomes, including overall attendance. At the same time however, as most marketers are aware, expectations need to be realistic. Hence, an event concept needs to establish a realistic vision of what the event is all about.

When developing the concept event managers need to consider the 5 Ws. They are important factors as they may influence guest satisfaction. These are:

- What (is the event about)?
- Who (will attend the event)?
- Why (are you having the event)?
- Where (will you run the event)?
- When (date of the event)?

Can you think of an event that you have attended in which your positive expectations have made it seem even more satisfying and more memorable?

What about the event magic?

In every event, but particularly in music festivals, we'd like to see and experience a bit of magic, the so-called WOW factor. But what it is and how to create or capture the almost undefinable quality that turns an event into a memorable, magical experience that distinguishes it from other events is the ultimate challenge for event designers.

When we think of events that appeared to be the most spontaneous, the most engaging and the most fun, they were often the product of well-thought-out planning and design, and the creation of unanticipated event elements or activities that transformed the usual into the unusual, the boring into the exciting, and the mundane into fun. Similarly, when we think about the most grandiose of wedding designs, aspects of that design that stand out as the most conspicuous in terms of spectacle and impact, are immersed in every element of the event, the invitations, the table settings, the lighting, the decorations, and so on.

This is the essence of great design, often a well thought out combination of a creative event concept and close attention to the detail that will bring that concept to life and produce the event magic or so-called WOW factor that makes an event unforgettable. Ultimately, the key objective is to design an event in a manner that will provide event attendees, individually and collectively, with a unique and memorable event experience.

Can you think of a memorable event in which those elements that had the greatest impact were those that related to details and features associated with the design?

Theming and event design

The event theme is a key aspect of the event concept and potentially one of the most important elements of the event design. There is no standard formula for an event theme. It may be a time in history, perhaps a medieval theme at a birthday party. It may have cultural or national significance, a Chinese, Italian or perhaps an ancient Egyptian theme. It may be a sporting theme, or even a religious or cultural theme. The theme could also be based a genre of music or some other special interest. Whatever is chosen, it is important that other aspects of the event support and reinforce that theme.

Benefits of theming

An important benefit of theming stems from the fact that almost any event will, in several ways, be similar to a number of other events that have been run or are running at the same time. It is the event theme that should most clearly differentiate an event from other events. Hence, if done properly, the event theme is what makes the event stand out from other similar events. The event theme will have the greatest impact if it is supported and reinforced by several elements of the event including:

- Event catering
- The location
- The event venue
- Decorations
- The music
- The lighting
- The audio system
- The overall ambiance of the event
- The physical layout of the event

Creating sensory experiences

There are several ways in which event designers can develop, support, and reinforce event themes. Considering the above models, event designers may choose sense-based experiences to highlight the five senses as follows:

- **Sight** – includes the colours, lighting, attire, the decorations, photos and pictures, fabrics, and even food presentation.
- **Sound** – includes ambient noise, musical entertainment, and even dialogue and dining sounds.

- ▪ **Taste** – the catering of the food and beverages provided at the event.
- ▪ **Touch** – includes surfaces, furnishings, fabrics, and even food texture.
- ▪ **Smell** – includes scented candles or incense, but also food aromas, as well as flowers and perfumes.

Case study 3.3: So Frenchy So Chic reimagined

Due to the pandemic and attendance restrictions, So Frenchy So Chic (a community event) had to transform their event concept to create an experience that was appealing to the So Frenchy audience and viable business wise – all within a very tight timeframe! So Frenchy So Chic normally brings a number of French artists to Australia to headline this festival. For the 2021 event, this was reimagined, with local artists engaged and a French flavour brought to the day through musical collaboration, French food, drinks and general 'joie de vivre'. The main aim of So Frenchy So Chic 2021 was to bring joy to the community after a difficult year – and to support local artists and the local hospitality sector.

While the event had to adapt to the restrictions at the time, including allocated seating pods and Covid Safe practices, So Frenchy So Chic achieved their goals – delivering a safe, joyful experience for guests – and was one of the first large scale community focused events to return to Melbourne.

Image 3.1: Supplied by Kate Stewart of EBC Advisory. Photography by Imageplay.

Case study supplied by Kate Stewart – for more information, please visit: http:// sofrenchysochic.com

Venue considerations and checklist

One of the key considerations when designing event experiences is the venue or site location. The decision to host the event indoors or outdoors or a combination of both may also be influenced by a number of factors such as weather conditions, budget and accessibility issues. It is advisable for event managers to create a venue checklist for each event as client needs vary.

A venue checklist helps event planners remember every detail especially when making venue decisions. Checklists can be useful for future reference and can assist with selling the event concept to the client. It is important to conduct site inspections early on, with subsequent visits closer to the time of the event. Some key questions to ask during inspections are below:

- What is the capacity of the venue / outdoor site?
- Is there a floor plan available?
- Are there any permits required for outdoor venues?
- What technological equipment is available?
- Is there staff support available if technology fails during presentations?
- How many staff are available to assist during your event?
- Is there disability access available?
- Indoor venues: Is catering inhouse or can it be outsourced? Is food sourced locally?
- What waste management systems are used for indoor venues?

Venue directories

There are various venue tools for use when looking for venues. Specific criteria are used to narrow down the choice and some are based on membership. For example, in Victoria (Australia), Business Events Victoria utilise a venue search tool to assist conference planners choose a venue in regional areas. Planners are able to select venue options based on meeting and accommodation capacity.

To review regional venue options in Victoria see: https://businesseventsvictoria.com/.

For international venue options visit https://www.venuedirectory.com/

> ## Case study 3.4: International Association of Venue Managers
>
> The international association of venue managers (IAVM) hosts an annual industry conference and brings together venue experts from all around the world to remain current, showcase innovations and exchange knowledge. Part of the commitment is to provide education and inspire venue leaders in strategic thinking while also offering certification options. Visit Venue Connect https://www.iavm.org/venueconnect

3

Designing virtual experiences

The pandemic led to many events adapting to the online world. While there is a plethora of software that may be utilised in the delivery of online events, there are key considerations when engaging audiences online. For example, Zoom (technology software) was widely used during and following the pandemic. The so-called Zoom fatigue led to event managers having to rethink their online engagement strategy. Key questions to consider are:

- How long should delegates be online?
- How can you keep them engaged?
- How can you encourage exchange of ideas in a virtual environment?
- What if technology fails?
- How can you create a WOW factor in an online event?
- How can you encourage delegate interaction virtually?

Use tools to create immersive experiences

Some event managers argue that conferences may not be as creative as festivals, however experts can take design one step further and create immersive conference experiences. There are various tools that can help to apply creativity in conference design. For example, menti.com is a technology tool that engages audiences in real time. Presenters log in with an email address, ask questions and the audience can enter via a 6-digit code to answer questions. For brainstorming, use padlet.com and miro.com.

Designing hybrid events

As event planners pivoted to virtual events in 2020, more and more professional conference organisers (PCOs) have started to think how to best design the next phase of hybrid event experiences. While companies still prefer to run their team meetings face to face, the reality is that the combination of virtual and face to face events is here to stay for a long time.

Some key considerations when designing hybrid events are:

- **Venue requirements** – What space do you need and what capacity. Request for the venue COVID safe practices. What style seating is available? What catering options? How far is the venue from transport options? What is the booking and cancellation policy? What Audio Visual is available for use?

- **Theming** – This will help theme your hybrid model. What is the main objective of your event? Will you need breakout rooms for team building exercises or networking? What speakers will you engage? Consider the diversity of speakers for all types of meetings, incentives, conferences, and exhibitions (MICE).

- **Logistics** – How will you manage the time? Consider the possible technology disruptions. Is it better to have some presentations pre-recorded and add the Question and Answer (Q & A) live? Will the chat rooms be separate? Make sure you adhere to the timeframes to keep the delegates satisfied.

- **Social program** – How will you engage your audience? Will this component be face to face or virtual? How can you create meaningful connections and reach a global audience at the same time? Will you include social options pre and post conference? Offer leisure opportunities for the families of delegates to boost local economies.

- **Marketing strategy** – How will you reach a global audience? What type of promotional tools will you use? Utilise hashtags and keywords to monitor the performance and use data analytics for ongoing marketing planning.

- **Brand activation** – Will you use innovative facilities to showcase your brand during the business event? Consider virtual galleries or face to face (F2F) exhibitions. How can you demonstrate your products and services and make your event memorable? Consider video recordings based on delegate experiences.

- **Financial strategy** – How can you measure the return on investment (ROI)? Utilise data analytics to make decisions on technology investment. Set your promotional budgets and customise your decisions based on the audience reach and target market strategies.

- **Evaluate, innovate and educate** – Evaluate all phases of your event planning, before, during and after. This will help improve event documentation, processes, and event planning. Stay updated with market trends and technology so you can confidently improve the delegate experience while you raise your company profile.

Case study 3.5: CAUTHE goes global

The 2021 Council for Australasian Tourism and Hospitality Education (CAUTHE) Conference Online utilised a range of software to execute their first virtual delegate experience. Following consultation with various companies the conference organisers decided to utilise *EventsAir* during planning phase, *OnAir* for the live experience and *Zoom* to host multiple sessions. The conference committee was delighted when their vision was achieved by engaging up to 300 global delegates, representing over 100 countries in an immersive online experience. See Table 3.1 how the association delivered the CAUTHE 2021 Conference Online. For more info visit cauthe.org/services/conferences/

3

Event design and sustainability

An area of transformation that is receiving renewed levels of interest and attention relates to event sustainability. However, sustainability has changed significantly over the past few years. A focus of recent research is on the application of the 'circular economy' to the events industry.

A *circular economy* is one that aims at eliminating waste and minimising the creation of carbon emissions, as well as continual use of resources, by creating a closed-loop system in which energy and waste materials become inputs for other processes. This approach provides a clear contrast to the traditional 'linear economy' approach of taking, making, using, and wasting materials and resources.

In the events industry, there is clearly a need to recognise the fact that the system is broken and move to fresh, proactive responses, to re-evaluate and reimagine strategies aimed at event sustainability. This involves moving from the 3 Rs, (Reduce Reuse and Recycle) to the circular economy's 6 Rs:

- Review
- Refuse
- Reduce
- Reuse
- Recycle, and
- Rethink

CAUTHE 2021 Conference: Draft Program Overview

Date	Times (AEDT)	Activity
Thur 4 Feb	13:00 – 16:00	TH&E Standards Workshop: *2021 Assessment Design workshop*
Fri 5 Feb		PhD/ECR Workshop
	13:00 – 14:00	☐ Panel Session: *Back to basics: How to get the most out of your PhD*
	14:00 – 15:00	☐ Small Group Mentoring Sessions: with Fellows & academics
	15:00 – 16:00	☐ Social Activity: *Business is Bliss* e-Mindfulness workshop
Tue 9 Feb – Thur 11 Feb	Throughout	The Marketplace: 1:1 appointments available at rostered times
		☐ Sponsor / Exhibitor displays
		☐ 'Ask a Fellow'
Tue 9 Feb		Plenary
	13:00 – 13:20	☐ Open and welcome
	13:20 – 14:00	☐ Keynote: Prof Ray Fisk *Tourism Services Elevate Human Experience*
	14:00 – 15:00	Concurrent paper session 1
	15:00 – 16:00	Concurrent paper session 2
	16:00 – 17:00	Social Activity: *Sprout Online* cooking demonstration
Wed 10 Feb	08:00 – 09:00	Interactive panel discussion *ServeCollab*	Chair: Prof Ray Fisk *Researching for wellbeing: How can you help?*
	13:00 – 14:00	Panel discussion with industry and academic speakers
		☐ *Restarting the tourism, hospitality and events industry: looking backwards to move forward*
	14:00 – 15:00	Concurrent paper session 3
	15:00 – 16:00	e-Poster visual paper session
	16:00 – 17:00	Panel discussion: Meet the Editors
		☐ *'Everything you ever wanted to ask an editor but were too afraid to ask'*
	17:00 – 18:00	Social Activity: *Adelaide Festival Centre* presentation and Q&A
Thur 11 Feb	11:00 – 12:00	ACSPRI Qualitative research methods workshop *Register via this link
	13:00 – 14:00	Panel discussion with industry and academic speakers
		☐ *Destination Management in the post-COVID era: How can we 'Build back better?'*
	14:00 – 15:00	Concurrent paper session 4
	15:00 – 16:00	The Great Debate
	16:00 – 17:00	Closing ceremony
		☐ CAUTHE Awards
		☐ Handover to CAUTHE 2022
	17:00 – 18:00	Social Activity: *Sydney Opera House* online guided tour and talk
Fri 12 Feb	10:30 – 12:00	Global hotel industry outlook, research brainstorming and SHARE center update
	13:00 – 14:00	Annual General Meeting
	14:00 – 15:00	Chapter Director catch up and Voting for 2021 Executive Committee (by invitation)
	15:00 – 16:00	Special Interest Group meetings
		☐ Critical Approaches
		☐ Event Studies
		☐ Information and Communication Technologies
		☐ Teaching and Learning
	18:00 – 19:00	JHTM Editorial Board Meeting (by invitation)
Mon 15 Feb	13:00 – 15:00	Special Interest Group meeting
		☐ Tourism Risk Crises and Recovery Management

Table 3.1: 2021 CAUTHE Conference Online program.

In an events context, most of this transformation needs to take place at the event design stage and involves reimagining sustainability with a focus that moves beyond neutral impacts towards a regenerative impact on our social, economic and ecosystems. Hence, the pandemic can be used as a major reset to restore and rejuvenate the environment. During the design stage, consideration of all potential sources of waste and pollution is critical, as is the need to collaborate with suppliers, sponsors, venue operators, contractors, and partners, and all key event stakeholders, to rethink ways in which events can be designed with an emphasis on regeneration.

How can you manage sustainability in event design?

To answer this question, Jones (2017) discusses the need to focus on:

- Issues
- Impacts
- Outcomes

Issues may relate to communication with the local community. **Impacts** may be positive or negative depending on how the issues are managed; while **outcomes** are the remains of the issues being managed. Examples of issues that need to be considered when designing events are:

- Use of natural resources
- Localised sound and light pollution
- Overcrowding
- Economic benefit for the local community
- Procurement choices
- Creation of social capital through the chosen event activities.

Stakeholders and sustainability

To successfully manage events and sustainability, it is important to consult and consider stakeholder perspectives. By involving key groups in sustainable event planning, event managers ensure the inclusion of effective management practices and a shared sustainability vision. Examples of stakeholder involvement may include: government, venue managers, community groups, volunteers and media.

For more visit Chapter 11.

Event outcomes, impacts and legacies

The initiation, design, and planning of an event generally takes place with specific impacts and outcomes in mind. These may involve the facilitation of social interaction, the achievement of political goals, or a range of other objectives. Certainly, when event organisers take part in the bidding process to secure a major or mega event, a key consideration is the anticipated event outcomes which include the short and medium-term impacts and the longer-term legacies.

Explain the short, medium, and long-term impacts on a city of being able to host the Commonwealth Games. To what extent do you think those impacts and legacies can be ensured through systematic and well-thought-out event design?

Regardless of the initial intention, the impacts of events may be positive or negative and while it is generally the economic, commercial and tourism impacts that are the source of most concern and analysis, they also include:

■ Socio-cultural impacts

■ Political impacts

■ Psychological impacts

■ Environmental and physical impacts.

Event design plays a key role in influencing these outcomes. In a way, event design is like a book, with a beginning and a middle and finally, an end, that is, the event outcomes. In the same way that event design can facilitate the magic that makes an event fun, engaging, stimulating or even surprising, it can also facilitate event impacts that are memorable and event outcomes that are constructive and positive.

Summary

Event design is a core function of event management with the potential to greatly enhance the impact of planned events. The emerging emphasis on transformational events coincides with a change in focus toward the design of events that provide life-changing experiences and reimagine approaches to event sustainability. Four frameworks are described that influence experience design. The extended framework by Pine and Gilmore (2011) brings the transformational elements together and can help event mangers design transformative and immersive experiences.

Events need to be designed in a manner that is consistent with the event theme and the overall event concept, and should by supported by all elements of the event including catering, location, venue, decorations, and overall ambiance. Another approach to supporting the theme is through sensory experiences focusing on sight, sound, taste, touch, and smell.

Event design generally occurs with specific impacts and outcomes in mind. A key element in event design is managing sustainability. When event organisers seek to secure a major or mega event, a key consideration in the bidding process is the anticipated event outcomes. These outcomes include economic, socio-cultural, and environmental impacts, in the short, medium, and long term. Additional outcomes relate to sustainability and include positive environmental and social outcomes for communities. Hence, as well as facilitating event impacts that are memorable, event design can also generate outcomes that are constructive and positive.

Industry profile: Kate Stewart, EBC Advisory

Kate is a hospitality and event expert with a passion for delivering memorable experiences. Founder of businesses including Bright Young Things catering and En Pointe Events, Kate currently consults via her business, EBC Advisory (Every Bit Counts).

Image 3.2: Supplied by Kate Stewart of EBC Advisory. Taken by Hikari Photography

Kate believes that the power of enlightened hospitality can help businesses stand out and stand the test of time. She shares her experience creating, growing and advising businesses through this hospitality lens, ultimately helping organisations define their purpose and deliver strategic events and experiences, with a little bit of magic – for all.

"Business, like life, is all about how you make people feel" – Danny Meyer, Shakeshack CEO, entrepreneur & author

Through her businesses, Kate has spent eight years working with the Melbourne Food & Wine Festival, first as a caterer supporting some of the world's best chefs and, over the past four years, as a design partner for the World's Longest Lunch and their Hub. The 2018 festival work resulted in selection as a finalist at two Australia-wide design awards. She has influenced the catering sector in Australia, revolutionised what healthy menus can look like and is leading the way in more sustainable event solutions and innovative business practices.

Business skills:

- Event experience design management
- Operations Management
- Catering – from conceptualisation to implementation
- Customer relations & marketing
- Hospitality management
- Sustainability in events.

How do you assist clients in event design?

I work with my clients to tease out what the best event strategy and customer experience can look like. I help businesses connect their goals with what is happening at a grass root level; inspire them so they can spend their money in meaningful ways and align their goals with sustainable solutions. There is often an educational component attached to my advice. I make sure I understand the demographics and client needs, so I am considerate of what I am actually planning.

Can you give an example of how COVID changed the way you run your events?

I normally work on a lunch event for a reputable university each year. Due to the pandemic, it shifted to an online format. I made sure to create an online experience that enabled smaller group discussions after the guest speakers had presented. By creating smaller breakout rooms and designating hosts to each room, we helped guests connect, feel comfortable to share their thoughts and engage. The online format provided safety for some audiences as they felt more comfortable to share questions via the chat function too.

Together with my partners we were pleasantly surprised by the positive outcomes of this event shifting to a virtual context. We were able to connect with a wider alumni audience across Australia – and some international alumni – rather than just those in Melbourne. We invited wonderful speakers from different cities such as Mumbai and Singapore. There was a real power in that experience. We have been able to test new ways of building connections. We are now looking at how we can move forward – reconnecting with physical events but continuing to use the opportunities that the digital world provides – and exploring what hybrid events might look like.

What skills and attributes are required in a COVID or post COVID world?

We are seeing more focus on risk management and Occupational Health and Safety procedures especially as we move into a COVID 'normal' world. Our top priority as event managers is to make people feel safe and comfortable. Event managers (EMs) need to be multi-skilled and creative.

- Make sure you know all the processes (there's no take two in events!)
- Make sure you consider your audience and how they might feel.
- Look at how things were before and know that expectations have shifted (i.e. check-in procedures, hygiene standards, sanitisation, event communications).
- Safety is everyone's obligation. We must provide a space that is safe for everyone.

I'm such a passionate believer of experience, but if it's not safe it's not on. Good EMs need to be able to look at the big picture and zoom in on the detail. Be cool headed when unexpected scenarios evolve, as they inevitably do! Be able to think creatively, manage the paperwork and be comfortable with being hands on and leading by example. Take the chance to gain as much experience as you can, as with every event, location and different group of guests, suppliers and stakeholders you can learn.

How are events being reimagined in the current world?

Events should be about joy and creating memorable moments for people. Whatever you're doing make it worthy of your audience – make them feel special. Events are an opportunity for vibrancy – be it through colour, entertainment or menu design. A sense of magic. That's how memories are made.

Some online events have been able to reach large audiences. For example, a lot of start-up pitch nights have gone online and been able to tap into a wider community in that digital format rather than be limited by venue capacities, budgets and people's locations. I think clients will consider whether they need to go back to an in-person 500-person lunch (for example) and interrogate what their events calendar may look like and how to best engage their audiences and reach their goals. COVID has created opportunities as people have been forced to innovate, adapt to technology and reshape how they connect. As such, we'll see a reset as to how events are managed moving forward. I also think that we're just at the precipice of what's possible with digital events. Successful digital events need extensive planning and consideration – just like physical events. Their duration, programming and format needs to be reshaped as people behave and respond differently to a virtual event. I think technological advances and further research will aid us and create greater possibilities for how we utilise these platforms for powerful storytelling and events.

Events will continue to evolve – and how lucky we are to work in such an inspiring, vibrant industry filled with talented, resourceful people and businesses.

Research questions

1. Explain how systematic efforts in event design can contribute to positive event experiences for event attendees.

2. Utilising the extended experience economy model by Pine and Gilmore's (2011) apply a combination of quadrants (educational, escapist, esthetic, entertainment) to events you have experienced.

3. Many events have an historical theme. How would you design the various elements of a birthday party to support a medieval theme?

4. Some events have a cultural or national theme. How would you utilise the 5 senses to support a cultural exhibition held at your local museum?

5. Watch the video on the 2021 ANZAC Day Dawn service on YouTube and identify the key elements that capture the type of experience. Given the COVID restrictions, how did the event try to capture the magic?

   https://youtu.be/v96z4vHXoH4

6. Utilising one of the experience design frameworks, design an event of your choice and interpret how each concept is applied.

Workshop activities (in pairs or small groups)

Using one of the venue directors listed above or your local one search for a venue that suits below scenario. Justify your venue choice:

Scenario A

A charity has approached you to recommend a venue for a social fundraising event. The main event objective is to bring people together for a fun and sociable evening. There will also be a silent auction to raise funds on the night. There will be music and opportunity for dance following dinner.

Task: Create a venue checklist with key requirements that will shape your event to your clients' needs, and conduct a venue inspection. Your recommendation must ensure the venue can deliver the magic and create a sensory experience. Search for venue layouts and discuss all possible sensory elements that can be included in designing the experience (sight, sound, taste, touch, smell). Upon your return update the checklist to include all key requirements. Make any adjustments to your checklist for future fundraising events.

Scenario B

You are a professional conference organiser (PCO) and a client has approached you requesting a suitable venue that can host a conference (up to 200 delegates) with three separate rooms to hold concurrent sessions. Consideration must be taken of additional accommodation needs. The conference theme is about discussing the future of events and the types of technologies that are currently being developed to facilitate future hybrid events. Delegate profiles are diverse, and all needs should be considered. Consider accommodation options, location, and access issues.

3

Task: Utilise a venue directory to search for a suitable venue that can deliver the required business event. The venue must be centrally located, easily accessible and cater for diverse needs. Recommend the venue and three accommodation options for your client.

References and further reading

Bigwood, G. (2020). The Regenerative Revolution: A new paradigm for event management. The IMEX Group. http://www.imexexhibitions.com/research (Visited 22 November 2021)

European Commission, An ambitious EU circular economy package 2015, European Union: Brussels.

Getz, D., & Page, S. J. (2016). Progress and prospects for event tourism research. *Tourism Management*, 52, 593-631.

Holmes, K., Hughes, M., Mair, J., & Carlsen, J. (2015). Events and sustainability (pp. 1-206). New York, NY: Routledge.

Jones, M (2017) *Sustainable Event Management: A practical guide.* Oxon: Routledge

Neuhofer, B., Celuh, K., &To (2020). Experience design and the dimensions of transformative festival experiences. *International Journal of Contemporary Hospitality Management*, 32(9), 2881-2901.

Orefice, C. (2018). Designing for events – a new perspective on event design, *International Journal of Event and Festival Management*, 9(1), 20-33

Pine, B. J., & Gilmore, J. H. (2011). *The Experience Economy.* Harvard Business Press.

Reed, B. (2007). Shifting from 'sustainability'to regeneration. Building Research & Information, 35(6), 674-680.

Robertson, M., Hutton, A., & Brown, S. (2018). Event design in outdoor music festival audience behavior (a critical transformative research note). *Event Management*, 22(6), 1073-1081.

Seligman, M. E. P. (2011). *Flourish*. New York, NY: Simon & Schuster.

Sheldon, P. J. (2020). Designing tourism experiences for inner transformation. *Annals of Tourism Research*, 83, 102935.

Steriopoulos, E., & Wrathall, J. (2021). Re-imagining and transforming events: Insights from the Australian events industry. *Research in Hospitality Management*, 11(2), 77-83. https://doi.org/10.1080/22243534.2021.1917809

Websites

www.nationalgeographic.org/activity/three-rs-framework/
businesseventsvictoria.com/
www.socialtables.com/blog/event-planning/site-visit-checklist/
www.eventmanagerblog.com
www.exdsummit.com/
ebcadvisory.co/
ebcadvisory.co/case-studies/so-frenchy-so-chic-reimagined/
eventsair.com
eventsair.com/onair/
ww.miro.com
www.eventbrite.com.au/blog/beautiful-event-design-ds00/
www.venuedirectory.com/
www.zerowastecenter.org/the-6-rs-of-sustainability-refuse-blog-3-7/17842/

Videos

youtu.be/czFr_kJCdKQ
youtu.be/CtAoq8mgFME
flippingthetin.buzzsprout.com/1735191/8624796-why-go-insights-into-attendee-motivation

4 Project management and logistics

Learning objectives

On completion of this chapter, you will be able to:

➤ Recognise the key benefits of utilising a project management framework in an events context

➤ Apply relevant project management concepts, principles and techniques to the planning and implementation of events

➤ Explain the key benefits associated with event logistics concepts and principles

➤ Apply relevant event logistics concepts and principles to the conduct of specific and general types of events

➤ Communicate the role and importance of logistical operational considerations.

Project management perspectives

Project management concepts, principles and techniques are commonly used for the completion of an extremely broad range of projects including roads, bridges, buildings, software packages and events. In the management of planned events the same principles apply. Even events held on a regular basis will be complex, given the broad range of uncertainties that exist, as well as the differences from one year to the next in terms of stakeholder activities, attendees' behaviours, marketing requirements, and a broad range of other contingencies. Hence, events will benefit from the application of a project management approach. Furthermore, events critically depend on progress that is made with careful planning and preparation prior to the actual staging of the event.

Accordingly, project management has become an essential element in the event manager's toolkit.

■ Project management provides a **methodological approach** to event management. In this way the event considers these factors;

Figure 4.1: Key factors to consider in project management

The first three of these factors, money, time, and quality are often referred to as the Triple Constraint or the Iron Triangle and have become a central concept in project management research and practice. They also represent *trade-offs* that the project manager can manipulate and utilise.

Consider this: What trade-offs exist in your local community event?

■ **Expandability** meaning that project management techniques can be used just as effectively on small or large events, or even on isolated parts of an event which can be regarded as stand-alone projects.

What elements of an event could be regarded as a stand-alone project?

■ As a **body of knowledge**, project management has been applied to a diverse range of large and small projects. As the scope and range of projects, including events, broadens, so too does the set of techniques, principles, and concepts that can be utilised. This has led to development of a standard system known as PMBOK (Project Management Body of Knowledge). Particularly for large, complex events, the event industry clearly benefits from the adaptation and application of this body of knowledge.

■ **Effective, on-going communication** is one of the most critical aspects associated with the conduct of a successful event. Event plans, key milestones, and on-going progress, need to be clearly communicated to key stakeholders in a timely and predictable manner. By providing a common terminology, project management facilitates communication that is, in fact, clear and unambiguous.

? *What approval processes do you have to manage communication effectively?*

Running sheets

Did you know? For each event it is important to create a running sheet for all stakeholders. An event manager can have a detailed running sheet during planning and operations phases and provide a brief running sheet to the stakeholders, so expectations are clear. Below is an example of a brief running sheet for an exhibition.

4

Time	Activity	Responsibility	Notes
7.30 – 10am	Bump in begins (event set up)	EM	EM opens door and all exhibitors bump in
10 am	Doors open for the public	EM	Guests arrive
10am-4pm	Exhibition operates	All	Event in full swing
4 am– 6pm	Bump out (shut down)	All	Event finishes and bump out begins. All stakeholders need to have left by 6pm.

Table 4.1: Brief running sheet for all exhibition stakeholders

- Widespread recognition of event management as a **profession** is strongly supported by the application of systematic approaches, such as project management, and the utilisation of associated processes and procedures.

- There is often a tendency for individuals to own a particular event and dominate the way in which the event evolves and develops. Project management serves to **formalise and depersonalise** event processes and procedures, establishing on-going documentation requirements, and avoiding the risks associated with long-term event success depending on one person.

? *What would you think are the main risks associated with one person owning or dominating a particular event?*

- The document requirements associated with project management provide specific event-related information, particularly in terms of event progress, and are developed according to a standard format facilitating **accountability to stakeholders.**

■ The project management approach provides a clear framework for systematic **training** for employees and volunteers. The more long-term **development** needs of employees may also be facilitated by the project management body of knowledge.

■ Event planning seldom gets the recognition it deserves but the use of a systematic, well-documented, project planning approach to events significantly **increases the profile of event planning**, making its importance more obvious to event stakeholders.

Developing event project plans

There are a range of project management principles that can be adapted and effectively utilised as part of the event management process. These principles and their relevance to event management are discussed below.

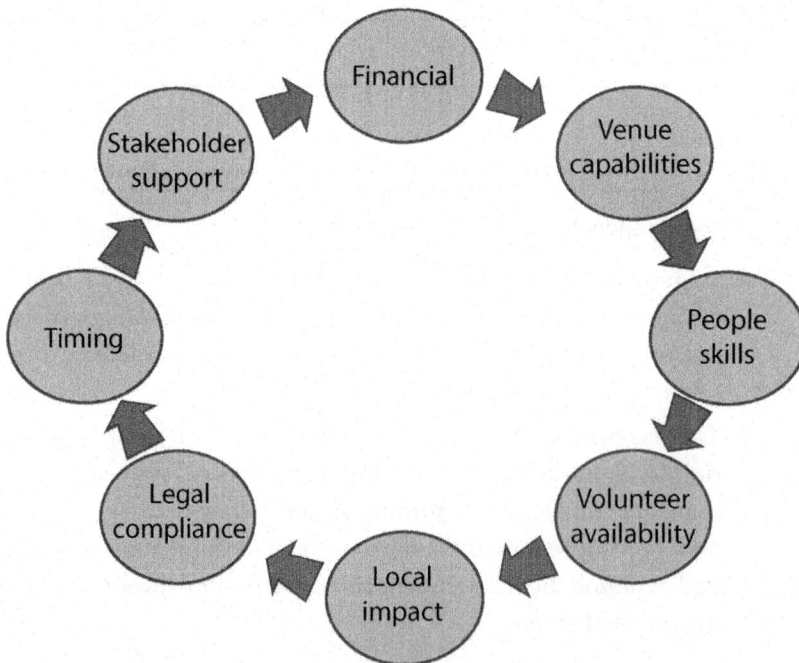

Figure 4.2: Feasibility considerations

Feasibility

Whether or not a project should proceed, or an event should be staged, gives rise to the obvious question: "Is it feasible?" A plausible answer to this question is particularly important when public sector approval is required or when external funding is sought. Relevant considerations from an events perspective include those in Figure 4.2.

Setting the project parameters

Salama (2021) discusses the traditional scope of project management as setting the parameters of the event to consider these critical factors:

- Time Frame
- Resources
- Budget
- Quality
- People
- Equipment
- Environment
- Corporate Social Responsibility (CSR) related factors

Particularly in terms of time and cost, limits to the parameters and scope must be clearly defined. Lack of attention in this regard may affect the parameters of the project and lead to scope creep. Scope creep takes place when the work required in staging the event, gradually expands, leading to project delays and budget issues.

Can you think of some examples of scope creep in an event context?

Work breakdown structure

Development of a work breakdown structure (WBS) can facilitate the analysis of work involved in the conduct of an event and support the task of defining its scope. As well as identifying what work is required it also provides a clear indication of what work is outside the scope of the event. The WBS also breaks up complex projects into smaller, more manageable, and easily identifiable tasks or units of work. Categorisation of tasks may be based on functions such as finance, administration, and so on. In this way, it can be used to clearly separate responsibilities and form a **work package** for a particular department, contractor, or organisational unit.

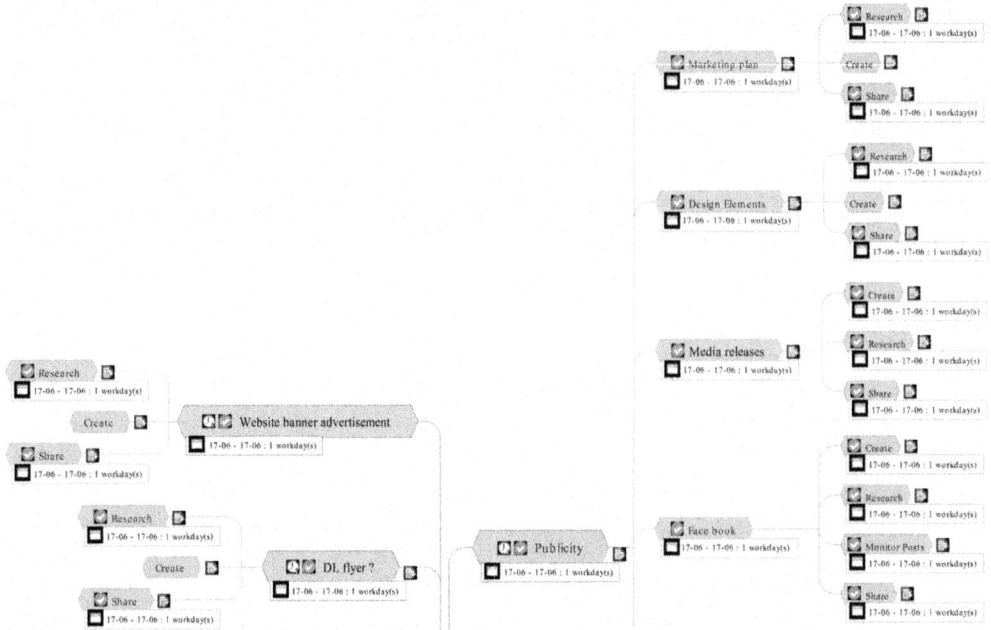

Figure 4.3: Sample WBS for marketing activities using mind map software.

Social media promotion	5 weeks out	4 weeks out	3 weeks out	2 weeks out	1 week out	Event day
Email campaign	✓			✓		
Facebook	✓	✓	✓	✓	✓	✓
Twitter		✓	✓	✓	✓	✓
Instagram			✓	✓	✓	✓
Monitoring engagement	✓	✓	✓	✓	✓	✓

Table 4.2: Scheduling promotional activities using Excel

Did you know? A well planned WBS helps event planners manage critical timelines and accountability. If there are task delays, the WBS shows who is responsible for each task and therefore planners can communicate any issues accordingly. There are various technologies that help create timelines. A simple linear WBS can be developed in *Excel* spreadsheet or as a visual, utilising mind map software.

Case study 4.1: Fyre festival

The Fyre festival, a party which was set in the Bahamas, was a logistical nightmare from the start, all due lack of planning. As the organisers did not prioritise logistics, the event led to numerous failures which resulted in hefty fines and imprisonment for the organiser. Read the case study and examine the key logistical issues that were ignored at:
   www.allynintl.com/en/news-publications/entry/logistical-fails-of-fyre-festival

Developing a communication plan

4

Research undertaken by Steriopoulos and Wrathall (2021) demonstrated the importance of communication in event planning. Accordingly, developing a communication plan (CP) is critical for event success. According to Salama (2021) the key elements of a CP include:

- **The aim of the CP**: why is it important to develop one?
- **Key stakeholders**: Who will the CP be directed to?
- **Frequency**: How often will reporting happen?
- **Channels**: What communication channels will be used for reporting? (virtual meetings, follow up emails, phone calls, social media etc).

Consider this: As the event gets closer, increase the communications and reporting tasks from monthly to weekly to daily.

Consider this: Develop a communication template which can be used and adjusted for each event type.

The five phases of project management

Projects go through five formal stages or phases and although the length and other details associated with each phase varies from project to project, the same basic framework applies. According to the Project Management Body of Knowledge, the five phases, followed either in succession until project completion or iteratively with the stages repeating in short bursts until satisfactory project completion has been achieved, are explained below.

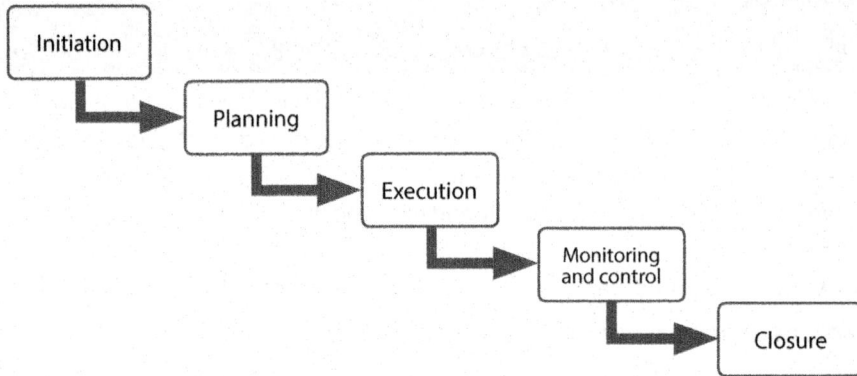

Figure 4.4: Phases of project management

- ■ **Initiation**, which generally involves:
  - ☐ The formation of a project team with roles and responsibilities assigned to team members;
  - ☐ Clarification of project goals and communication of expectations amongst the project team;
  - ☐ Stakeholder analysis ensuring that all key players are identified and given due consideration;
  - ☐ An examination of feasibility prior to commencement of detailed planning;
  - ☐ A formal meeting to commence the project.
- ■ **Planning**, which for major and mega events involves a substantial period of time. It generally involves:
  - ☐ Establishing the project scope;
  - ☐ Creating a plan for engagement of, and communication with, stakeholders;
  - ☐ Development of a Work Breakdown Structure (WBS);
  - ☐ Assessment and analysis of risk and development of mitigation plans;
  - ☐ Identification of resource requirements;
  - ☐ Development of schedules, Gantt charts, etc.;
  - ☐ Identification of project dependencies and resource constraints;
  - ☐ Utilisation of Gantt charts and other project management tools and packages to identify a critical path.

Why is it important to establish the project scope?

- **Execution**, which generally involves:
  - ☐ Carrying out work requirements (or staging the event) in accordance with the project definition and scope;
  - ☐ Maintaining high levels of communication to ensure clear direction;
  - ☐ The 'moment of truth' when the quality and rigour of the planning process, and of the people involved in staging the event, are tested.

In an event context, what do you think is meant by 'the moment of truth'?

- **Monitoring and control**, which needs to reflect the reality that if things go wrong, they may go wrong quickly and unexpectedly. It involves:
  - ☐ Adherence to communication plan;
  - ☐ Measuring performance against expectations and monitoring activities against the critical path;
  - ☐ Taking corrective action when necessary;
  - ☐ Monitoring and controlling budget and resource use;
  - ☐ Monitoring and mitigating risks.
- **Closure**, which generally involves:
  - ☐ Delivery of the project;
  - ☐ Evaluation and review of lessons learned;
  - ☐ Development of plans for continuous improvement;
  - ☐ Adjournment of the project team;
  - ☐ Clean up.

What are some key risks associated with staging a local fun run event?

Event logistics

Event logistics may be described as the planning, implementing and controlling of all of the transport, supply, storage, communication and other flow activities that facilitate the achievement of a positive and memorable event experience for event attendees. The importance of logistics to a range of projects including events, is undeniable. While other aspects of an event, including its popularity and its broad social, community, and cultural impact may seem more compelling, logistical considerations may have a profound impact on the extent to which staging the event turns out to be feasible and realistic.

What aspects of event logistics would you regard as being the most important in terms of positive event outcomes?

In fact, event logistics, and logistics generally, often go unnoticed. And it's when logistics goes unnoticed that you know it's been successful. It's when something goes wrong, that most people really notice logistical issues and develop an awareness of their importance. At the same time, well thought out and well managed event logistics can significantly enhance the event experience of attendees.

While many of the basic principles remain, several of the key elements of event logistics have changed significantly over recent years, partly as a result of changing technology and partly due to the impact of the pandemic. Traditionally, the most critical concerns of event logistics included:

- **The venue**, particularly in terms of its location and capacity, whether the venue is indoor, outdoor or a combination, and security considerations.
- **The transportation** of supplies and equipment, as well as customers, performers, and VIPs, to, around and from the venue.
- **The provision of hospitality and catering**, which generally differs depending on whether the food and beverage (F&B) services are managed in-house or contracted out to one or more external caterers.
- **The provision of event technology**, particularly audio, presentation and registration technology.
- **The supply of event merchandise**, souvenirs, giveaways, and perhaps on-site food stalls.

Recent transitions toward online and hybrid strategies have impacted substantially on the relative importance of all of the above elements. While, for example, online events may have far less to do with venue, physical transport, traditional hospitality and catering, or event merchandise, considerations about event technology have become paramount. At the same time, while virtual events have become far more commonplace in recent years they are, by no means, a new phenomenon.

Considerations of venue, transport, hospitality and catering, and merchandise take on a totally different focus with hybrid events. However, they remain incredibly important considerations. It may be useful to examine each of the key concerns of event logistics in terms of traditional face-to-face, virtual and hybrid approaches.

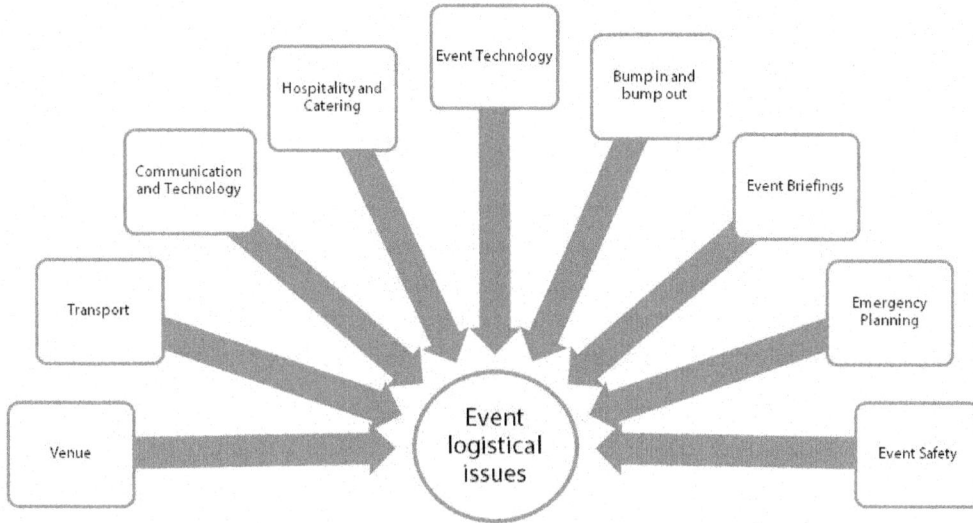

Figure 4.5: Event logistics

Venue

For traditional face-to-face events the selection of an appropriate venue is a critical determinant of positive event outcomes. Given current and emerging concerns about event sustainability, location is an important consideration. Every effort must be made to avoid the need for attendees and other participants to use private vehicle transport. If possible, venues that are close to public transport, and that provide better opportunities for active transport (ie. walking, cycling, etc.) should be selected. Appropriate information, including public transport timetables, as well as information about active transport options, should be provided. In addition to making the event more environmentally friendly, the provision of this type of information has a positive marketing impact. While adequate parking for private vehicles has been a traditional concern, the focus needs to change. Car parking can be minimised, perhaps in favour of the provision of space for bicycle parking.

The capacity of the venue should adequately accommodate but not greatly exceed the anticipated number of attendees. Hence, a reasonably accurate estimate of the likely number of customers needs to be established. That may be based on previous levels of attendance, the extent to which customers have expressed an interest, or comparisons with other similar events.

? *Can you think of any other approaches to forecasting event attendance?*
For a business conference?
For a sporting event?
For an outdoor music festival?

Reliable estimates of event attendance are important for financial and marketing purposes, as well as operational. For indoor events, a reasonably accurate estimate of event attendance is particularly important from an operational perspective. And while it is less important for outdoor events, efforts should be made to establish reasonably reliable forecasts.

Another important concern relates to security and emergency procedures that focus on the protection of assets, the health and safety of participants, the maintenance of control, and the avoidance of disorder. In terms of cash resources, ticket sales at the gate can be a particular concern. The exchange of relatively large amounts of cash may also occur prior to and during the event as a result of catering operations and the sale of merchandise. Following the staging of an event, the temptation to unwind and relax may heighten the potential for cash or expensive equipment to go missing.

In the current environment and in the foreseeable future, venues are likely to adopt and maintain a range of procedures that minimise the possible transmission of infections. These event specific interventions may include:

■ The wearing of face masks

■ The use of barriers

■ Hand hygiene

■ Distancing measures

■ Improved ventilation

■ Structuring attendees into social bubbles or cohorts

For virtual events, venue considerations relate primarily to the needs of the event product and associated requirements, in terms of the performance for music events, the competition for sporting events, or the presentations for business events. For several events, including sporting, this has meant that the venue remains unchanged, but the competition or performance takes place in an empty venue or stadium. However, concerns about venue capacity, anticipated numbers, and security issues are going to be far less relevant. Key concerns relate to making the event experience as real and memorable as possible despite the absence of a physical crowd.

For a sporting event with a virtual audience, can you think of any strategies that can be applied to ensure that the event experience doesn't suffer due to the absence of spectators at the physical venue?

Hybrid event requirements may be similar to face-to-face events but on a different scale. This is likely to make interventions aimed at minimising the possible transmission of infections easier and less problematic. A different, smaller venue may be selected depending on the number of attendees at the physical venue. Security issues are still relevant but perhaps less problematic as a result of lower levels of attendance. Considerations about location and sustainability issues will also still apply.

4

Transport

For traditional face-to-face events, transport is requited for supplies and equipment that are not transported to the site by event suppliers. Transport is also required to move customers, performers, and VIPs, to and from the venue. For outdoor venues, transport around the venue may also be an important consideration.

Environmental sustainability and hence, the need to minimise the use of petrol vehicles, perhaps utilise electric vehicles, and minimise distances travelled, are all important concerns at face-to-face and hybrid events. Given a greatly reduced need for any form of transport for virtual events, environmental sustainability as well as reduced transport cost become key benefits.

Can you think of any other benefits of virtual events when compared with face-to-face and hybrid events?

Event merchandise

A broad range of merchandise, souvenirs, giveaways, and on-site food stalls are often a key feature and an important logistics concern for face-to-face and hybrid events. For virtual events, online transactions may replace physical transactions.

In summary, while approaches to event logistics have changed as a result of the pandemic, as well as the emergence of new technologies to support virtual and hybrid events, the importance of event logistics to the successful planning and staging of events, remains undeniable.

Case study 4.2: Glastonbury music festival

The Glastonbury festival, spreading across a 900 acre site, is the largest greenfield music festival in the world, with up to 203,000 in attendance in 2019. In 2020 the festival reached its 50th birthday but the COVID restrictions did not allow for a festival celebration. In 2021 the festival was delivered virtually. Its success creates over 1000 jobs in the community, however this comes with an increase in logistical considerations that required ongoing management and monitoring. These include:

- Increased number of staff and volunteers;
- Number of market stalls;
- Increased infrastructure;
- Minimise impact to the environment.

An example of the key logistics to operate Glastonbury include:

- The length of the fence;
- Number of security people, volunteers, stewards;
- Number of loos, showers, sewerage waste;
- Number of rubbish bins;
- Waste recycling.
- Composting

For more visit **https://www.glastonburyfestivals.co.uk/**

Hospitality and catering

A key event logistics issue involves the set-up, service and clean-up associated with the catering process. A key issue with regard to catering and the provision of F&B service is whether it will be managed in-house or contracted out to an external caterer or caterers. Other issues include:

- The extent to which it is a central feature of the event and whether or not alcohol is included
- The number of staff and scale of resources required
- Sustainability issues, particularly in terms of food wastage
- Minimising possible transmission of infections
- Minimising other risks including contamination of food

At face-to-face and hybrid events these are all key concerns. At virtual events, F&B services won't be provided, and the key problem becomes how to make up for the absence of F&B in terms of the event experience.

? *Can you think of any creative ways in which an alternative to the normal F&B service can be utilised for a virtual event?*

In view of the fact that food is central to many events and, in fact, represents a particular important element at cultural festivals and events, the inability to provide normal F&B services at virtual events is a key issue that needs to be considered.

Event technology

A range of technologies have been developed to assist the event management process and enhance the event experience. However, for the planning and staging of virtual and hybrid events, the utilisation of a broad range of technologies becomes a paramount concern. Key types of technology include:

- Customer friendly, **event registration** technology that is seamless and secure and allows attendees to register and pay for the event.
- A dedicated **virtual event website** that engages customers, provides up-to-date information, and seeks to make the virtual experience a little more tangible.
- Reliable **WiFi**.
- **Webinar or video streaming** platforms such as Zoom.
- Software that allows for **live streaming** for part or all of the event.
- **Digital video camera** and other equipment for capturing key elements of the event.
- Event **planning and marketing software.**
- Perhaps a **virtual reality camera** and associated equipment to provide the WOW factor and enhance the virtual event experience.

Did you know? Visio is an effective technology tool to assist planners when thinking and negotiating venue layouts. Visio is useful for all types of events (weddings, product launches) but also used for exhibitions, festivals and other major events where logistics are involved. Event planners can design layouts and communicate positions of exhibitors and include in visitor maps. Visit Microsoft Visio to explore the floorplan feature or watch a simple video on how to drag and drop elements to develop your event floorplan design. https://youtu.be/jXX9Pbfy3YI

Communication and technology

Developing communication plans as part of logistics is an essential part of any event plan throughout all phases of event management. The use of technologies has made communication alot easier in recent years especially with the use of social media.

During pre-event stage, communication strategies may include specific messages to stakeholders to keep them informed. Examples include marketing strategies, key messages, sponsor alerts etc. The key elements of a communication plan may include and not limited to:

- Who the message is directed to:
- Key message
- Preferred medium
- Frequency of message

Organising monthly or weekly meetings including agenda items and follow up reports ensures your relationship with stakeholders is managed and any ideas can be examined in relation to possible logistics.

Consider this: Client communication is key in securing a successful event. In your role as a wedding planner, how often should you maintain communication with your bride and groom leading up to their special day?

During the event teams may wish to adopt social media to maintain communication throughout the event. Examples include WhatsApp, messenger or related social media. The key consideration is for the whole team to be on the same platform to ensure any logistical issue can be dealt with immediately.

In post event phases, communication strategies can be reflected upon in terms of general improvement. As a team develop effective communication plans for future planning.

What communication channels do you use for corporate communication? Given recent advances in technology, what additional communication options do you use for client communication?

Developing emergency and safety plans for crowds

Different types of events require different types of emergency planning and often event security companies are hired as external contractors. It is advisable to consider event security companies as a primary stakeholder and work closely with them as key partners in ensuring patron safety. The key elements in an event safety plan include:

■ Strategies for effective crowd control (marshalling, managing entry and exit points)

■ Managing vehicle traffic

■ Cash handling

■ The use of alcohol or drugs

■ The number of staff required to assist with evacuation procedures

As each event venue has its own evacuation plan it is important for event managers to be aware of these plans and include them in event briefings. Educating all stakeholders on safety and emergency procedures allows managers to effectively manage crowds. More on crowd behaviour can be found in Chapter 7.

Bump in, bump out and event briefings

Bump in and bump out refer to the set up and shut down of the event. Often there is limited time in between events for bump in/out and therefore this presents a logistical issue. The timings for bump in and bump out need to be included in running sheets and plenty of time should also be given for final event briefings.

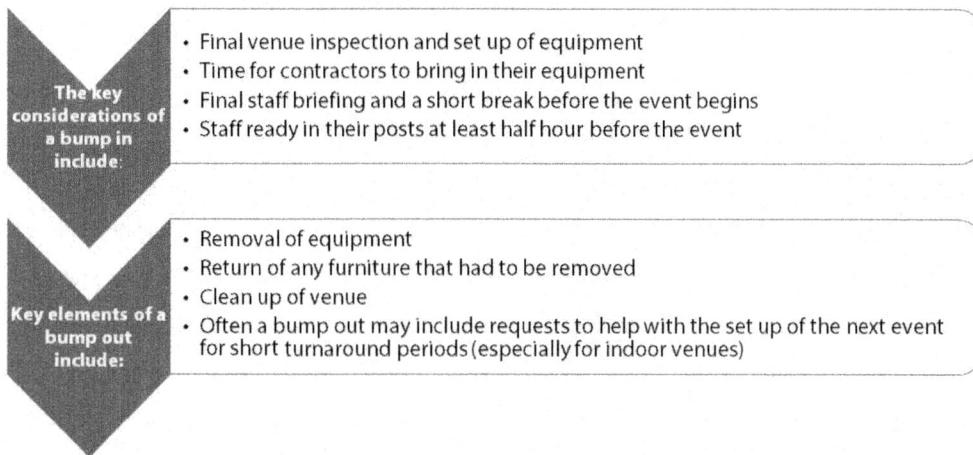

The key considerations of a bump in include:
- Final venue inspection and set up of equipment
- Time for contractors to bring in their equipment
- Final staff briefing and a short break before the event begins
- Staff ready in their posts at least half hour before the event

Key elements of a bump out include:
- Removal of equipment
- Return of any furniture that had to be removed
- Clean up of venue
- Often a bump out may include requests to help with the set up of the next event for short turnaround periods (especially for indoor venues)

Figure 4.6: Bump in and bump out responsibilities

Where possible bump out takes place immediately after an event. This is due to possible future bookings which require event managers to clean the site or venue before the next event. Major events may require days of cleaning and this is normal. Volunteers can also be used for event clean-ups, especially at festivals where they tend to be rewarded with free entry tickets. Similarly with clean up, event debriefs form part of the event process of finalising thoughts and event successes or failures. Often event de-briefs get postponed or neglected due to potential burnouts. However, it's key to conduct event debriefs with all stakeholders and report on key reflections which will help with the future planning of events.

Case study 4.3: World Vegan Day

World Vegan Day is an annual festival that is promoted around the world on the first day of November. There are various activities that take place to celebrate healthy living and promote a sustainable environment. The festival attracts many stall holders and activities all around the world. It is therefore important for each stall holder to know the exact set up location. Here is a sample of a detailed bump in running sheet for a World Vegan Day event.

Image 4.1: © Garth Lategan, The Event Network Australia

Table 4.3: Bump in Running Sheet Friday 18th October 2019

Date	Time	Task	Area
18/10/19	08:00-12:00	Tread & Pedals	Grand Pavilion Stall 121
18/10/19	08:00-12:00	Those Girls Beverage Co.	Grand Pavilion Stall 127
18/10/19	08:00-12:00	Bailey Beau Pty Ltd	Grand Pavilion Stall 160
18/10/19	08:00-12:00	Phils Original	Grand Pavilion Stall 179
18/10/19	08:00-12:00	VegVic	Ancestry Stall 2
18/10/19	08:00-12:00	Paleo Zone	Ancestry Stall 5

18/10/19	08:00-12:00	Grateful Harvest Activities	Ancestry Stall 6
18/10/19	08:00-12:00	Happy Happy Poo	Ancestry Stall 7
18/10/19	08:00-12:00	doTERRA	Ancestry Stall 9
18/10/19	08:00-12:00	Botanical Spritzer	Ancestry Stall 12
18/10/19	08:00-12:00	Grateful Harvest	Ancestry Stall 13
18/10/19	11:30-12:15	Roshni lunch break	
18/10/19	12:00-15:00	Remedy Kombucha arriving in fridge to be signed for (20 cases of 330ml)	
18/10/19	12:00-17:00	Forklift items for Pana Chocolate	Ancestry
18/10/19	12:00-17:00	Forklift items for Loving Earth	
18/10/19	12:00-17:00	Forklift items for BSKT	
18/10/19	12:00-17:00	Forklift items for Paleo Pure	
18/10/19	12:00-17:00	Forklift items for PRANA ON	
18/10/19	12:00-17:00	Forklift items for The Vege Chip Company	
18/10/19	12:00-17:00	Amaroo Wildlife Shelter & Project Triceratops	Grand Pavilion Stall 2
18/10/19	12:00-17:00	Lord of the Fries	Grand Pavilion Stall 20
18/10/19	12:00-17:00	Twistto Pty Ltd	Grand Pavilion Stall 65
18/10/19	12:00-17:00	Adorn Cosmetics	Grand Pavilion Stall 89
18/10/19	12:00-17:00	PRANA ON	Grand Pavilion Stall 99
18/10/19	12:00-17:00	Heart of Chocolate	Grand Pavilion Stall 104
18/10/19	12:00-17:00	BSKT	Grand Pavilion Stall 108
18/10/19	12:00-17:00	Orgone effects Australia	Grand Pavilion Stall 111
18/10/19	12:00-17:00	banting food co	Grand Pavilion Stall 128
18/10/19	12:00-17:00	St.Gerry's	Grand Pavilion Stall 130
18/10/19	12:00-17:00	Paleo Pure	Grand Pavilion Stall 130
18/10/19	12:00-17:00	Loving Earth	Grand Pavilion Stall 131
18/10/19	12:00-17:00	Get Ya Yum On	Grand Pavilion Stall 133
18/10/19	12:00-17:00	Tupperware	Grand Pavilion Stall 134

4

Crowd control

Crowd control is a necessary function not only in times of emergency but also for the entry and exit of large crowds. However, it is generally more important during the exit of crowds, because during shutdown:

- Most crowds leave all at once.
- Consumption of alcohol during the event may increase the probability of behavioural problems.
- Sections of the crowd may want to stay and 'party on'.
- Crowds tend to be in more of a hurry when leaving an event, and frustration and anger may be more of a problem.

What risks may be associated with the management of crowds?

Successful online events

Running online events come with many logistical issues. These begin with possible technology failures and also include issues during event execution. To ensure your online event is successful ensure the following:

- Your event goals are clear;
- Limit breakout rooms to a reasonable number of delegates;
- Have enough staff to allocate one as host in each virtual breakout room;
- There is technical support available;
- Request presentations beforehand in case presenters have technical issues;
- Test the online platform beforehand;
- Any issue can be communicated during the event immediately;
- Manage the online time efficiently; start and finish on time to avoid unexpected technical costs;
- Limit the virtual event experience to no more than 3-4 hours to avoid online fatigue;
- Keep each session to no more than one hour;
- Allow 5-10 minutes for delegates to move into other sessions;
- Provide online instructions to your presenters and delegates prior to event including training videos and a phone number for issues.

Summary

Over recent decades, the growth in the number, size and complexity of events has led to a greater need for more systematic approaches to the management of events. While it may be argued that event management is more of an art than a science and imagination rather than systematic planning is what leads to the successful staging of events, there no reason to believe that an organised, structured, and systematic approach reduces the level of creativity and imagination. In fact, getting rid of the clutter and chaos that goes with lack of organisation may be conducive to greater levels of creative thinking. The key potential benefits associated with the application of a project management approach include:

■ The provision of a systematic approach to event management;

■ Scalability;

■ Establishment of a rich and practical body of knowledge;

■ Facilitation of clear communication with all internal and external stakeholders;

■ The professionalisation of event management;

■ Formalising and depersonalising the event management process;

■ Ensuring accountability to stakeholders;

■ A framework for training and development;

■ Increasing the profile of event planning.

Some project management principles are directly relevant to events management. These include:

■ Feasibility;

■ Scope and the avoidance of scope creep;

■ Work Breakdown Structures;

■ Stakeholder analysis;

■ Milestones and deliverables;

■ Risk management.

There are five phases of event management. These are initiation, planning, implementation, the event itself, and closure. The application of relevant project management principles, practices, and techniques at each of these stages can help to ensure that events are run on time, within budget, according to specifications, and in a manner that meets stakeholder expectations.

Event logistics may be regarded as the essence of a well organised and successful event. Key issues associated with event logistics include the event venue and whether it is an indoor or outdoor venue. Other important logistical issues include: the movement of customers to, from, and around the event venue; the movement, accommodation and care of performers, artists, athletes and speakers; the movement and storage of equipment and materials; and the supply of facilities and amenities. Special attention needs to also be given to the transport, accommodation, and the care of VIP guests. Each of these groups require different catering arrangements.

Communication and information flows are vital before, during and after the event. At the event, employees and volunteers need clear direction, customers need to know what's on offer and where to go, and performers and artists need to be aware of what's happening. Other stakeholders also need to be kept informed. Security and emergency procedures are also major concerns during the set-up, staging and shutdown of an event, and require thorough planning. Finally, shutdown or bump-out presents the event logistics manager with another broad range of responsibilities.

Industry profile: Garth Lategan, The Event Network Australia (TENA)

Garth Lategan is the director of The Event Network Australia (TENA) and manages festivals such as World Vegan Day while contributing his expertise to additional music events held at various venues including night clubs. Garth's expertise ranges from utilising technology to planning events, managing all stakeholders and delivering projects within key timelines.

Following the pandemic, Garth's role pivoted to consultation and development of safety management plans for music (Esoteric) and sustainability (Looped) festivals. A key transformation included producing digital events. Some examples include: digital music festivals, trivia and bingo virtual events and online men's mental health workshops. Garth uses various technologies for his projects such as Microsoft suite and mind mapping tools. Whether running a small function or a major festival he claims the process is similar, in that there is an initial work breakdown structure (WBS) based on consultation with all stakeholders and then this is followed through to execution. Garth prides himself in managing people throughout his events and believes relationship management is an important aspect of every project manager. He makes people feel empowered and this helps retain ongoing relationships.

What key skills and attributes are required for project management and logistics?

Being flexible and adaptable to situations are important attributes of any event manager. Key skills to run festivals include:

- Communication (oral, written)
- Active listening
- Excellent organisational Skills
- Developing budget sheets
- Adopting technologies
- Understanding and managing people needs
- Collaboration
- Problem solving

What are some key challenges you face in your role and how do you overcome them?

Attracting volunteers

Major festivals depend on volunteers to be viable, and it is not always guaranteed that events will attract volunteers. For example, music festivals may be attractive as volunteers work for a high-priced ticket to the event. Other festivals require creating meaningful experiences to attract volunteers. As an example, on Vegan Day I make sure I give volunteers a sense of learning and I assign key responsibility, so they feel part of the event's success. With repeat volunteers I make sure I give them bigger authority and in some cases I allow them to run the event, so they develop expertise in stage management. Having a level of responsibility becomes an attraction to securing volunteers in future festivals.

Seasonality of festivals

As you know, festivals are seasonal. We spend a lot of time and energy training volunteers and then we lose them. Along with people we lose the intellectual property, and we need to re-train new volunteers and invest in the same resources repeatedly. This becomes a financial issue and may affect the viability of an event. Small businesses face issues when training staff in technology and this becomes a costly exercise when staff and volunteers leave, and re-training is required.

Communicating the key timelines to stakeholders

From an event manager's perspective, creating event timelines is key but communicating these timelines to all stakeholders is even more important. Sometimes people don't think that their actions have consequences and may affect the next person. For example, when producing a flyer, the graphic designer may not realise that, delaying the delivery of the design will affect the promotion and selling of the event. The designer might get precious about the detail of the flyer and hold on to the task past the due date. This however affects the critical path of the festival such as the promotion of the event and the selling timelines. The result is, we don't sell as many tickets, and this affects our cash flow. Lack of cash means there is no upfront money to pay venue deposits, as some stakeholders require them in advance.

How do you deal with unexpected situations?

I use my relationship skills and work with people. I can see where the roadblocks are and can clear the runway. I sit with them and have regular meetings; I see what the needs are so the team does not miss any deadlines. My focus becomes managing people's personalities. People may be going through personal issues but at the same time the show must go on. I mostly provide emotional support rather than technical support. Further staff have different perspectives and see the event issues differently. Sometimes volunteers or contractors lose focus of the patron experience. I then step in and voice my view so the event can continue as per the timelines.

What steps do you take to manage critical timelines?

1   I use a mind mapping software to map out the whole event by myself. This way I make sure I am across everything. I understand each job – how to do it step by step and how to complete it. From the concept development of an area to bumping out the area, I create the WBS for all areas.

2   In meetings I discuss the WBS and make any adjustments based on stakeholder consultation. Once agreed we sign off on the plan.

3   The WBS helps me carry out the event every step of the way. I can ask questions along the way and if contractors can't give me an answer, then I know they are falling behind the plan. When this happens, I sit with them so I can see where the roadblock is.

4   I work together with all stakeholders to get them up to speed. Where there are signs of lack of transparency, I deal with it straight away, so everyone is kept up to speed. It's a logical process which everyone must follow. This usually ensures timelines are met and the event becomes successful.

Discussion questions

1. Discuss the benefits of developing a WBS from an event planner's perspective.

2. Discuss the importance of allocating clear roles from initiation phase and give an example of what can go wrong where there are not clear tasks.

3. Give three examples where things can go wrong when critical timelines are not met.

4. View the Fyre festival documentary on Netflix (or read the story on https://www.allynintl.com/en/news-publications/entry/logistical-fails-of-fyre-festival). Discuss how the event organiser could have avoided key logistical mistakes with effective planning. Create a WBS starting 12 months ahead of the event day outlining all five phases of project management (initiation, planning and execution, monitor and control, close the event).

4

Workshop activities (in pairs or small groups)
Scenario A

It is four weeks until event day and your graphic designer has not delivered the event flyer to you. It is two days over the agreed delivery time and the designer texts to say there are other priorities at the office. Meanwhile you need the flyer to promote the event on all social media channels, so you can start selling tickets. Making sales is really important in this phase, as you need the cashflow to pay a deposit to the venue supplier (as this was part of the contract agreement). How can you approach the issue with the graphic designer (who is holding on to the flyer for some fine-tune detail)? Negotiate the consequences and the critical issues that will arise if you don't receive the flyer that same night.

Scenario B

You were scheduled to run a fundraising event for a charity of your choice at a venue in the city on Friday evening for 50 attendees. However, (7) days prior to the event new COVID restrictions were imposed because of an outbreak. You now need to move the event to a virtual platform. Discuss how you will move the event online and how you will deliver and manage all event elements that were included in the face-to-face event including the fundraising component.

References and further reading

Burghate, M. (2018). Work Breakdown Structure: Simplifying project management. *International Journal of Commerce and Management Studies*, 3(2), 7-11.

Creazza, A., Colicchia, C., & Dallari, F. (2015). Designing the venue logistics management operations for a World Exposition. *Production Planning & Control*, 26(7), 543-563.

Duignan, M.B. (2020). Utilising field theory to examine mega-event led development. *Event Management.* https://doi.org/10.3727/1525995 20X15894679115583.

Geraldi, J., & Soderlund, J. (2018). Project studies: What it is, where is it going. *International Journal of Project Management*, 36(1), 55-70.

Gomes, J., & Romao, M. (2016). Improving project success: A case study using benefits and project management. *Procedia Computer Science*, 100, 489-497.

Jalil, E.E.A., Liau, S.H., Ku, E.N., & Lee, K.F. (2019). Event logistics in sustainability of football matches. *International Journal of Supply Chain Management*, 8(1), 924-931.

Jinquan, Z. (2016). Special event project management and marketing: a case study of the 59th Grand Prix 2012 in Macau. *Asia Pacific Journal of Sport and Social Science*, 5(3), 187-201.

Liang, C-C., (2016). Queuing management and improving customer experience: empirical evidence regarding enjoyable queues. *Journal of Customer Marketing*, 33(4), 257-268.

Locatelli, G., & Mancini, M. (2015). Controlling the delivering of projects in mega-events: An application on EXPO 2015. *Event Management*, 18(3), 285-301.

Nadkarni, S (2019), The pre- and post-event planning roadmap for Expo 2020: Dubai's coming-out-party, *Worldwide Hospitality and Tourism Themes*, Vol. 11 No. 3, pp. 259-265. https://doi.org/10.1108/WHATT-02-2019-0009

Nunkoo, R., Ribeiro, M. A., Sunnassee, V., & Gursoy, D. (2018). Public trust in mega event planning institutions: The role of knowledge, transparency and corruption. *Tourism Management*, 66, 155-166.

Salama, M., & Raffaelli, Y. (2021). *Event Management: A sustainable project management perspective.* Goodfellow: Oxford

Sox, C. B., Sox, M. M., & Campbell, J. M. (2020). Giving light to mega-event planning: residents' perceptions on total eclipse weekend. *International Journal of Event and Festival Management.*

Zerjav, V. (2021). Why do business organizations participate in projects? Toward a typology of project value domains. *Project Management Journal*, 52(3), 287-297.

Websites

www.allynintl.com/en/news-publications/entry/logistical-fails-of-fyre-festival

www.glastonburyfestivals.co.uk/

www.theeventnetwork.com.au

www.seasidescavenge.org/

www.mindmanager.com/

https://cscmp.org/

https://sapartners.com/glastonbury-festival-lean-operations-management-challenge/

Videos

youtu.be/jXX9Pbfy3YI Creating a Basic Floor Plan in Microsoft Visio 2019

youtu.be/vaAhJW7pNzw Fyre Festival: The World's Most Infamous Music Festival - 4 Years Later (Documentary)

4

5 Event budgeting and financial health

Learning objectives

On completion of this chapter, you will be able to:

➤ Appreciate the importance of budgets and explain the budgeting process in an event management context.

➤ Explain the influence of cash flow considerations and identify key strategies for addressing cash flow problems.

➤ Identify and explain the key considerations associated with the development and application of income strategies.

➤ Explain how financial statements and financial ratios can be utilized in an events context.

➤ Recognise the benefits of financial analysis and explain its application to financial decision making.

➤ Understand the concept of financial health and the key determinants of the financial health of an events enterprise.

A critical determinant of successful event management is the capacity to predict and monitor event costs and revenues. Cost blow-outs or lower than expected revenues can significantly impact an event's financial performance, turn an anticipated profit into a loss, create major cash flow problems, and impair the financial health of an events business.

What event costs do you think are more likely to increase unexpectedly?

The nature and importance of an event budget

While budgets can vary in terms of type and level of sophistication, the key purposes of any event budget are to:

■ Forecast, monitor and facilitate the management of event costs and revenues.

■ Provide quantifiable and useful financial objectives for the evaluation of financial performance.

■ Establish early warning systems to alert event managers of potential financial problems.

■ Generate a greater awareness of areas of financial uncertainty and vulnerability.

■ Facilitate the planning of future events through a more informed understanding of event finances.

Even for experienced event managers, it's not uncommon for event costs to be far greater than originally anticipated, particularly when key aspects of the event have been adjusted or upgraded. And while event budgets have their limitations in terms of accurately and reliably forecasting future costs, they generally represent a simple and relatively effective planning and control mechanism. In terms of revenue, sluggish ticket sales, the withdrawal of sponsors, or poor performance with other revenue-raising strategies, can create serious financial problems that can be ameliorated through the development and utilization of a well-thought-out budget.

A budget seeks to provide accurate forecasts of future streams of revenue and expenditure. Which of these two elements would you think is the most difficult to accurately determine in an events context?

Wrathall and Gee (2011) note there are two types of budgets that are generally used in an event management context. These are:

■ **Line-item budgets** that provides an estimation of all cost and revenue items for the overall event.

■ **Program budgets** that are developed for specific programs or program elements. For example, an academic conference may have a special program for PhD students. Specific programs are isolated allowing for analysis of the financial aspects of these individual programs.

Consider this: When deciding on additional elements to include in your program ask below budgeting questions:

1. What is your event budget strategy? Will you use event management software? Consider the key phases of event management:
    a. Planning the event
    b. Conducting the event
    c. Evaluating the success of the event

2. What lessons were learnt from past event spending? Were there areas that you overspent previously? Have you monitored the areas that needed more attention or higher budgets?

3. What are recent trends in budgeting? Recent blogs stress the need to utilise event planning software and/or use cloud-based systems. Have you researched benefits and calculated monthly costs for using cloud-based systems?

4. What are your event goals and objectives? Are the objectives linked with customer relationships; teambuilding or driving sales? Be clear about your SMART (Specific, Measurable, Actionable, Realistic and Timely) based goals

5. How well are you supported by your stakeholders? Do you have partners such as media or sponsors to support you throughout the phases of event planning? Have you explored setting up partnerships and shared arrangements for utilising event software?

6. How customised is your budget to your event? Each event has different needs. For example, charity events may attract higher promotional costs than team building events. Therefore, create budget sheets that cater for the event type.

7. Are there additional experiential and technology costs? Some events may attract higher technology costs. Consider international exhibitions which attract global delegate markets.

8. What are your promotion costs? How much will you invest in social media marketing and promotional tools? Specific tools attract a cost to conduct promotion by utilising one place for all, for example **hootsuite** (https://www.hootsuite.com/solutions/social-marketing)

9. Do you have an emergency fund?

10. Have you calculated the breakeven point and considered the return on investment? Utilising the breakeven formula, calculate how many tickets you need to sell in order to break even. Use this formula to calculate the breakeven point:

> At which point does revenue exceed costs?
>
> $$\text{Breakeven number} = \frac{\text{Fixed Costs}}{\text{Contribution margin (or Price - Variable costs)}}$$

Setting your registration fee for conferences

When planning a conference, you need to decide on setting the registration fees. What criteria do you use to set the registration fees?

1. Calculate your expenses
2. Build your event profile so it becomes an attractive proposition
3. Consider what your target audience can afford to pay
4. Be aware of how many delegates you need to break even

Example

At a business panel dinner the minimum variable expense per person is $60. This includes the registration fee and the food/beverage package. Tickets sell for $100. The event owner needs to calculate the number required to attend the event in order to break even. Any extra attendees after that translate into a profit. Use the formula to calculate the breakeven point.

ITEM		Number of guests		
		80	97	100
Registration Fees	100	8000	9700	10000
FIXED COSTS				
Venue Hire		1000	1000	1000
Speaker transport		960	960	960
Stage		500	500	500
Audio Visual		1000	1000	1000
Marketing costs		270	270	270
Speaker gifts		150	150	150
Administration costs		0	0	0
Total fixed costs		3880	3880	3880
VARIABLE COSTS				
Food/Beverage package	55	4400	5335	5500
Registration	5	400	485	500
Total Variable Costs	60	4800	5820	6000
Total Costs		8680	9700	9880
Registration less Total Costs		-680	0	120

Table 5.1: Fixed and variable cost calculation example

Breakeven	=	$\dfrac{\text{Fixed Costs}}{\text{Registration fee - Variable costs (Contribution margin)}}$
Breakeven	=	$\dfrac{3880}{100 - 60 \ (= 40 \text{ contribution margin per attendee})}$
	=	97 guests need to attend to break even

Table 5.2: Breakeven formula and example

> *If fewer than 97 people attend, the event owner will make a loss. Above 97, the owner will make a profit. Based on this information, what would your advice be?*

Consider this: When budgeting, calculate a projected amount and the actual amount. Look for any variations. Look also for high costs. See this sample marketing budget for Vegan Day. How can you reduce marketing expenses in the future?

Marketing	Projected	Actual
Media & Advertising	4,500	4,500
Facebook	2,700	2,700
Half price printing	2,500	2,500
Google Adwords	880	880
Poster distribution	2,000	2,000
Total Marketing	12,580	12,580

Table 5.3: Marketing budget sample

In the above example the projected budget matched the actual. This is unusual, as mostly the actual budget tends to vary.

The budgeting process

The development and utilization of a budget is often a balancing act between the need for control and the need for flexibility. In this regard, the budget should be viewed primarily as a mechanism to facilitate sound decision-making and hence, whilst financial control is an obvious budget objective, that need for control should not override or constrain creative decision making. There may in fact be times when the budget needs to be modified in light of unforeseen circumstances or unanticipated opportunities. These modifications should, however, be made in consultation with the relevant stakeholders.

Providing quotations based on accurate calculations

One key consideration is to provide an accurate quote for your event.

Calculate all expenses

Consider all items: for example, if the event is interstate, don't forget to estimate distance and cost of transport. Additionally, consider the number of staff you will hire per hour; transport of staff; renting additional equipment and vehicles. Some events may attract higher costs due to the complexity of the requirements, especially when it relates to the menu design and food delivery. When costing a food and beverage package, consider the number of staff, buffets and food truck.

> **Consider this:** The biggest challenge with a wedding relates to cancellation, especially because of Covid restrictions. This is probably one of the events that cannot pivot to online platforms. Be prepared to postpone and provide alternative dates and venues, while remaining flexible in communications with all clients and stakeholders.

5

Providing financial quotes for weddings

Wedding planners may be individual consultants or employed by venues. Each case is different. Accordingly, the process for providing a quote to a potential client may vary. The scenario below is based on individual consultation, where event planners start out as small businesses, probably home-based to avoid large overheads:

Steps to providing a quotation:

1. Provide an initial quote including all costings (fixed and variable).
2. Once the client agrees, quotation must be signed, and the event planner should seek a deposit.
3. If the number of guests increase, adjust requirements accordingly.
4. If the couple change their mind and number of guests drop significantly, then this poses an issue for the viability of your business. Decisions need to be made about whether or not to cancel.

> **Consider this:** Cancellation terms should be clear in your quotation. Terms and conditions could be listed at the end of the quotation. They should also be discussed with the client prior to signing so all aspects are clear.

What to include in a quote

Fixed costs (venues, staging, entertainment, decorations, materials).

Food and beverage. As this may vary, include the cost *per person*. Note any changes to the price if the number changes. Some companies stipulate that a minimum spend is required as this guarantees you are not losing out. For example, some large venues may ask for a minimum spend of $5,000 and this may include tables, chairs, decorations, styling etc. The minimum spend can also vary according to the season (winter versus summer). This is due to the nature of seasonality in our event industry.

The key thing to remember is to arrange for final payment to occur a couple days before the event. Due to Covid and uncertain times as small businesses we understand and can be flexible, but we need to make sure we manage the financial wellbeing of our business.

As well as considering whether the emphasis is on control or flexibility, a range of other factors need to be considered, including:

■ **Environmental factors** such as the general economic environment, current trends for the type of event being staged, and the costs and revenues associated with previous similar events. Minor changes in terms of ticket prices, program content, and marketing issues, also need to be considered, as well as major environmental changes that may be associated with technology, legislation, health crises or other disasters.

(?) *In seeking to develop a realistic budget, which of these environmental factors would you regard as the most problematic?*

■ **Levels of uncertainty** about future costs and revenue streams. Uncertainty or financial vulnerability can, of course, be disturbing and may prompt a need for creative decision making and efforts to broaden revenue bases or become more efficient. When considerable uncertainty exists, alternative budgets representing different financial scenarios may need to be developed. This may, for example, involve the development of a 'most likely' scenario plus development of more pessimistic and optimistic scenarios.

■ **Levels of detail** and the need for categorization of various types of revenue and expenditure will generally vary depending on the level of control that is required. For event budget elements, where considerable uncertainty or vulnerability exists, levels of detail and categorization will generally be greater.

- The need for **ongoing communication with key stakeholders** should be built into the budgeting process ensuring that stakeholders are kept up to date with all aspects of event planning. This is an important by-product or benefit of the budgeting process.

- **Budget review** should also be an ongoing part of the budgeting process. Hence, if a particular category of expenditure starts to significantly exceed budgeted levels, corrective action can be taken. For regular events, accuracy should improve over time and hence the need to monitor and review may gradually decrease.

To what extent should stakeholders be informed of, or participate in, various aspects of the budgeting process? Does this depend on the type of stakeholder?

Cash flow considerations

An event budget may indicate that over the course of a year, revenues will cover costs comfortably. But the revenues and expenditures associated with events are often uneven and significant expenditure may be required well in advance of revenues being received. Furthermore, borrowing money to overcome a temporary shortfall may, at times, be difficult and hence, cash flow problems can occur even for relatively successful event enterprises.

In efforts to avoid cash flow problems, a key principle is to get revenue as early as possible and delay expenditure for as long as possible. But given the nature of events, this principle will not always be easy to apply.

Administration	Budgeted	Actual	Variance	
Hosting	300	300		-
Envato Market Invoice	450	450		-
Meeting	500	500		-
Volunteer Thank You	2,000	2,000		-
Caps and Aprons	1,200	1,200		-
Sched Event app	1,200	-	-	1,200
APRA	85	85		-
Website	2,800	2,800		-
Postage	600	600		-
Competition	500	500		-
Total Administration	9,635	8,435	-	1,200

Table 5.4:. Administration budget example

? *What potential problems could be anticipated for an event company that tries to delay expenditures? What actions could be taken to mitigate against these?*

Consider this: Staffing costs per hour vary depending on expertise and license requirements. Consider the rate payable in your country and identify the increase in administration cost. Is your event viable with paid staff only?

The planning phase of the event management cycle, in which expenditure is likely to significantly exceed revenue, can be lengthy and the bulk of revenues may not occur until tickets are sold at the gate. Hence, addressing cash flow problems may require a more systematic approach. In general, this requires the following five steps:

1. Develop a cash flow timing chart that illustrates the pattern of cash flows on a weekly, monthly, or yearly basis. Potential cash shortfalls can then be anticipated and addressed.

2. Delay expenditure streams to the extent that is possible without gaining a poor reputation amongst actual or potential creditors or losing the goodwill of suppliers.

3. Seek ways of gaining the most attractive terms with suppliers. Here, the first steps are to develop good business relationships and gain as much information as possible about the terms that are generally on offer.

4. Be vigilant and maintain close control over expenditures. Administrative efficiency and effective control over purchasing decisions are relatively straightforward approaches to reducing cash flow problems.

5. Design income strategies in a manner that brings revenue steams forward as much as possible. Tickets may for example, be paid for in advance, online rather than at the gate, reducing logistics problems as well as cash flow problems.

Consider this: See the sample expenditure for Vegan Day. What streams can produce additional revenue? How can you reduce expenses?

Items	Actual budget	% expense
Total Stalls and others	112330	36
Total Sponsorship	83370	27
Total Reimbursement	6500	2
Total Administration	4085	1
Total Design	5000	2

Total Marketing	5580	2
Total Operations	83500	27
Risk management	9850	3

Table 5.5: Distribution of costs (%)

> **Consider this.** Notice how your expenses can be visually represented in team discussions. Decide which areas need attention for future planning.

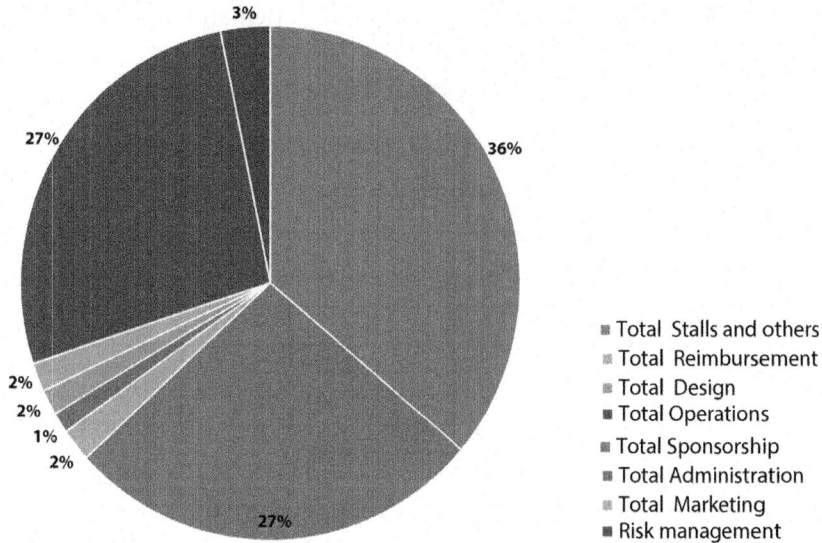

Figure 5.1: Distribution of costs

Are there any potential revenue streams you can recommend moving forward?

Income strategies

Event income can be derived from a range of sources and hence, the revenue forecasts utilized in an event budget depend critically on the income strategy that has been developed. However, even for smaller events, the development of an income strategy can be a relatively complex task. Key sources of event income may include:

- **Sponsorships** which, in recent decades, have become one of the most important sources of income for several events. However, attitudes to sponsorship vary. For example, the Rainbow Serpent Music Festival accepts no commercial sponsorships.

- **Grants** that for various types of events, can be gained from a range of private and public sector bodies.
- **Ticket sales** which are often the most important source of income. Key decisions involve when and how they should be sold, and how much they should sell for. The timing and method of sales should take account of cash flow as well as logistics issues including queuing problems, crowd control difficulties, and other customer service and safety concerns. In determining prices, the price sensitivity of potential attendees, or 'the price elasticity of demand' must be considered.

Sponsorship packages as additional income strategy

When creating sponsorship packages consider below:

- Calculate your marketing costs.
- Make sure there are key differences across package levels
- Ensure sponsor implementation reflects the cost of the package

GOLD (3000)	SILVER (1500)	BRONZE (500)

Logo to be displayed on all material:
  Banner
  Website
  Conference bag
  PowerPoint presentation
  Tables
  Full page advertisement in event program
	Logo to be displayed on:
	  Banner
	  Website
	  Conference Bag
	
	Half page advertisement in program
		Logo to be displayed on:
		  Website
		  Conference Bag
		
		Quarter page advertisement in program

4 social media posts per week over a 5 week campaign. Use of 4 social media tools Acknowledgement of Gold sponsor in all marketing material Flyer inclusion in conference bag Acknowledgement at opening and closing ceremony Creation of digital brand story Design of digital flyer Flyer inclusion on website 3 complimentary registrations 1 x complimentary stand at exhibition hall for the duration of the event	2 social media posts per week over 5 week campaign Use of 4 social media channels Acknowledgement of sponsor (at silver level) in all marketing material Flyer inclusion in conference bag Acknowledgement at opening and closing ceremony 1 x complementary registration 50% reduction stand hire at exhibition hall	1 social media post per week over 5 week campaign Use of 4 social media channels Acknowledgement of sponsor (at bronze level) in all marketing material Flyer inclusion in conference bag Acknowledgement at opening and closing ceremony

Table 5.6: Sponsorship package design

See the example of how to cost sponsorship packages for conferences. Make sure the packages represent bigger value than the monetary amount, so it can be an attractive proposition and add extra value to the relationship.

Sponsorship Income	Budgeted	Quantity	Actual	Variance
Platinum	24,000	5	16,570	-7,430
Gold	5,000	2	15,000	10,000
Calendar	1,000	13	2,500	1,500
Showbag insets	1,000	10	1,500	500
Area Sponsors	1,000	10	2,000	1,000
Photo Booth	600	300	800	200
Show Bags	20,000		25,000	5,000
Grant	20,000		20,000	-
				-
Total Sponsorship	72,600		83,370	10,770

Table 5.7: Sample sponsorship income by Vegan Day

? *What type of event do you think would be the most price sensitive?*

- **Licensing of product sales** which, particularly at large, popular events, can generate a significant amount of revenue.
- **Other sources of income** which include:
  - ☐ Sales of programs, fixtures, or other event-related information
  - ☐ Merchandise and souvenir sales
  - ☐ Parking fees
  - ☐ Food and beverage sales
  - ☐ Rental for stalls, rides, stands, and exhibitions

Budget table for music design and theming elements

Design element			
Music	Projected	Actual	Variance
Stage	3,000	6,000	3,000
Marquee 6x3	500	550	50
Marquee 3x3	300	500	200
Sound and Lighting	3,000	3,000	-
Projections/TV	600	600	-
Decore	300	300	-
Total Music	7,700	10,950	3,250

Table 5.8: Theming budget

Risk Management	Projected	Actual
Event Insurance	2,500	2,500.00
Volunteer Insurance	750	750.00
Security Hire inc Equipment	5,500	5,500.00
First Aid	1,100	1,100.00
Total Risk	9,850	9,850

Table 5.9: Budgeting risk

Case study 5.1: Revising a financial strategy – Gala event

Shannon, an engagement marketing officer at a secondary school had to cancel the Year 12 formal in 2020. It was decided the event will be delivered instead in 2021. Shannon focused her energy on delivering the event to 'alumni' since the audience was no longer in Year 12, and an event positioned as a 'gala' or 'ball' would be more attractive to the guests who were mostly at university, or at a minimum considering themselves to be more 'adult' and beyond the construct of 'school'. With this in mind, she offered alcohol as part of the package and created a theme around connecting with past teachers and peers.

To meet her contracted amount, she needed to sell 180 tickets. However, due to the uncertainty of Covid and ongoing restrictions, consumer confidence dropped and there were only 156 tickets purchased. Shannon was determined to make the event happen so following close communication with the venue supplier, she was able to change the catering format to include a more substantial stand up canape offering for the first hour, which also facilitated social connection with teaching staff, without the requirement for these staff to be in attendance all evening. This was part of a revised budget strategy to make sure the event went ahead without a loss.

The outcome was outstanding by achieving a balanced event budget that delivered the hallmarks of a traditional 'formal' with the addition of reunion elements and greater freedoms than the students would have experienced. That same night lockdown began midnight. The only difference was the event had to finish at 11pm rather than midnight. Shannon commented:

It's an event manager's job to be prepared, have robust discussions with suppliers and present flexible solutions to create the magic in any event.

Financial statements

Financial statements can provide a clear overview of the financial health of an events enterprise. They provide a formal record of the financial activities of a company or enterprise and in so doing, they quantify the financial strength, financial performance, and liquidity of an enterprise. The information obtained from financial statements is important for:

- **Taxation purposes**
- Answering **fundamental questions** about how an event enterprise is going, how much it is currently worth, and what is required to improve its financial health.
- **Optimal decision making**

While hiring an accountant can help to address the first two issues, the last one requires the event professional to have a basic understanding of financial statements and the capacity to interpret them in a manner that facilitates the best possible decision outcomes.

Four types of financial statements reflect the financial impact of various transactions and activities on an events company. They are:

1. The **Balance Sheet** or Statement of Financial Position
2. The **Profit & Loss Statement** or Income Statement
3. The **Cash Flow Statement**
4. The **Statement of Retained Earnings** or Statement of Changes in Equity

Balance Sheet

The **Balance Sheet** presents the financial position of a company at a specific moment in time. It provides a snapshot of a company's assets, liabilities, and shareholder equity.

- An **asset** is something of value that the business owns or controls. It may be a **current asset** such as cash or bank deposit that the business requires for its ongoing operations but is likely to use up within a year, or a **fixed asset** such as a building or office, that the business is unlikely to sell or otherwise use up within a year. Furthermore, in addition to assets that are physical or tangible, **intangible assets** are things of value that are not physical. If, for example, an event business has developed a solid reputation for providing a good customer service then that reputation, otherwise known as goodwill, is an intangible asset.
- A **liability** is something that the business owes to someone external. It may be a **current liability** such as a creditor or short-term bank loan, or some other debt that is incurred for the purpose of running the business,

where repayment is anticipated to take place within a year. Or it may be a **non-current liability** such as a long-term bank loan or mortgage where repayment is not anticipated to take place within a year.

■ **Shareholder equity** is what the business owes to its owners. It represents what the business is worth at any point in time and equals the difference between the total assets and total liabilities of the business.

From a decision-making perspective, how could the information contained in an event company's balance sheet be utilised?

Profit & Loss Statement

The **Profit & Loss Statement** indicates the financial performance of the business in terms of net profit or loss over a specified period of time. The period may be monthly or quarterly but is usually annual. Net profit or loss is calculated by deducting expenses from income.

■ **Income** is the revenue that has been earned over the specified period.

■ **Expenses** are the costs incurred by the business in earning its income.

Income: stalls and others	Budgeted	Quantity	Rate Average	Actual	Variance
Food Stalls	34,000	40	850	39,010	5,010
Regular	47,700	90	530	50,880	3,180
Non-profit	9,900	55	180	9,360	- 540
Subsidised	500	10	50	430	- 70
Extra Stall fees, power,hire	10,000			12,000	2,000
Gold Coin Donations	600			650	50
Total Stalls and others	102,700	195		112,330	9,630
Sponsorship Income					
Platinum	24,000	5		16,570	- 7,430
Gold	5,000	2		15,000	10,000
Calendar	1,000	13		2,500	1,500
Showbag insets	1,000	10		1,500	500
Area Sponsors	1,000	10		2,000	1,000
Photo Booth	600	300		800	200
Show Bags	20,000			25,000	5,000
Grant	20,000			20,000	-
Total Sponsorship	72,600			83,370	10,770
Total Income	**175,300**			**195,700**	**20,400**

Table 5.10a: Part of the Profit and Loss statement Vegan Day sample, showing the income. Contribution by The Event Network Australia (TENA)

Consider this: If you make informed budgeting decisions, you may end up with a positive variance, which translates to additional profit. See the example Profit and Loss Statement for Vegan Day.

Expense	Budgeted	Paid	Balance		
Reimbursement					
Garth	1,500			1,500	-
Mark	1,500			1,500	-
Emily	1,500			1,500	-
Rici	2,000			2,000	-
Total Reimbursement	**6,500**			6,500	-
Administration	**Budgeted**			**Actual**	**Variance**
Hosting	300			300	-
Meeting	500			500	-
Volunteer Thank You	2,000			2,000	-
Caps and Aprons	1,200			1,200	-
Sched Event app	1,200			-	- 1,200
APRA	85			85	-
Total Administration	**5,285**			4,085	- 1,200
Design					
Music					
Stage	3,000			**6,000**	3,000
Marquee 3x3	300			**500**	200
Sound and Lighting	3,000			**3,000**	-
Projections/TV	600			**-**	- 600
Sound and Lighting	500			**500**	-
Total Design	**3,700**	-		5,000	1,300
Marketing					
Facebook	2,700			2,700	-
Google Adwords	880			880	-
Poster distribution	2,000			2,000	-
Total Marketing	**5,580**			5,580	-
Operations					
Table & Chair Hire	15,000			17,500	2,500
Venue Hire	40,000			40,000	-
Cleaner	8,000			9,500	1,500
Electrician	15,000			15,000	-
Signs	1,200			1,500	300
Total Operations	**79,200**			83,500	4,300
Risk					
Event Insurance	2,500			2,500	-
Volunteer Insurance	750			750	-
Security Hire inc Equipment	5,500			5,500	-
First Aid	1,100			1,100	-
Total Risk	**9,850**			9,850	-
Total Expenses	**110,115**	-	-	114,515	
Total Income	**175,300**			**195,700**	**300**
Total Expenses	**110,115**			**114,515**	**4,400**
Total Profit or Loss	**65,185**		-	**81,185**	**16,000**

Table 5.10b: Remaining part of Profit and Loss statement Vegan Day sample, showing Expenses and the bottom line. Contribution by The Event Network Australia (TENA)

Cash Flow Statement

The **Cash Flow Statement** indicates the movement in cash and bank balances over a specified period of time. It highlights problems resulting from the pattern of cash inflows and outflows during that period. The movement in cash flows can be classified as follows:

- **Operating activities** representing the cash flow from core activities such as the marketing and conduct of a festival or event.
- **Investing activities** representing the cash flow from the purchase and sale of assets.
- **Financing activities** representing the cash flow spent or generated as a result of raising and repaying of share capital and debt, as well as interest and dividend payments.

How can a Cash Flow Statement highlight potential problems that may be ignored by a Profit & Loss Statement?

Statement of Retained Earnings

The **Statement of Retained Earnings** provides details of the movement of owners' equity over a specified period of time and is derived from:

- **Net profit or loss** reported in the Profit & Loss Statement.
- **Share capital** that is issued or repaid during the period.
- **Dividend payments.**
- **Gains or losses** due to revaluation.
- Effects of **changes in accounting policies or procedures.**

The link between financial statements

The link between the various financial statements can be illustrated diagrammatically as shown in Figure 5.2.

Financial analysis and decision making

Once developed, the financial statements provide a wealth of information about the financial health of an events enterprise. Further insights can be gained from the development of financial ratios that are introduced at the end of this chapter. Decisions made while running an events enterprise will always have financial implications and hence, a clear understanding of how to interpret financial statements and financial ratios is essential.

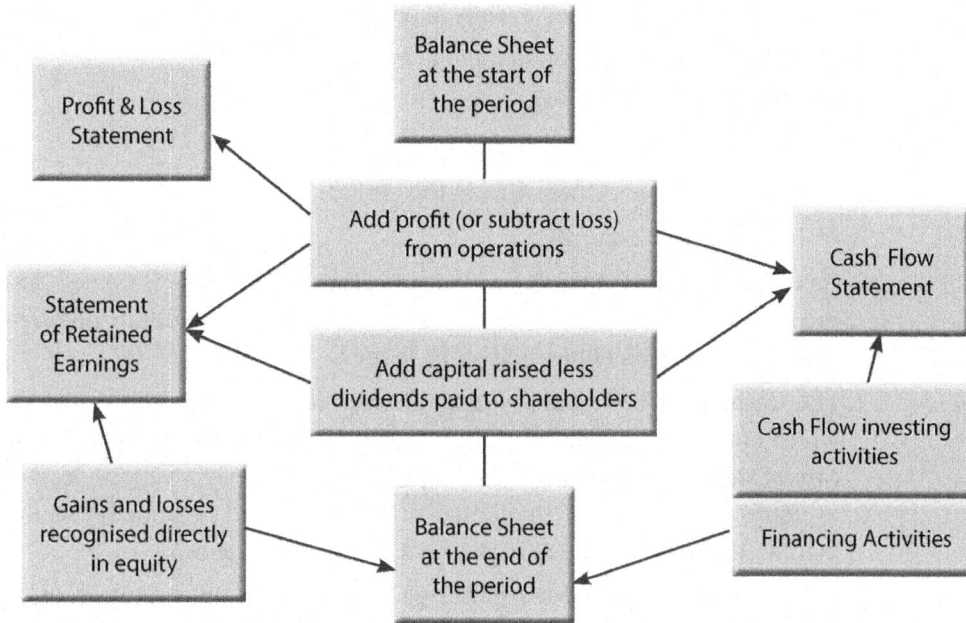

Figure 5.2: The link between financial statements

The **Balance Sheet**, for example, reveals the overall financial health of a business. Although it is just a snapshot at one point in time, it is a result of every transaction that the business has ever made. In addition:

- Changes in a balance sheet over time reveal whether or not the business has progressed and by how much.

- A deteriorating balance sheet may reflect an overall reduction in the business's core activity, reductions from other sources of revenue, increased expenditures, or poor financial control.

- It may therefore signal a need for further investigation via other financial statements and ultimately, the need for strategic intervention.

- Information in the Balance Sheet can also be utilised to calculate the **Current Ratio**, discussed below, as a means of measuring liquidity.

- A current ratio below 1.5 may signal a need to convert some of the business's fixed assets into current assets.

Do you think that an unusually high current ratio signals the need for any corrective action?

The **Profit & Loss Statement** reveals how the business has performed over the last reporting period, generally a year. A poor result in terms of net profit margin, return on assets or return on equity may result from:

- Postponed or cancelled events, as occured during the recent pandemic;
- A temporary reduction in income from events;
- The withdrawal of key sponsors;
- A reduction in income from other sources;
- Increased expenditures during the period;
- Poor financial control.

As well as revealing the net profit or loss, the Profit & Loss Statement also provides details in terms of costs and revenues and can therefore highlight areas of concern on either side of the ledger.

The **Cash Flow Statement** is essential for signalling liquidity problems which often arise as a result of the pattern of cash flows. Particularly in the case of start-up event companies, expenditures precede revenues, leading to liquidity issues. These potential problems should be anticipated in a manner that allows time to implement financing strategies.

The **Statement of Retained Earnings** also provides an indication of the financial health of a business and as with other financial statements, can be utilised to monitor financial performance and progress over time.

Financial health

There are four key indicators of the financial health of a business or enterprise. These are liquidity, solvency, profitability, and operating efficiency. Each of these indicators are discussed below.

Liquidity

The liquidity of an enterprise is its capacity to meet short-term obligations, i.e, debts that need to be paid within one year. The **current ratio**, which equals current assets divided by current liabilities, measures liquidity.

$$\textbf{Current ratio} \quad = \quad \frac{\text{Current Assets}}{\text{Current Liabilities}}$$

In an event industry context, the current ratio should generally be in the range of 1.5 to 3.0. A current ratio below 1.5 signals possible problems in the enterprise's capacity to meet creditor demands while a current ratio that exceeds 3.0 may indicate a lack of efficiency in the way that the enterprise is using its current assets or its short-term financing facilities.

? *In an event industry context, how important do you think it is for an enterprise to maintain adequate levels of liquidity?*

Solvency

Solvency is similar to liquidity but on a longer-term basis. It is the capacity of an enterprise to meet debt obligations on an ongoing basis. It can be measured by the **debt-to-equity ratio** which is equal to total debt divided by shareholder equity.

$$\textbf{Debt to equity ratio} \;=\; \frac{\text{Total debt}}{\text{Shareholder equity}}$$

A relatively low debt-to-equity ratio means that operations are being financed largely by shareholders rather than creditors. A downward trend over time tends to indicate solid financial performance. Conversely, an upward trend signals potential problems.

What actions do you think an event company should consider if its debt-to-equity ratio increases significantly over time?

Profitability

Net profitability, the difference between net revenue and net expenditure, represents a company's bottom line and in the longer term, attaining and maintaining profitability is essential for survival. According to the great author, professor, and statistician, William Edwards Deming, *"Profit in business comes from repeat customers, customers that boast about your project or service, and that bring friends with them."* Simply put, achieving profits in any business, including events, is determined primarily be the achievement of high levels of customer service. However, measurement is essential for determining whether a profit has actually been made and if so, how much.

All the following measures provide an indication of an event company's profitability and financial health, as well as their capacity to commit to growth and expansion.

Profit can be measured in several ways:

$$\textbf{Net profit margin} = \frac{\text{Net profit}}{\text{Total revenues}}$$

Net profit margin indicates the rate of profit from total revenue.

$$\textbf{Return on assets} = \frac{\text{Net profit}}{\text{Total assets}}$$

Return on assets indicates the rate of profit from the company's assets.

$$\textbf{Return on equity} = \frac{\text{Net profit}}{\text{Equity}}$$

Return on equity indicates the rate of profit from the company's equity.

5

? *To what extent do you think that the abovementioned quote by William Edwards Deming can be applied in an events industry context?*

Operating efficiency

Operating efficiency measures the event company's ability to deliver high quality events in a cost-effective manner. It provides an indication of how well the company can control costs without compromising on quality. It measures the company's operational profit margin after deducting the variable costs associated with conduct and marketing of events.

? *What are the likely long-term implications of poor levels of operational efficiency?*

Case study 5.2: Business set up by Allison Anderson

Allison Anderson is the founder and principal consultant of Episteme Consulting which focuses on consulting in strategy planning, based on art and science.

Additional services

- Tourism planning (cities and regional)
- Market research (primary and secondary)
- Strategy (marketing and branding)
- Use of events as a strategy tool to boost local economies.

Allison's work varies from marketing and strategic planning to branding and destination management.

Clients:

- Primary: state government, businesses, regional organisations (private/government)
- Secondary: businesses (small size).

Partnership strategy:

Having partners is crucial for financial viability, therefore it it highly advisable to create collaborators. To achieve this, extend to your existing networks and invite them as collaborators. Key partners can secure a shared knowledge and image library. They can give you access to additional resources and help you build your projects.

Tips for startup businesses

- Be aware of your value in the market and be flexible.
- Set a daily rate, usually higher for short term work and lower for long term work. As you are more in demand, you can increase your rate to manage your workflow.

- Be prepared to subcontract to other providers.
- Think carefully about the timeframe for project completion.
- Never start work without an agreed contract.
- Understand how government procurement works versus the private sector.
- Understand the true cost of doing business: Be aware of administrative costs that you don't get paid for (for example, bookkeeping and accounting data entry).

Financial set up:

- Use accounting software to manage your daily expenses.
- Shop around for a good accountant.
- Set up a separate bank account.
- Invest in accounting software and learn how to use it.
- Invest in cloud software to secure your work and perform reconciliation in real time.
- Set up a password for data security.
- Learn your deductions.
- Track your hours and profitability [billable hours versus administrative hours].
- Use a simple software such as Excel to track your hours and profitability.
- Record your hours against each project.

One key advice by Allison is to know your costs and be aware of how you manage your finances from initial quotation to project completion.

Further information: https://www.episteme.com.au/

Summary

The financial health of an events business is a key concern of events professionals, as well as most key stakeholders. The four principal indicators are:

- **Liquidity** or the capacity of the business to meet short-term debt obligations. The current ratio (current assets divided by current liabilities) provides a measure of liquidity and the Cash Flow Statement can signal potential problems arising because of the pattern of cash flows.

- **Solvency** or the capacity of the business to meet debt obligations on an on-going basis. It is measured by the debt-to-equity ratio with any upward trends signally potential problems.

- **Net profitability** or the difference between net revenue and net expenditure, is an essential determinant of business survival. It can be measured in terms of net profit margin, return on assets, or return on equity. Revenue and cost elements that impact on the profitability of a business can be examined using Profit & Loss Statements.

■ **Operating efficiency** or the event company's ability to deliver high quality events in a cost-effective manner.

Event budgets can either be line-item budgets that relate to the event as a whole, or program budgets that relate to specific programs or program elements. They provide early warning systems that alert event managers to potential financial problems.

During the budgeting process a balance must be struck between the need for control and the need for flexibility. Other considerations are:

■ Environmental factors

■ Levels of uncertainty

■ Levels of detail required

■ Ongoing communication with key stakeholders

■ Ongoing budget review.

Given the nature of events and the fact that associated revenues and expenditures are often uneven and significant expenditure may be required well in advance of revenues being received, cash flow problems can occur. These problems may be addressed by:

■ Developing a cash flow timing chart

■ Delaying expenditure streams

■ Seeking ways of gaining attractive terms with suppliers

■ Being vigilant and control costs

■ Developing income strategies that bring revenue streams forward.

Income strategies should consider a range of income sources including:

■ Sponsorship and grants

■ Ticket sales

■ Licensing of product sales

■ Sales of programs, fixtures, merchandise, souvenirs, etc.

■ Parking fees

■ Food and beverage sales

■ Rentals for stalls, exhibitions, etc.

Financial statements that can provide a better understanding of the financial health of an events enterprise include:

■ The Balance Sheet

■ The Profit & Loss Statement

■ The Cash Flow Statement

■ The Statement of Retained Earnings

A clear understanding of the purpose, content, and use of each of these financial statements, as well as the way in which they are linked, can facilitate a broad range of financial decisions in an events industry context.

Industry profile: Nicholas Kalogeropoulos

Nicholas Kalogeropoulos is the Director of Calibre Feasts with over 30 years' experience in hospitality and events. The type of events Nicholas manages vary from sporting and corporate events to private functions. His reputation as a hospitality expert extends internationally, having been involved with international sporting events such as the 29th Universiade Games in Taiwan (2017) and the Rugby World Cup in Japan (2019). Nicholas often lectures at educational institutions where he continues to inspire students with his enthusiasm about the industry and the key messages he conveys.

During the pandemic Nicholas ventured into consulting for small to medium businesses for post pandemic recovery. As a business coach, he assists businesses with their post pandemic recovery and consults on problem solving, reviewing expenses, assisting generating new income streams and generally contributing towards sustainable business models. His entrepreneurial mind and thirst for ongoing knowledge makes Nicholas one of the key experts on managing and assisting a large range of industries, including event businesses, during challenging times.

Key skills and strengths:
- Operational (hospitality and events)
- Communication
- Small to medium business management
- International logistics and management
- Procurement
- Stakeholder management and engagement
- Sales proposals.

What influenced you to become a business coach?

I have always had a genuine interest in helping others. As an alumni of hospitality programs I have shared my knowledge to students and extended my expertise to future hospitality professionals. My affiliation with local councils means that I have been able to pass on my knowledge to local businesses and assist them in adapting to current situations.

During the pandemic my operations ceased like any other business in Victoria. This led to my greater involvement with coaching as there was a need to provide consultation to small businesses and help them navigate their recovery as we came out of lockdown. The mental health issues that arose from the pandemic meant that assisting people and business coaching became my priority during business recovery.

What are the key areas that small to medium enterprises struggle with?

Business survival

The key area that most business owners faced during the pandemic was business survival. One key consideration was to assist owners in hibernating their business during lockdown to minimise costs during times of closure or limited trade. Other considerations included controlling costs so businesses can remain viable during and after lockdown. Recovery may be slow and this also depends on the level of government support. Sometimes owners have to make hard decisions when there are cash flow issues. For example, do business owners have an exit strategy? The reality is that sometimes businesses may have to stop operations when there is not enough working capital to maintain the business during its recovery.

Accountability

Coaching ensures business owners remain accountable when running their business and preparing plans and carrying out administrative tasks. The mechanisms of running a business may vary across the globe, with small business owners having to execute tasks by themselves, and not able to share the burden of responsibility. Owners know their craft but may not have full understanding of the pragmatics of running their business. At the same time being a business owner can be lonely. Once the operational side of business is completed for the day the administration side begins. There are key responsibilities that need to continue once staff leave, such as ordering and bookkeeping, so the ability to administer the business is important.

How can business owners strengthen their position in the industry?

Transform you mind

The pandemic influenced different lines of thinking. Business owners need fresh thinking to win the customer back. They also need innovative strategies to secure new customers. Be creative in your approach and at the same time strategic. Understand what the customer wants, what your stronger point of difference, is in order to become an attractive value proposition.

Build an online profile

If your business does not have an online profile, this is now the time to create one and transform digitally. A good starting point is a personal profile on LinkedIn. Build your personal brand – who you want to be perceived as – and connect with associations, networks, and various societies. Having an online presence is instrumental in business growth. Establish an online communication and sales strategy that will highlight your business and place it 'on the radar' of customers. Businesses should decide which social media tools suit them best. Understanding the channels, their strengths and targeted audiences can assist with tailoring campaigns, and maintaining an ongoing digital profile.

Create a workforce recovery plan

To survive, businesses need to prioritise their future viability. Running a business is not easy; it's hard. You have to make some unpopular decisions sometimes because if you don't the business will fail. Think about its sustainability. As an employer, I make difficult decisions and some with a heavy heart, such as the inability to pay casual staff during lockdown. Having open and honest communication with staff also helps them make their own choices. Ensure the mental health of your workforce as staff will have their own issues to deal with. Staff totally understand in times of crisis that difficult decisions can be made. So look after your employees but also your business.

Review the supply chain

Conduct regular reviews of your costs and supply chain. Identify opportunities for alternative and more cost effective suppliers with greater value proposition. There are many suppliers out there who can deliver the same result but with more efficiency. Consider how your business model can deliver outputs in a cost effective manner.

Finance and liquidity

Business activities may be slow to come back, and with that costs may increase due to the change in government support. If not done already, draw up a strategic recovery plan with a worst-case scenario on the cash position and revenue/cost projections. This will need to be revised often. Ensure you get all relevant government support.

Review questions

1. Explain the key indicators that you would utililise to measure the financial health of an events business and discuss the factors that may cause its financial health to deteriorate over time.

2. Explain the importance of liquidity for an event business, identify how it can be measured, and discuss the problems associated with low levels of liquidity.

3. Explain the various ways in which the profitability of a business can be measured and discuss the key differences between profitability and operating efficiency in an events context.

4. In view of the uncertainties and difficulties that are often attached to forecasting the costs and revenues associated with planned events, how would you justify budgeting as a worthwhile activity? In what ways can the uncertainty associated with financial forecasts be addressed?

5. Discuss the differences between line-item budgets and program budgets and explain the contexts in which each type of budget is useful.

6. How should an event business communicate financial information with key stakeholders? Which are likely to have the greatest interest in the event budget?

7. Why may cash flow concerns be of particular relevance in an events context? How can these cash flow concerns be addressed?

8. Discuss the key issues to be addressed in the development of an income strategy for a large outdoor music festival and identify the major components.

9. Discuss the use and value of the four key types of financial statements and explain how they relate to each other in an events context.

10. Explain the main difference between a Profit & Loss Statement and a Cash Flow Statement. Why are both of these necessary for a business?

11. What is the value of the Balance Sheet in terms of financial analysis and event management decision making?

12. How can each of the four financial statements be utilised to provide a meaningful picture of the financial health of an event business?

Workshop activities

1. Set up a marketing budget, **projected vs actual**. Decide which expenses can be reduced and how you can compensate with alternative marketing strategies.

2. Create three tier sponsorship packages for an event of your choice: Gold, Silver, Bronze. Calculate the marketing expenses for each package and make sure the gold package offers the best value and maximum promotional benefit. Compare the three tiers and discuss any possible variances that can leverage the marketing effort.

3. Consider how you can reduce staff expenses by balancing the use of staff and volunteers. First, calculate how many staff you need, hours and days. Then calculate the amount of savings (%) by incorporating volunteers. Include gift costs for volunteers as part of the alternative operational expense. Ensure volunteers also receive a certificate of appreciation, therefore include any additional printing costs.

4. Consider this scenario: a client has approached you as the event manager (EM) for a quotation to their wedding. The client will have 80 guests and is looking for a regional venue to save costs. The couple have a limited budget and are seeking advice on the best value offer.

a) Referring to the above case study on how to quote for weddings, design a quotation including all relevant costs such as venue, staffing, vehicle expenses etc.

b) Roleplay the client – event manager scenario where the EM presents the quotation, but the client is asking for ways to minimise cost.

c) Roleplay the client where the client agrees on the revised quotation which is a savings of 10% from the initial quote.

References and further reading

Atrill, P. & McLaney, E.J. (2019*). Accounting and Finance for Non-Specialists*, 12th ed., Harlow, UK: Pearson Education.

Carstens, D. S., & Richardson, G. L. (2019). *Project Management Tools and Techniques: A practical guide*. CRC Press.

Drury, C. (2018). *Management and Cost Accounting*, 10th Ed., Cengage Learning EMEA

Dwyer, L., Jago, L., & Forsyth, P. (2016). Economic evaluation of special events: Reconciling economic impact and cost–benefit analysis. *Scandinavian Journal of Hospitality and Tourism*, 16(2), 115-129.

Janjusevic, J. & Mathur, S. (2021). Financial Planning and Budgeting of Events. In: Salama, M. (ed), *Event Project Management: Principles, technology and innovation*, Oxford: Goodfellow Publishers

Jiménez-Naranjo, H. V., Coca-Pérez, J. L., Gutiérrez-Fernández, M., & Sánchez-Escobedo, M. C. (2016). Cost–benefit analysis of sport events: The case of World Paddle Tour. *European Research on Management and Business Economics*, 22(3), 131-138.

Knardal, P. S., & Bjørnenak, T. (2020). Managerial characteristics and budget use in festival organizations. *Journal of Management Control*, 31(4), 379-402.

Knardal, P.S. & Pettersen, I.J. (2015). Creativity and management control – the diversity of festival budgets, *International Journal of Managing Projects in Business*, 8(4), 679-695.

Quick, L. (2020). *Managing Events: Real challenges, real outcomes*. Sage.

Solberg, H. A., & Preuss, H. (2015). Major sports events: the challenge of budgeting for the venues. *Event Management*, 19(3), 349-363.

Wrathall, J & Gee, A (2011). *Event Management: Theory and practice*. McGraw-Hill.

Websites

https://www.eventbrite.com.au/blog/event-budget-guide

http://www.leoisaac.com/budget/

http://www.nicholaskalogeropoulos-businesscoach.com/

https://globalhospitalitygroup.com.au

5

6 Event marketing and brand strategy

Learning objectives

On completion of this chapter, you will be able to:

➤ Understand the meaning, scope and nature of event marketing and brand strategy

➤ Explain what is involved in the process of marketing and the development of marketing communication strategies

➤ Identify key issues associated with communicating and promoting the not-for-profit sector

➤ Discuss the growth of event sponsorship, explain the concept of sponsorship fit and identify the various sponsorship packages that can be developed

➤ Appreciate the importance of leveraging sponsorship

➤ Identify and explain other key marketing issues including ambush marketing

The term 'event marketing' has been used in a range of different ways and given a range of different meanings. While all of these meanings may be appropriate in various contexts, the term utilized in this chapter refers to that part of the event management process that involves the marketing of events and hence, to the market research, promotion and advertising that aims at increasing the number of customers that pay to attend the event. The American Marketing Association defines marketing as *"the set of activities, institutions, and processes for creating, communicating, delivering and exchanging offerings that have value for customers, clients, partners, and society at large"* (www.ama.org).

In this vein, event marketing includes the activities, tactics and tools used to communicate and promote the value of events to prospective attendees.

When thinking about marketing, it's not uncommon for people to adopt a product focus and emphasise those aspects of marketing that involve advertising and personal selling. However, a real marketing focus, particularly with the marketing of services, or events which may be regarded as a service experience, involves an emphasis on the customer. This customer emphasis or focus necessitates conscious efforts aimed at identifying, anticipating, and satisfying the needs and wants of customers in a manner that is commercially viable. In an events context, the emphasis is on seeking to provide an event experience that event attendees will find satisfying, perhaps surprising, but certainly memorable.

Why is a customer focus as distinct from a product focus, more effective as a means of marketing events?

The scope and nature of event marketing

As discussed earlier, event marketing can be viewed from different perspectives. In terms of the marketing of events, this involves all activities that are associated with market research, that is, identifying the needs and wants of prospective attendees, promotion and advertising of the event, and development of all aspects of the event that contribute to a positive and memorable event experience.

6

When considering the nature of marketing in an events context, it is important to recognize major differences between the marketing of services and the marketing of tangible products. These differences include:

- **Intangibility** or the fact that physical products can be seen, felt, and touched whereas services can't. In an events context, previous events may provide an indication of what can be anticipated, but every event is unique and different.

- **Simultaneity** or the fact that the customer receives a particular service, or experiences an event, at the same time that the service is produced, or the event is staged.

- **Inseparability** or the fact that the service provider is inseparable from the service. In the case of events, the event provider is inseparable from, and is a major influence on the event and the event outcomes. Customers or event attendees are also part of the process and have a major impact on outcomes.

- **Heterogeneity** or the fact that it is extremely difficult, if not impossible, to standardize the quality of a service or an event. An event that is staged at a particular time by particular people for a particular group of event attendees, is unique.

■ **Perishability** or the fact that services and planned events cannot be produced and stored before consumption. Events exist only at the time in which they are being staged and experienced.

Which of the above differences do you think is the most important when considering the marketing of events?

A major implication of these differences relates to the importance of human resources. While the quality and value of tangible products can be worked on, improved, and tested well before it is offered for sale, the quality and value of an event is only tested when it is staged and experienced, at the so-called 'moment of truth'.

Service quality and event quality depends on human resources, the talent, ability, attitudes, and motivation of the people involved in providing the service or staging the event. How event employees and volunteers perform and respond to various circumstances has a major impact on expectations regarding future events and the capacity of event organisers to effectively market those events.

The marketing process

Traditional theories posit that the key steps to a marketing process includes: marketing analysis, marketing planning, implementation and control. In an events context, the marketing process has been described in a number of ways but given the need for a customer focus, generally starts with the research required to identify and understand the needs and wants of event attendees and finishes with the creation of customer satisfaction and customer equity in a manner that is profitable. The key steps to a marketing process in events mainly include those shown in Figure 6.1.

Understand the marketplace and customer needs and wants

As indicated in the model, the first stage involves development of an understanding of the marketplace and the customer. In an event context, understanding the customer involves developing:

■ An understanding of the needs and wants of prospective event attendees
■ Knowledge of the tangible and intangible benefits that attendees want to gain from the event
■ An appreciation of the likely motivations of prospective attendees
■ An understanding of the decision-making processes of prospective attendees

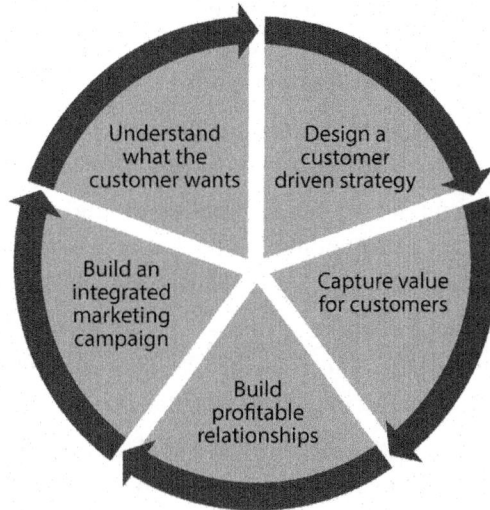

Figure 6.1: Customer value process

How might you describe the wants of attendees at an academic conference? What benefits are they likely to gain from it? What are their key motivations for attendance? What other factors may impact on their decision to attend?

Design a customer-driven market strategy

The second stage involves designing a customer-driven marketing strategy. Key components of a marketing strategy are:

- **Identifying a target audience.** This may be based on demographic (age, income, gender, etc.), geographic (location, culture, language, etc.), psychographic (values, lifestyles, opinions, etc.) or behavioural (actions, website activity, etc.) factors.

- **Developing goals and objectives.** Goals and objectives should be SMART (Figure 6.2)

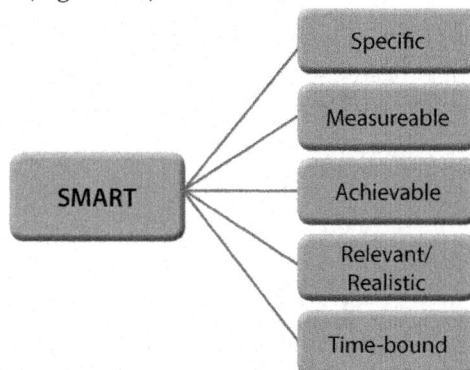

Figure 6.2: SMART based objectives

A sound basis for understanding the event business and the goals and objectives that need to be pursued can be obtained through a competitor analysis or a SWOT analysis. This involves identifying:

- The **strengths** that the event business exhibits. For example, do you have event experts working on your event? Are your volunteers trained?
- The **weaknesses** or vulnerabilities of the event business. This may include lack of technology expertise and a sound registration option. Lack of staff training may result in productivity issues.
- The **opportunities** or external conditions that may contribute to business success. This may include little competition or time availability where no other event is scheduled.
- The **threats** or external conditions that may have negative consequences on the event business. In contrast to above, this may include strong competition. Also, weather conditions may pose a threat especially if there are no contingency plans.

Two types of strategies can be developed through an understanding of these factors. Whenever a *strength* lines up with an *opportunity*, a competitive advantage exists that can give rise to the potential for a **matching strategy.** For example, an events business with extensive international and cross-cultural expertise may identify a need for corporate team building events that has arisen as a result of increased cultural diversity.

The opposite situation arises when a *weakness* lines up with a *threat* giving rise to the need for a **conversion strategy**. For example, event businesses that had concentrated their efforts on live events were faced with the need to transition to online and hybrid strategies during the COVID-19 crisis.

- **Conducting a competitor analysis.** Here, the focus is on identifying brands that are a potential threat and gaining as much knowledge as possible about the strategies, strengths, resources, capabilities, and vulnerabilities of actual and potential competitors.

    These competitors may offer events that compete directly or indirectly. Knowledge needs to be gained about their events, market share, websites, social media presence, and the strategies that they have relied upon. It's important to be able to stage events that are distinctive and different, and this is only possible with a thorough knowledge of what competitors have on offer.

- **Creating content** that is authentic, projects thought leadership, and goes well beyond simple slogans or promotional articles. Content marketing has become an important mechanism for communicating important aspects of the brand and gaining customer acceptance and a competitive edge. Content should be a key element in the event's website but may also be a part of blogs, podcasts, infographics, or in a range of other forms.

■ **Establishing measurements** that provide knowledge about the impact of marketing activities and whether those efforts have actually paid off. Collecting data may start simply through an analysis of things like website traffic, social media activity, email bounce rates, and so on.

The marketing mix

Whilst events can be viewed differently to traditional product offerings, the key principles of Ps still need to be considered. In events there are 5 Ps that unite in order to create value:

Product   Place   Price   Promotion   People

Figure 6.3: The 5 Ps of event marketing

Consider this: Do you know the 5 Ps of your event?

6

Example: The 5 Ps of Edinburgh music festival

☐ **Product** may be the type of event you are offering, e.g. festival

☐ **Place** is the location where the festival takes place, e.g. Edinburgh in Scotland

☐ **Price** refers to the ticket (this may vary)

☐ **Promotion** includes the mix of activities to spread the word about the festival (e.g. website, social media, public relations, etc.)

☐ **People** refers to the target audiences that attend your event, music lovers, social enthusiasts, etc.

What about the Ps of online events?

Due to the nature of hybrid events, it is important to look at the relevant Ps of online marketing:

■ **Planning:** Consider the event and attendee goals. Do they want to learn or simple network? Compare your goals with previous events. What about your budget goals? How will you design the event? What format? How many guests are you expecting? Will you record the virtual experience?

- **Promotion**: How will you promote online? What is your key message? What combination of tools will you use? Website? Social media? Emails?
- **Production**: How will you engage the audience and the stakeholders (e.g. sponsors?) Will you have space for exhibitors? Live chats? How will you record the attendee data?
- **Post Event**: How will you measure client satisfaction? Surveys? Blogs? How will you share the feedback?

Case study 6.1: Bastille Day French Festival (Melbourne)

The annual **Bastille Day French Festival** brings together the French-Australian community to celebrate the French National Day. This vibrant and authentic festival of all things French brings a little slice of French summer to Melbourne winter. With a wide variety of Melbourne-based French businesses and associations who are passionate about French culture, food, history, literature and technology, the Festival, running since 2015 prides itself on delivering a free multicultural community event.

In 2019, the event attracted over 16,000 visitors to Fed Square. After a hiatus in 2020, plans were underway in 2021 to bring the joie de vivre back to Melbourne in July with a live, in person two day festival at Fed Square. The event was positioned to 'Escape to France, right here in the heart of Melbourne as the Bastille Day French Festival brings the joie de vivre to Melbourne this winter. A free community event full of French culture, music, food, history, art and fashion, the Festival was set to transform Fed Square with the spirit of the French Revolution'.

On the eve of the Festival, a snap lock down was announced – giving organisers less than 24hours to adapt. Whilst this news was devastating for organisers, the event was prepared and had planned for this scenario, allowing a swift switch to virtual for some of the festival elements as well as leveraging the existing free online program.

The festival co-ordinator had curated a comprehensive free online program, in tandem with the in-person event format. Initially designed to be played on the Big Screen at Fed Square and as a secondary format on the Festival website, this suddenly became the main focus, which allowed for a speedy adaptation to a virtual delivery.

Key events that were delivered online included:

- Free online program (including musical performances, French cooking demonstrations, documentaries and sponsor content)

- Les Lumières talks (moved from an in person format at Federation Square to Zoom):
  Les Lumières Blanc; A Revolution in Painting – The French Impressionists
  Les Lumières Vert; Can we achieve net zero carbon emission without decline?
  Les Lumières Rouge; The French Revolution and its relevance to today
  Les Lumières Bleu; Demystifying the French cliché
- Caudalie, A Guided Online Wine Tasting (always planned for online delivery)
- The Art Embroidery Revolution with French couturier, Delphine Genin (always planned for online delivery)

With these online options, the community was able to stay connected while staying at home. Bastille Day French Festival Vice President, **Georgie Stayches**, discusses the quick adaptation to virtual platform:

"We always knew that this scenario could happen and while the live event format, particularly the French Winter Market and entertainment program are key, we had contingencies of what could be moved online if Public Health Orders changed. In fact, in all our communication regarding the Les Lumières, we noted that they would move online if the event couldn't be held in person. We had already set that expectation."

In addition, we already had a free online program in place for three reasons:

- Provide content for the festival screen at Federation Square;
- Provide access to the Festival via the website for people who weren't comfortable coming to a live event; and
- Have a format ready, should a lockdown happen.

Key marketing learnings from the online delivery are:

1. **Communication is key**. As soon as lockdown was a possibility, we had our messaging ready to go for all stakeholders – and this included the transition to an online format. We kept in touch with our audience throughout the process across all channels to keep them informed. In other words, we didn't go dark.

2. **Put your audience first.** Our audience appreciated the offer of online program elements, while they were stuck at home. With so much disruption due to the lockdown, we wanted to provide some stability and certainty for our community by proceeding with a Festival, albeit a slightly different Festival.

It was important for us to still stay connected and we chose Zoom, as that allowed for easy delivery - and we knew our audience would be accustomed to it. In fact, **sales** for our online elements increased, once we announced the shift online. Feedback included:

"Thank you to you and Bastille Day organisers for your great work in organising and then adjusting at the last minute so the audience could still participate in so many aspects of the celebrations for this special day. Please can you pass our thanks on to all involved, and for adjusting so readily to the changed circumstances."

3. Don't forget the elements that can't pivot. While we could move Les Lumières online and promote our free online program, we couldn't fulfil the French Winter Market or utilise our performers online. This is where our social media ramped up and we shared and promoted the takeaway services our stall holders were now providing as well as featuring videos of some of our performers.

Case study supplied by Georgie Stayches. For more on Bastille Day in Melbourne as a cultural and community event visit https://www.bastilledaymelbourne.com/

Event branding and brand strategy

Event branding is the collection of elements that make an event different, unique, more easily recognizable, able to stand out and be distinguished from other events, and ultimately more memorable. It is a clear set of attributes, and benefits that characterize the event. However, it must be more than just a logo, slogan, or catchy tagline. It should integrate all elements of communication into a coherent and consistent message. In general, the easier it is to describe the event brand in a single word or single phrase, the more powerful and more useful it is likely to be. It should also be:

- **Unique**, promising something that other events can't promise
- **Meaningful** and relevant to the needs and wants of event attendees
- **Authentic**, capturing trust and credibility amongst attendees
- **Creative** and perhaps building on the unexpected which adds to uniqueness
- **Consistent** with every detail and all elements of communication reinforcing the brand promise

An effective brand strategy contains core elements that include purpose, vision, and values. The clearer the purpose of an event, why it is being staged and why people should attend, the easier it is to attract customers. Development of a bold but realistic vision makes an event more compelling and more attractive in the longer term. However, being able to define, articulate, and display clear values is central to determining how the event will be perceived in the marketplace.

How would you describe the brand values of the Bastille Day?

Positioning the brand involves understanding the target audience, carrying out a market analysis, and defining the marketing goals. All of these elements combine to more effectively differentiate the event from other events. They also create direction in terms of new event features and attractions, reinforcing the event brand and making the event more attractive and more recognizable. An ultimate aim is to create a recognizable brand persona helping to cement relationships with customers and build customer loyalty.

What features have been added to the virtual adaptation of Bastille Day? Has the brand been showcased in the online platform?

Brand activations

Events can build brand reputation by activating brand experiences.

These days brand need to be more creative due to increased competition. Event managers can create unique brand activation experiences by engaging audiences and giving them something to remember about the brand. Here's how you can create a brand activation campaign;

1. **Set your goals and objectives**. What do you want to achieve?
2. **Have a campaign budget.** Clearly understand the resources you have to create your campaign
3. **Develop the experience around your audience.** Understand what ticks their passion. Then work around that
4. **Create a call to action.** In the end consider your goals. What do you want your audience to do?
5. **Amplify your activation**. Create a story and notify the community to spread the word so your brand can achieve results

For more on how to create a brand activation campaign visit: youtu.be/BrssVgheZnk

Construct an integrated marketing program that delivers superior value

Following on from the design of the marketing strategy, the third stage involves construction of an integrated marketing program for the event and the event's brand. An integrated marketing program is one in which the various elements come together to deliver superior value through the provision of a consistent, seamless, multi-dimensional, brand experience for event attendees. Regardless of the communication channels that are utilized, each branding element should be presented in a manner that reinforces the brand's ultimate message. If designed properly, the whole will be greater than the sum of the various elements.

At the same time, efforts to develop and maintain consistency in terms of the brand's key message, should not be at the expense of creativity. All elements of the marketing program need to be developed with the aim of achieving maximum impact. All of the below elements need to support each other in a consistent, integrated manner, reinforcing the key aspects of the event's brand.

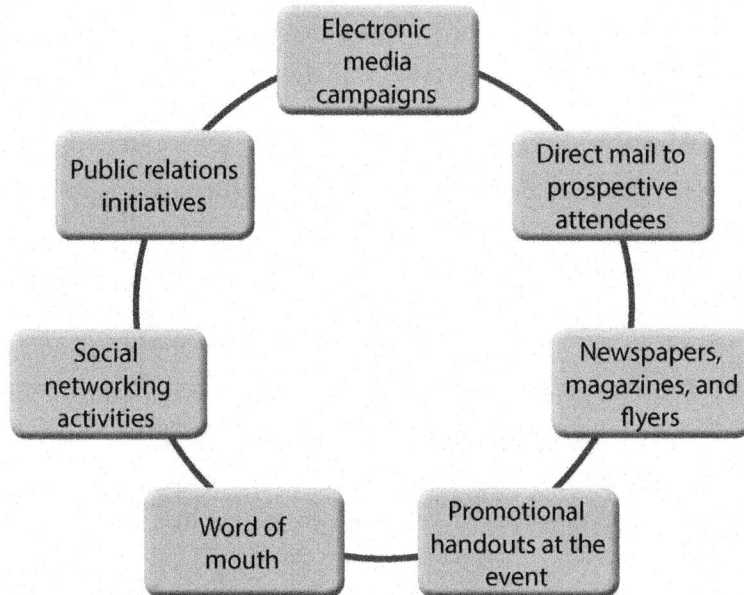

Figure 6.4: Marketing program elements

Build profitable relationships and create customer delight

Profitable relationships develop as a logical extension of a well-thought-out marketing program that is backed up by successful events in which the expectations of attendees are met or exceeded. Those relationships need to be maintained and nurtured through on-going communication and promotional activity. However, creating expectations that are realistic and can be either met or exceeded during the 'moment of truth' when the event is staged, is critical to the development of customer satisfaction or better still, customer delight.

While the problems associated with over-promising and under-delivering are obvious, what are the potential problems associated with under-promising?

In an events context, it is often the unexpected, the surprise elements of an event, that move the event experience from 'customer satisfaction' to 'customer delight'. Sound marketing communication that is supported by the provision of service excellence during the staging of events has the potential to transform first time attendees into loyal, regular attendees. And hence, one-off transactions become profitable relationships.

Capture value from customers to create profits and customer equity

The capacity to achieve customer delight repeatedly leads to high levels of customer equity. Customer equity can be regarded as the potential profit that all of the customers of an event business can bring during the business-customer relationship. It underpins the level of loyalty that an attendee has to an event, or a customer has toward a brand. Hence, customer equity defines the financial success of a business and represents the value that attendees add to an events business. Capturing this long-term financial benefit is the ultimate aim of the marketing process.

Marketing and communications planning

Getz (2021, p. 192) defines marketing and communications planning as the action where the event manager gathers data from primary and secondary sources to develop a complete strategy plan. This analysis may also include targeting audiences as well as stakeholder analysis such as volunteers and/ or sponsors. The main objective is to create an action plan to guide the wellbeing of the business.

In order to prepare your marketing plan, key steps are below:

1. Analyse the market
2. Set goals and objectives
3. Outline the marketing mix
4. Set the marketing budget
5. Monitor and control the marketing plan

Marketing communication strategies

The critical role that communication plays in effective marketing is obvious. It engages prospective customers, maintains their interest, directs their attention, and ultimately impacts on their decisions to attend events.

What aspects of the communication message would you regard as the most important when promoting an outdoor music festival?

As the usage and popularity of various communication channels change, and as new forms of communication emerge, marketing communication must adapt to remain relevant and effective. Clearly, the importance of web pages, electronic media campaigns and social networking activities have been elevated in recent years. In fact, the capacity to effectively communicate and influence others impacts on all aspects of event management.

Case study 6.2: World Dubai Expo

The world Dubai Expo promises cultural immersive experiences by participating countries. In 2021 the expo includes separate pavilions for the participating countries. This creates a sense of identity and uniqueness and gives the opportunity for each country to highlight their strengths. The business event becomes a hub where participants can exchange ideas and deal with the current challenges while also nations can identify future collaborative opportunities.

For more on the expo visit www.expo2020dubai.com/en/experiences/theme-weeks

? *What other event management functions can you identify in which the role of communication is critical?*

There are various communication and persuasion models. These are drawn from communication and consumer behaviour theories. The key concepts in persuasion are:

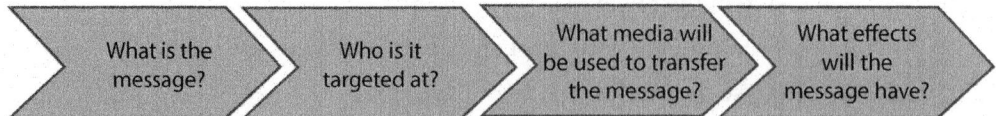

What is the message? → Who is it targeted at? → What media will be used to transfer the message? → What effects will the message have?

Figure 6.5: Key persuasion concepts

Consider this. How does the Dubai world expo attempt to influence event participation? What key issues do they highlight for collaboration and communication?

Online marketing

Online marketing, also known as e-marketing, internet marketing, or digital marketing, is a broad term that refers to the process of using internet-connected services to promote a product, service, or event.

The internet has become the primary source of information for most customers. However, despite its popularity, reach, and cost effectiveness, it may, at times, be limiting or risky to rely entirely on online marketing. It may often be better to utilise an online approach in tandem with traditional forms of communication, given the reluctance that some market groups may have to fully embrace online concepts. The internet is in a constant state of change and hence, event marketers need to stay abreast of new innovations. The process of online marketing is as follows:

1. Develop a budget.
2. Select appropriate communication channels.
3. Define the purpose of each channel.
4. Link social networks with websites, adverts, and promotional material.
5. Develop online communication strategies.
6. Execute strategies through the provision of information.
7. Monitor various channels and provide feedback to users.
8. Continuously review and adapt as required.

Creating a social media strategy

Creating a social media strategy ensures you understand how your audiences uses the various digital tools to receive and accept information. This is important for events as well as customizing your strategy according to your targeted profile. Different generations may use social media tools differently, therefore understanding how consumers behave is important. Baby boomers (born between 1946-1964) are slowly embracing technology. Generation X (born mid 60s till and 1980) may prefer to use Facebook over Instagram. The millennials (born between 1981 and 1999) focus on innovation. The year of birth may slightly vary according to the country and the influences these generations received. To see targeting strategies for each generation see www.wordstream.com/blog/ws/2016/09/28/generational-marketing-tactics.

To learn how to create a social media plan the key steps include:

1. Pay attention to our own behaviour. How do we engage?
2. Understand the goals you have for your social media.
3. If you wish to build trust with customers, share customer testimonials.
4. Choose the tools according to your customer profile.
5. Create your plan.
6. Execute your plan.
7. Monitor usage. Count the likes and shares.

8. Study the data analytics and evaluate usage.

9. Adjust your tools and methods according to your evaluation.

What changes to the internet have you noticed over the last couple of years?

The not-for-profit sector

The relevance and use of marketing communication extend beyond those events that are staged in order to make a profit. In an event context, marketing is broadly concerned with understanding and serving customers regardless of the purpose of the event. In the not-for-profit sector it is still necessary to engage diverse groups of stakeholders and market events, as well as the event organisation. The effort involved may be as great as, and sometimes more complex than, for commercial events. The communication effort can include:

■ Stakeholder engagement

■ Broader community engagement

■ Promotion of the event

■ Delivery of the events purpose and strategic priorities

■ Advocacy activities

■ Liaison with public sector bodies

■ Communication and elevation of the organisational brand

■ Social marketing and initiatives designed to influence behavioural change

■ Raising public awareness of the event and its cause or purpose.

Event sponsorship

For many events, sponsorship represents a key source of income. However, it is important to understand the motives of event sponsors and the difference between patronage and sponsorship. With patronage the motives may be altruistic, and a donation may be provided with no expectation of any commercial advantage. However, the same is not the case with sponsorship where clear commercial benefits are anticipated, particularly from a marketing communication perspective.

Hence, event sponsorship provides mutual benefits. From the event organiser's perspective, the key benefits of event sponsorship are the income or 'contra' (in-kind support through the provision of goods or services) that is received from the sponsor. Other advantages may also arise from the development of a closer partnership with the sponsor in which the image and awareness of both the brand and the event benefit from the sponsor – creating an *event relationship*.

Case study 6.3: Yellow Ladybugs – Creating a more inclusive world for autistic girls

Yellow Ladybugs is a not-for-profit organisation dedicated to acknowledging and celebrating autistic girls and women. The charity was set up by Katie who first recognised the need to highlight diversity in autism. The charity runs several events from girls' movie nights to educational conferences, with the aim to bring a voice to the issue of autism, remove the stigma and promote acceptance for individuals of all genders. Autism is presented in different formats across all genders; therefore, the charity seeks to highlight the issue of diversity and how to best manage it across various contexts. The various events bring people together in a sensory friendly setting with the additional objective to foster a sense of belonging and connection.

For more on Yellow Ladybugs visit www.yellowladybugs.com.au/

6

? *Can you think of a suitable sponsor for the Yellow Ladybugs charity? How can the not-for-profit organisation raise its profile through the development of sponsorship arrangements?*

From the sponsor's perspective, key benefits may include:

- **Promoting brand awareness** which can be particularly effective when the brand is given a high level of exposure at a popular event which has gained significant media attention.
- **The creation of goodwill amongst event attendees** which is likely to enhance the sponsor organisation's image and translate into positive attitudes towards the sponsor's brand.
- **Promoting brand image** particularly when there is a 'good fit' between the event and the sponsor's brand, for example Slazenger's sponsorship of the Wimbledon Tennis Championships.
- **Demonstrating product features** at the event. The tennis balls used at Wimbledon are always supplied by their long-term sponsor, Slazenger.
- **Repositioning a company or brand image** may be regarded as necessary and my be facilitated through sponsorship arrangements.

■ **Enhancing the effectiveness of other marketing activities** such as advertising, merchandising, and retail promotions through integration with the sponsorship arrangements.

■ **Rewarding employees** with tickets and access to key parts of the event.

? *Can you think of other benefits for sponsors affiliating their brand with an event?*

Sponsorship fit

As indicated earlier, some of the benefits of sponsorship only accrue if a good 'sponsorship fit' has been attained. In fact, the quality and appropriateness of the fit between the sponsor and the event is critical.

The appropriateness of the fit may not always be obvious. Beer manufacturers often sponsor major sporting events which begs the question about the relationship between drinking alcohol and gaining sporting prowess. However, the demographic that attends major sporting events is often similar to, or overlaps with, the demographic that consumes a particular brand of beer. For example, Guinness became the title sponsor for the Six Nations, one of rugby's greatest championships. Similarly, Jim Beam is a sponsorship partner of the Australian Football League and Repco Supercars Championship.

As well as seeking an event in which the audience has similar characteristics to the sponsor's target market, the sponsor may also look for the type of event in which there is a perceived fit with organisational values. For example, the digital currency firm, LIFElabs has partnered with Sky Sports British Masters and while the connection between digital currency and golf seems strange, both organisations may be regarded as highly creative, forward thinking, and innovative.

Case study 6.4: Rugby World Cup, Japan 2019

Global Hospitality Group won the rights to run the Heineken bars for the spectators of the sporting event. In addition to providing the bar service, the global group provided additional hawking solutions for up to eight stadiums. This placed GHG as a leading hospitality leader at an international scale.

For more visit: http://globalhospitalitygroup.com.au/our-work/rugby-world-cup-japan-2019

Ensuring a good sponsorship fit is beneficial for both the sponsor and the event and hence, sponsorship arrangements should not be entered into lightly. The event organiser needs to be confident that the sponsorship arrangement will have a positive impact on the events reputation and image, and sponsoring organisations should have a sound awareness of the event organisation's values, the environment in which it operates, and the nature of the event that it plans to sponsor.

> **Consider this.** What criteria would you use to evaluate the sponsorship fit of a major sporting event?

Sponsorship packages

While financial or cash sponsorship is the most common and well-known form of event sponsorship, other types of sponsorship arrangements may, at times, be more appropriate and better suited to the needs of the event and the sponsor. In-kind sponsorships may be useful when the sponsor is a producer of goods that can be used in the event. The Slazenger - Wimbledon partnership is an obvious example. Naming rights or title sponsorships often appeal to a sponsor that wants to ensure that their sponsorship arrangement is not undermined or overshadowed by arrangements with other sponsors. On the other hand, a broad range of tailor-made sponsorship packages have been developed with the aim of bringing together the unique requirements of the event and sponsor.

? *What type of arrangements could be included in a sponsorship package to maximise the impact on brand awareness?*

Depending on the sponsor's contribution to the event a range of different levels of sponsorship may also be developed. For example:

- Platinum
- Gold
- Silver
- Bronze

> **Consider this.** Each event has different partnership needs, therefore naming the levels can be customized to the event. Accordingly, the cost of each package will vary.

Sponsor leveraging

The funds or in-kind value that is provided to an event by a sponsor may merely represent the starting point for an effective and fruitful sponsorship arrangement. A broad range of other marketing activities may be initiated that complement, support, and extend the event-sponsor relationship. This additional investment is referred to as 'leveraging' or 'activating' the sponsorship with the primary aim of more effectively communicating the link between the brand and the event.

Leveraging may greatly extend upon the initial sponsorship agreement but is generally encouraged by event organisers as it raises the profile of the event as well as the sponsor's brand. Coca-Cola's sponsorship of the Olympics dates back to 1928 and provides a good example of the mutual benefits associated with sponsorship leveraging. At the 2016 Rio Olympic Games Coca-Cola launched the #thatsgold campaign. Two TV commercials that formed part of the campaign featured archive footage from past Olympics as well as images of current athletes. The campaign successfully promoted the Coca-Cola brand but also broadened the reach and appeal of the Olympic Games. Both the sponsor and the event benefited significantly from the leveraging initiative.

Case study 6.5: The Australian Open

Australian Open is an international mega event which attracts a number of sponsors at different levels. These levels are named as: major partners, associate partners, partners, broadcast partners. When creating sponsorship packages consider the type of event and customize your packages to the needs of the event.

See video on creating sponsorship packages: https://youtu.be/bvBC841km-Q

Can you think of any events where you automatically think of the sponsor at the same time? What is the impact on your attitude to the event?

Key marketing issues associated with sponsorships

When implementing sponsorship arrangements, several issues may arise that can be problematic. These include:

The potential for **ambush marketing.** Also referred to as 'guerilla marketing' or 'parasite marketing', ambush marketing occurs when the official sponsorship of an event is undermined by a company with no sponsorship agreement that still attempts to conduct a marketing campaign around the event. Often these companies find creative ways to connect their brand to the event without actually breaking any laws. A good example is the legendary marketing campaign which was undertaken by Nike in 1996 at the Atlanta Olympics in which Adidas had paid for exclusive sponsorship rights. If event organisers are unable to prevent ambush marketing the integrity of the event is undermined and the capacity to attract future sponsors is greatly reduced.

Consider this: At the 2012 London Olympics Games, Adidas was the main sponsor. However, Nike managed to create an impactful campaign which went viral, giving the impression that somehow the company was associated with the games whilst they were not. See video: https://youtu.be/kydKkwNjb80

What brand strategies did Nike use to create the perception they were affiliated with the 2012 Olympic games? What strategies can the event organiser use to reduce the possibility of ambush marketing?

Other implementation issues may include:

- Incompatibility between two or more of the sponsors
- The use if title sponsorships
- Perceptions of inequity amongst sponsors
- The utilisation of sponsor logos.

6

Summary

Event marketing involves the market research, promotion and advertising that aims at increasing the number of customers that pay to attend the event. A real marketing focus, particularly with the marketing of events, involves an emphasis on the customer. This necessitates the provision of event experiences that event attendees find satisfying, perhaps surprising, but certainly memorable.

It is important to recognize major differences between the marketing of services and the marketing of tangible products which include: intangibility, simultaneity, inseparability, heterogeneity and perishability.

A key implication of these differences relates to the importance of human resources. The quality and value of tangible products can be worked on, improved, and tested well before they are offered for sale, but the quality and value of an event is only tested when it is staged and experienced, at the 'moment of truth'. It depends on the talent, ability, attitudes, and motivation of the employees and volunteers involved in staging the event.

Event branding is the collection of elements that make an event different, unique, and more easily recognizable. Branding needs to be:

- Unique
- Meaningful
- Authentic
- Creative
- Consistent.

The marketing process involves:

- Understanding the marketplace and customer needs and wants;
- Designing a customer-driven market strategy;
- Making an integrated marketing program that delivers superior value;
- Building profitable relationships and creating customer delight;
- Capturing value from customers to create profits and customer equity.

Marketing communication strategies are critical to the effective marketing of events. Over recent years online marketing has become increasingly important and involves:

- Developing a budget;
- Selecting appropriate communication channels;
- Defining the purpose of each channel;
- Linking social media with websites, adverts, and promotional material;
- Developing online communication strategies;
- Executing strategies through the provision of information;
- Monitoring various channels and provide feedback to users;
- Continuously reviewing and adapting as required.

Event sponsorship has become an increasingly important aspect of event marking in recent years. Mutual benefits apply to the event and the event sponsor. From the perspective of sponsors, key benefits include:

- Promoting brand awareness;
- The creation of goodwill amongst event attendees;
- Promoting brand image;
- Demonstrating product features;
- Repositioning a company or brand image;
- Enhancing the effectiveness of other marketing activities;
- Rewarding employees.

Important sponsorship issues that need to be considered are:

- Achieving sponsorship fit;
- The design of appropriate sponsorship packages;
- Initiatives aimed at leverage or activating sponsorship;
- Implementation issues including the potential for ambush marketing.

Industry profile: Georgie Stayches, Fetching Events and Communications

Inspired by the 1992 Barcelona Olympic Games and kicking off her life in events at the 1997 Australian Open Tennis, events has always been in Georgie Stayches' DNA. From major international events, including the 2000 Sydney Olympic and Paralympic Games and 2002 Commonwealth Heads of Government, to community events, including the Pioneer and Working Horse Festival and Teddy Bear's Picnic, to national roadshows, including taking Winnie the Pooh and Tigger around Australia to national conferences and graduations, Georgie's experience has covered the spectrum.

Combining this with her communications experience of working at Channel Nine (Melbourne), Granada Television (London) and various PR agencies, Georgie brings the knowledge and the know-how. As the Chief Engagement Officer at Fetching Events & Communications, an organisation she founded in 2009, she is passionate about not just nailing the run sheet but identifying the event purpose and understanding human behaviour to create the best event experience.

Fetching Events & Communications was founded to provided specialist advice and support in the areas of events, communications and volunteer management and works with organisations including associations, peak bodies, community services, education, tourism and sporting sector. During COVID-19, Fetching's core purpose remained the same while the delivery changed. Fetching Events & Communications was created to help organisations engage with their audiences and create events that influence and inspire. While that was usually done in a hands on role, it became a strategic and training role while events were paused.

Georgie believes the event industry will require graduates to work smarter, work together, share information, share insights, have a strong curiosity, collaborate with people they previously saw competitors, thus generating better results and creating a stronger and more robust industry. During 2020, Georgie took time to play a larger role within the industry to provide peer support and mentorship, create collaboration and advocate for the power of events, in a positive way.

She is characterised by her passion for the industry; her versatility and adaptability and believes events is not all about time and logistics. It's about meeting your event purpose; asking whether you have engaged with your audience and whether you have successfully engaged with your staff and event volunteers.

What are some key considerations that have arisen over the past year?

"As events professionals, we set the tone. While we were (and are) faced with unprecedented challenges, we also have the opportunity to shape the narrative.

Language and communication have never been so important than during a crisis of this nature; language we use within the industry, language we use with our clients and language we use externally. During COVID, there's been a stream of "we've been decimated", "events are dead", "events must run" (regardless of the health risks) sentiment. This use of language is damaging. It sends the wrong signal. How do we expect our industry to recover when we keep telling people we have been decimated? We need to be our own champions and advocates and show our versatility and adaptability, focus on what we can do, not what we can't do.

The truth is, events never went away, they just adapted and adjusted (and perhaps hibernated) for the situation. While live events are returning, each event needs to be planned and developed based on the objectives, purpose and most importantly, audience. Audience behaviours and priorities are changing, and events need to adjust accordingly.

The pandemic has forced us to do things differently and that's not a bad thing. Let's take this opportunity, let's re-imagine how we do things; let's really make the most of it. We can't rely on being handed solutions, it's up to us to create our own solutions and opportunities."

How have your services changed as a result of the pandemic?

"Every event and project we are working on is different and tailored to the audience. There is no one event size fits all. It is important that organisations don't make the mistake of rushing live events back to the format just because they can – it is crucial to reassess and reimagine the event in the new world. It is important to ask ourselves "What do our audiences want? What do our audiences need? How can our events deliver experiences that influence and inspire? What are the COVID considerations and scenario planning we need to make?"

We used to help our organisations engage with their communities by planning and delivering meaningful events. We now also help them by providing strategic consulting and training workshops. Our training, research and development arm of the business has increased, and our services now include keynote speaking, training workshops, data driven research and consulting."

Can you tell us how you adapted your marketing strategies?

"We knew immediately that we couldn't 'go dark' during this time. Research shows that companies that invest in marketing during recessions, not only survive but also thrive (Johnnie Walker is a classic example of this!*). We invested in time. In fact, it was one of the busiest times of our career as we poured all our time and resources into business development. We knew we needed to stay visible but also have a clear purpose. If we could stay visible and build a strong network during this time, we would be (hopefully) top of mind when people were ready to run events.

Our starting point was to understand our audience's challenges and be their solution. It wasn't about focusing on our own challenge of being an event agency during a pandemic. We looked at where the gaps in knowledge and support were and stepped up to fill those. We created online Huddles for event professionals to join. A safe space where they could talk through their challenges, their experiences and their personal journeys, with their peers.

We ran free webinars and panel discussions to create industry collaboration, which in turn opened us up to new audiences. It also increased our website visitation, e-news subscribers and connections. These webinars also acted as practical examples of our work to prospective clients. In fact, we picked up several virtual event management contracts because the webinars also demonstrated we were virtual savvy – that was completely unexpected and a lovely bonus.

We wrote blogs to establish our knowledge, our research, but also our authenticity. We connected with and collaborated with other event and industry professionals. We looked at each month, what the consumer sentiment would be, what the major challenges would be, and we adjusted our marketing accordingly. It was no use to promote and push our event management services when events weren't running.

The story goes that Johnnie Walker advertised throughout World War 2, even when Whiskey was not available. Once the war ended and Whiskey could now be purchased, there was pent up demand. And of course who was top of mind from advertising through-out? Johnnie Walker!

Collaboration was such a positive of 2020 and there is an amazing community out there to help and support each other. The more you can engage authentically, the more relationships you can create and build."

What kind of skills do you think event managers should have in relation to digital marketing and communications?

"Curiosity and adaptability. Whether it is live events, virtual events, communications or digital marketing, curiosity and adaptability will be the key soft skills for event managers. Be curious of your own event, be curious about audience behaviours, be curious about which platform is best for each event. It's not about the best technology, it is about find the right technology fit for your event to deliver on it's purpose."

To read more on Fetching Events visit http://www.fetchingevents.com.au/about.html

Industry profile: Jenny Mitten, Brand strategy and leadership expert

Jenny develops strategies for destination brands. Currently her focus is positioning Melbourne as a city which offers opportunities to host major business events. The creation of events as part of branding a destination is an essential element especially for cities such as Melbourne which is renowned for its events as opposed to landmarks. It is therefore important to showcase the city's unique selling point with the creation of major events. Her advice to event planners is to innovate and utilise some of the city's new products such as hotels, precincts, and key centrepieces as part of their event concepts. Having a sound knowledge of the key marketing principles or four Ps (product, place, price and promotion), in addition to having an open and broad mindset helps create a full picture of what Melbourne has to offer.

During strategy development Jenny leads small teams from initial conceptualisation to delivering final strategy solutions. As a passionate leader, Jenny allows small teams to contribute ideas as they are easier to develop into meaningful outcomes based on united goals.

What are your key principles when leading small groups into strategy development?

We often establish matrix teams across the business to breakdown silos and foster team accountabilities. For example, if you have 30 people divide them into three groups with various skill sets, set a problem or task for each group, who then report back to the brand strategy manager. This gives a chance to every person to fully explore and test an idea, it can also break down hierarchies.

How do you diversify your strategy in order to create new products?

We work closely with stakeholders and analyse the markets. We then create products for each market segment. Due to COVID we had to diversify and focus our attention to our national markets. This is now a key priority. In order to attract business events domestically we have to create customised programs for each segment. We are a city that hosts amazing major and business events; so, our supply chain is very strong. We need to think differently to showcase the city's creativity when we sell Melbourne as a business event destination. We want to showcase innovative event experiences to set ourselves apart from other cities. All cities have meeting spaces, but where else can you organise a corporate event on the court of a Grand Slam arena?

What is your key advice when developing brand identities?

Test identity with small focus groups to provide confidence when positioning the brand on the national and international agenda. Use relevant digital marketing and social media channels and tools. There are many tools out there. It's about researching and understanding your audience, and how your business fills that need for them.

What are some tips when events have to suddenly adapt to online platforms?

If an event was meant to be delivered in-person and instead had to go virtual, it is important to monitor delegates' intentions and embrace opportunities. Do they still plan to visit Melbourne in the future? Can we convert the cancelled business trip to a future leisure visit? Can we create some leisure experiences and re-market the city to this target group? Virtual and hybrid events are here to stay. Hence, it is now easier for business delegates to attend their business meeting virtually but hopefully visit the place in person at a later date so try and think of the online experience as a way of increasing your reach to larger audiences.

What are the key skills and attributes in team leadership and strategy development?

Lead diverse teams

Focus on group work with different personalities and working styles. Understand and accept that there are different people hence ideas will vary. Each person is different, but the ideas may be complementary. My advice is to find people who complement personalities and bring different skill sets to create the work. This helps build collaboration. You don't know it all and you need the different perspectives hence the diverse backgrounds are important. Have patience, as it may take a while to understand how people work.

Ask questions

In brainstorming sessions give the chance for the introverted personalities to think and respond to creative ideas; make them comfortable when contributing ideas. Don't assume you know peoples' background and experience. Ask them if they have experience; you would be surprised what you learn by asking the right question. Often the person that is quiet has the most relevant things to say.

Be curious

Show interest in listening to other people, show empathy. Ask questions about industry partners (especially if you work in a government organisation), try and understand how they operate. It goes back to empathy, asking questions and good listening skills.

Be flexible and adaptable

You need to be flexible, and able to think quickly and adapt to situations. Become someone that has a vision and is able to communicate it. Rather than saying how you want it done, demonstrate the vision and revert to questions.

Collaborate with partners

Increase your collaborators as it will help when developing proposals and pitching ideas. We can't win events if we don't have strong partnership with industry. Some of our key partners include Melbourne Convention and Exhibition Centre, Melbourne Airport, Harry the Hirer and others in the events world. You need a strong local industry, confidence and attendees to position yourself as an event capital. Look for shared objectives with your partners and leverage the benefits. Event businesses want to raise their profile via our channels while we want to showcase our city via their efforts. We market to win the event, then work closely with our partners to deliver it.

Explore the value of digital events

From a government perspective, events are often valued based on economic impact. The travel and event gathering restrictions during the COVID pandemic have the potential to change the way events are evaluated. Do participants attend digital events? What value does this provide a destination, if any? This is important to explore as online participants may still wish to visit Melbourne in the future. What is their intention? Will they visit Melbourne? How do we capture that data? If you think of public events that are broadcast by the media, for example the Australian Open, part of its value is how many people are watching it globally and how it promotes Melbourne and Victoria via that content. Is there a way we can do that with virtual events? Find ways to add value to your event other than just delegate attendance.

Ongoing learning and improvement

Event planners need to commit to ongoing learning and improvement. Digital skills are becoming more important for event planners. Show your client or employer that your investment in ongoing learning will enable the shared objective of putting on an amazing event.

Research questions

1. What are the keys steps in marketing planning? Use an event as an example.
2. Choose the best promotional mix for an event of your choice. Consider the target market.
3. Before you develop a marketing mix for your event, develop event aims and objectives. Once you set your goals, then decide on the 4 Ps.
4. How do you use social media and for what purpose? Conduct a self analysis of your social media behaviour. How active are you on each social media tool? Create a table to record your responses for each social media you use. Compare your social media behaviour with others.

5. How can you market your event online to create awareness and increase competiveness?

6. Discuss the differences among social media sites and the tools used by audiences. Refer to generational usage and behaviour patterns.

7. Select an event and discuss how it is perceived as a brand by audiences.

8. What are elements of your personal brand? What do you want to be known for in events? Brainstorm and discuss.

9. How do you think technology may influence event promotion?

10. Discuss the different strategies used in social marketing networks to influence decision making and event participation.

Workshop
Marketing planning exercise

You have been approached by a charity to deliver new marketing concepts in relation to their next fundraising event. The charity needs new income to survive, and this includes a new marketing plan. Follow below steps:

1. Based on the selected charity:

   a) Conduct a market analysis (scan the environment including websites, social media, publications, etc). Key aspects to consider are the 5 Ps of event marketing. Note down the findings.

   b) In groups, discuss any market gap and provide any recommendations that arise from your secondary research.

   c) Recommend a new target profile that may be suited to that event.

   d) Provide a social media strategy plan for the new target market.

   e) Provide key tips on how the charity can monitor social media usage and re-share of information.

2. Select an online event and prepare an online marketing mix based on the 5 Ps of online marketing.

3. Events are seasonal offerings. Consider the local events in your area. Conduct a competitor analysis over a selected period (e.g. for January or July) and note opportunities that are offered during non peak seasons.

Brand activation exercise

Since COVID, city centres have been vacant and businesses struggling to survive. As an event marketing consultant, you have been approached by the local council to activate experiences in the city.

■ Prepare a strategy plan for how you can engage businesses and customers in shopping experiences.

■ Highlight branding activities that promote collaboration.

■ Develop a promotional timeline to present to council.

■ Present a monitoring plan which will assist businesses control customer activity.

References and further reading

Altschwager, T., Goodman, S., Conduit, J. & Habel, C. (2015). Branded marketing events: A proposed 'experiential needs-based' Conceptual Framework. *Event Management, 19*(3), 381-390.

Chang, C. H., King, B. E., & Shu, S. T. (2020). Tourist attitudes to mega-event sponsors: Where does patriotism fit? *Journal of Vacation Marketing,*

De Pelsmacker, P., Van Tilburg, S., & Holthof, C. (2018). Digital marketing strategies, online reviews and hotel performance. *International Journal of Hospitality Management, 72*, 47-55.

Getz, D. (2021) *Dictionary of Event Studies, Event Management and Event Tourism*, Oxford: Goodfellow Publishers.

Hoyle, L. H. (2016). *Event Marketing*. John Wiley & Sons.

Koo, J., & Lee, Y. (2019). Sponsor-event congruence effects: The moderating role of sport involvement and mediating role of sponsor attitudes. *Sport Management Review*, 22(2), 222-234.

Winsor, R. D., Sheth, J. N., & Manolis, C. (2004). Differentiating goods and services retailing using form and possession utilities. *Journal of Business Research*, 57(3), 249-255.

Wood, M (2017). *Essential Guide to Marketing Planning*, (4th ed.). Harlow: Pearson Education.

Wrathall, J., & Gee, A. (2011). *Event Management Theory and Practice.* McGraw-Hill.

Websites

http://www.fetchingevents.com.au/about.html

https://www.cvent.com/au/blog/events/four-ps-online-events

Videos

https://youtu.be/kydKkwNjb80 Nike Find Your Greatness - 2012 London Olympics Commercial

https://youtu.be/bvBC841km-Q What are sponsorship packages

https://youtu.be/iyJ4fN-Xh0 How to create effective social media strategy

7 Legal compliance, risk and crisis management

Learning objectives

On completion of this chapter, you will be able to:

➤ Recognise the importance of legal compliance in the events industry

➤ Identify and explain key issues associated with legal compliance in an events context

➤ Understand the importance of crisis management and the need for an emergency response and evacuation plan

➤ Recognise the realities associated with the existence of risk at planned events and explain the steps involved in the risk management process

➤ Analyse and mitigate the risks associated with outdoor events

➤ Provide an understanding of theoretical issues associated with crowd behaviour, as well as the practical implications in terms of event security

➤ Explain the role and the challenges faced by event security staff.

In the current environment, it is more important than ever for event professionals to recognise and understand their legal obligations and be able to ensure compliance. While many of the associated issues are complex, a sound understanding of their implications is an essential part of the event manager's toolkit. In fact, issues associated with legal compliance represent one of the most significant areas of risk for practitioners in the events industry.

Legal compliance

Legal compliance in the events industry generally involves adherence to a range of legislative and regulatory requirements and obtaining appropriate licenses and permits. From an event enterprise perspective, it is important to have a compliance culture, that is developed and sustained around the core dimensions of legitimacy, permeability, and control.

How would you describe a compliance culture in an event company context?

Relevant legislation, regulations, licenses, and permits vary from country to country, region to region, and state to state. In broad terms though, legal compliance in the events industry involves a focus on:

- **Doing business** which generally includes:
  - ☐ Business registration either as a sole trader, partnership, or company.
  - ☐ A broad range of issues related to trade practices including the advertising of events.
  - ☐ Taxation issues.
- **Employees** which generally includes:
  - ☐ Occupational health and safety and ensuring that employees, contractors, and volunteers have a safe working environment.
  - ☐ Worker's compensation which generally covers employees for treatment and rehabilitation if injured on the job. Volunteers and spectators are often covered by public liability insurance.
  - ☐ Industrial relations, which are concerned with the employment relationship and hence, the workplace rights and responsibilities of employers and employees.
- **Operating requirements and procedures** which generally include:
  - ☐ Security and the need to provide appropriate staffing, training, and equipment for crowd control and the protection of people and assets.
  - ☐ Pyrotechnics licences for events in which pyrotechnics will be used and appropriate safety procedures will need to be applied.
  - ☐ Copyright.
  - ☐ Catering issues and the need to ensure food safety and acquire appropriate licences, including liquor licences for events that involve the sale and consumption of alcohol.
- **Compliance with legislation and regulations specific to the event,** e.g.:
  - ☐ Entertainment events and the need for licenses for managers, consultants, and agents in the entertainment industry.

☐ Sporting events and the need for adherence to relevant sports legislation and licensing requirements.

? *Can you think of reasons why sporting events have different legislation and licencing requirements from other events?*

Case study 7.1: Alumni ceremony event

The Le Cordon Bleu alumni ceremony was held at the Melbourne Convention and Exhibition Centre in February 2021. To adhere to the safe Covid practices, multiple food stations were made available with easy access and space for guests. The event followed strict food safety processes with extra precautions including sanitising procedures. Staff received multiple briefing and training sessions to ensure processes were adhered to. To see the flexible solutions that were adopted while ensuring the event was memorable, visit https://mcec.com.au/news-and-awards/2021/4-april/case-study-le-cordon-bleu-graduation-ceremony.

Permits and licences

There are a broad array of permits and licences that impact on operations in various sectors of the events industry. In general, they authorise event organisers to provide a range of special activities during the staging of an event. However, the scale, nature, and scope of permits and licences that apply to events varies significantly from country to country and even across state borders within many countries. Hence, it's important for event managers to be aware of local requirements and act accordingly.

For example, legislation that covers liquor licencing generally specifies, amongst other things, the age of drinkers. In the United Kingdom, Australia, and several other countries the drinking age is set at 18 but can vary between 13 and 25 years of age in other parts of the world. Liquor licencing may also cover the venues in which alcohol can be served, as well as the situations such as, in some cases, only with meals. It may also specify the hours in which alcohol can be served which again, varies significantly depending upon location.

Other liquor licencing issues relate to requirements that providers display drinking age, ask patrons for proof of age, and so on. In several locations, pop-up licences may also be provided allowing for alcohol to be served for low-risk licenced activities, including a range of special events.

7

? *What are the liquor licencing regulations in your location with regard to:*
- *Drinking age?*
- *Venue hours?*
- *Pop-up licences?*
- *Other requirements?*

Permits and licences may also be required for other special activities at events. These include:

■ The handling of food

■ The use of pyrotechnics

■ Road closures

■ The use of recorded music.

Consider this: What food permits and licenses do you need for your local community event of up to 5000 people?

Case study 7.2: Yo India

Yo India is a food truck company that participates at local community events, one example being the Queenscliff music festival. Conan, the owner, submits a request for a permit via the local council. The request goes through the respective health department and then Conan receives the permit to attend and cater for the event.

See https://www.qmf.net.au/apply/stall-holder

Did you know? When you wish to film at a designated place you need an event permit. Currently there are strict rules to follow during filming. These relate to how many types of equipment film crew can carry, to how many people can work in a group. Check the local government rules for further information.

See the permits required to film in Melbourne: https://www.melbourne.vic.gov.au/arts-and-culture/film-music-busking/filming-in-melbourne/filming-permits/

Insurance cover

Event managers are generally required to obtain appropriate insurance cover for all planned events. In addition, they are generally required to refrain from any conduct, behaviour or activities that would disqualify them from their insurance cover. When obtaining insurance cover, it is essential for event managers to disclose all relevant details including the expected number of attendees and details about any high-risk activities such as the use of pyrotechnics, that may be part of the event. Failure to do so may void the insurance contract.

There are generally three types of insurance policies that are relevant to planned events. These are:

- **Public liability** to cover accidents involving other people where liability rests with the event manager.
- **Property insurance** to cover damage to the venue during the period in which the venue has been hired.
- **Professional indemnity** to cover loss associated with advice provided to a client by the event manager.

Copyright

Event managers need to comply with copyright, particularly with regard to the use of sound recordings. Hence, if sound recordings are planned for use at an event, the organiser needs to apply for licences from relevant bodies. The licencing bodies vary between countries and regions but in general, two copyrights are required, one in the sound recording of the performance and one in the song or the lyrics of the song.

From the event organiser's perspective, the benefits associated with playing music at the event are fairly obvious. This is particularly the case with dance and music festivals where the music is a vital and intrinsic part of the event and recorded music may be used extensively by DJs. It is, however, up to the event manager to obtain appropriate licences.

What events have you attended that have made extensive use of recorded music?

Did you know? The Australasian Performing Right Association Limited can help its members manage their music rights. It has partnered up with the Australasian Mechanical Copyright Owners Society Limited so members deal with one body especially when reproduction of music is required. The licenses cover music that is communicated or performed publicly. For more see https://www.apraamcos.com.au/

Contracts

Entering into contract arrangements, either on their own or their client's behalf, is a regular and on-going occurrence for event managers. Hence understanding contracts and accurately interpreting them in terms of the associated requirements and responsibilities, is an essential event management skill. The most common types of contracts in an event context are:

- **Indoor or outdoor venue hire agreements** which generally specify a broad range of considerations including details of parties to the agreement, venue hire fees, deposit required, other associated costs, the rights of event managers in terms of how the venue is used, liability and indemnity issues, car parking rights, and hiring period.
- **Ticket agency agreements** which allow the ticketing agency to prepare, promote, and conduct presale of tickets prior to commencement of the planned event. These generally include details about the event, the event manager, the price, the venue, and performance schedule.
- **Stakeholder agreements** which outline key expectations of the organiser and the specifics of each additional stakeholder involved in the event.

Negligence

Negligence litigation is, as a result of the transient nature of events and the unpredictability of attendee behaviour, possibly the greatest ongoing legal concern for event managers. Hence, an understanding of negligence and what it implies in terms of the legal ramifications of potential negligence claims, is an essential requirement for event managers.

A *tort* relates to a negligent or intentional civil wrong which brings with it the capacity for the injured party to sue the wrongdoer for damages. Negligence is the omission of some action that a reasonable person would carry out, or the action that a reasonable person would refrain from carrying out. In an events context, these three elements of negligence apply:

- The event manager owed a duty of care to the injured party.
- The duty of care was breached by the event manager.
- The injured party sustained the injury as a direct result of the event manager breaching that duty of care.

For the staging of an outdoor music festival, do you think it's ever possible for an event manager to achieve zero risk of a negligence claim? What actions can the event manager take to minimise the risk?

Duty of care

There are two tests that are utilised to establish duty of care. These are:

- The *reasonable foreseeability test* which establishes the extent to which an action and associated injury was predictable or foreseeable.

■ The *vulnerability test* which establishes whether or not there was a reliance that existed between the injured party and the event manager.

The concept of risk

The concept of risk and a recognition of the need to assess and manage the risks associated with virtually all aspects of human activity and endeavour has a long history. Furthermore, the conduct of major and mega events involves a broad range of attendees and stakeholders whose behaviour is often difficult to predict. Exposure to the elements, political risks, and the potential for emergency situations, make planned events particularly vulnerable. Other aspects of the planning, design and conduct of events are also fraught with difficulty, uncertainty, and risk. Event risks in terms of finances, resources, and health and safety, make assessment and management of that risk essential.

What event types would you regard as the most vulnerable in terms of health and safety risks?

Zero risk is not achievable and the only way to ensure no loss of property and no injury or loss of life, is to refrain from the staging of large events and perhaps, even small ones. However, although this is the case, a key responsibility of event organisers is to minimise risks and take action to mitigate their severity. The importance of these dual objectives was highlighted in April 2013 with the Boston Marathon bombing. Despite efforts to minimise the risk of terrorist activity, several people died due to the Boston bombing. However, the initial casualty count could have been far worse if not for immediate action to move spectators from the location of the initial blast. Furthermore, at least partly due to the effective and efficient transport of victims to local hospitals, 264 victims, many with serious injuries, survived the attack.

More recently, the failure of organisations to predict and respond to risk was highlighted by the Covid-19 crisis. While the impact in terms of major and mega events was obvious, the real economic impact was far broader. The crisis heavily impacted all planned events including business events, which have a significant economic impact and could be described as the hidden engine of the economy. Whether or not the Covid-19 crisis could have been predicted is still open to debate. However, there is a strong argument to suggest that measures to minimise the impact of that type of crisis could have been far more advanced.

Case study 7.3: Drive-in concert planned for Flemington Racecourse, Melbourne

This event was scheduled to be delivered in July 2020 however got cancelled due to Covid. The main features of the sample emergency evacuation plan are:

- A snapshot of the event site - usually little detail about the infrastructure on these
- The location of emergency assembly area(s). The number, location and distance of emergency assembly areas required are guided by a combination of factors, but primarily the nature and landscape of the site itself, and the event capacity.
- The paths of travel from the event site (both front of house and back of house) to the assembly area(s)
- The access points and paths of travel for emergency vehicles.

Image 7.1: Contribution by Leo Gester, Safety Officer & Risk Assessor

What, if anything, do you think could have been done to minimise the impact of the Covid-19 crisis on the events industry?

For risk management to be effective, it needs to be far-sighted and proactive. Furthermore, key risk-related responsibilities must be assigned to specific people who will take appropriate action to:

- Establish and progress the risk review process;

- Maintain required registers and related documentation including a risk management plan, an incident register and a post-event review;
- Monitor and review risks and risk-related activities;
- Ensure that all stakeholders are aware of the risk management process;
- Liaise, communicate and consult as required; and,
- Where required, provide appropriate training.

The risk management process

Risk management involves the generally following nine steps:

1. **Identification of the event and the internal and external stakeholders.** For first-time events, their key elements need to be identified, along with stakeholders. For events that have been held before, these details need to be reviewed and updated. Key elements of the event include:

   - The type of event – sport, business, cultural, entertainment, community, fundraising, etc.
   - Local, regional, national or international?
   - Purpose of the event.
   - Anticipated frequency – one-off, regular, monthly, annual, etc.
   - Size, anticipated impact and public profile.
   - Internal and external stakeholders.

2. **Identification of associated risks and their likely causes**. This involves:

   - An assessment of what can go wrong;
   - Establishing the causal factors.

   Details about risks and their causes can generally be established with the use of a broad range of sources including: experience from previous events; other event practitioners and industry contacts; relevant government departments and agencies; risk consultants; published and unpublished materials; and, internal and external stakeholders. These details must then be recorded on an *event risk register*.

When organising an in-house Christmas party for a medium sized company, what possible risks would you identify? What are the causal factors?

3. **Establishment of controls for all risks.** Establish which people are the most appropriate to accept responsibility for addressing each of the specific risks associated with the event and ensuring the safety of attendees, staff, volunteers, and all other stakeholders.

4. **Conduct a risk analysis**. Identify all possible risks. These may include:

☐ Existing risks associated with the venue or event site;

☐ Additional risks that the event creates;

☐ External risks that event staff have little control over but still need to be identified and managed as well as possible.

Further consideration of various elements of the event may highlight some activities that are clearly too risky. Options may be to:

☐ Avoid the activity altogether;

☐ Isolate the hazard that is likely to give rise to the risk;

☐ Find a way to reduce the risk and hence, its likelihood of happening;

☐ Transfer or contract the risk to another party;

☐ Share the risk;

☐ Insure against the risk.

At an outdoor music festival, event attendees may risk injury due to exposure to the elements. What steps can be taken to minimise that risk?

5. **Evaluation of all risks.** This may involve a relatively simple qualitative approach in which probability and impact are rated. Risk probability and impact ratings may use categories such as low, medium, and high, or may involve rating the probability and impact on a scale, perhaps 1 to 10. Multiplying the two together provides an overall risk rating.

6. **Completion of a risk management plan.** A plan is an essential element in the event planning process. Its key purpose is to identify all potential risks associated with the event and develop plans for reducing or mitigating those risks. A risk is anything with the potential to cause:

☐ Personal injury or loss of life;

☐ Loss or damage to assets, including infrastructure, equipment, venues or event site;

☐ Financial loss;

☐ Harm or damage to the environment;

☐ Harm to the reputation of the event or event organisers.

Many risks are beyond the control of event staff or event organisers. In such cases it is still essential to establish which people need to accept responsibility for addressing risks associated with the event and ensuring the safety of attendees, staff, volunteers, and all other stakeholders.

The risk management plan should include details regarding:

- ☐ The task, issue, or hazard;
- ☐ What could go wrong;
- ☐ The people and locations that could be affected;
- ☐ The risk rating – probability and impact;
- ☐ Risk control measures;
- ☐ People responsible for implementing risk control measures;
- ☐ The timing of risk control measures;
- ☐ How control measures will be monitored;
- ☐ Any other notes, comments, or guidelines.

7. **Implementation, documentation, and communication of the risk management plan.** The risk management process needs to be as transparent as possible and understood by all event stakeholders. Responsibilities must be clearly assigned for all aspects of implementation and the plan must be documented and communicated to all stakeholders.

8. **On-going monitoring and review of the risk management process.** As the environment changes over time, the risks associated with the conduct of planned events also change. Hence, all aspects of the risk management process, the extent to which key elements of the process still reflect current realities, and the capacity of the organisation to realistically identify potential risks and respond in a timely and effective manner, need to be monitored and reviewed on a regular basis.

In what ways have the risks associated with running a three-day business conference changed over the past decade?

9. **Immediate response to mitigate the severity of incidents as they occur.** As discussed, a key element of the risk management process is the capacity for immediate response to minimise negative outcomes. Hence, remaining vigilant, and constantly on the lookout for anything that can go wrong, is essential. This applies not only to those risks that are well known and regularly dealt with, but also the risks that are unexpected. In fact, learning to expect the unexpected is perhaps one of the most important characteristics for a risk manager.

When an outdoor cultural festival experiences unusually high temperatures, how can the associated risks be mitigated?

Risks and hazards

In risk management we talk about risks and hazards: *Hazards* are things that can go wrong (like a tripping hazard), and *risks* are consequences of hazards (injury).

The following tables and case study have been contributed by Leo Gester, Safety Officer & Risk Assessor.

Table 7.1: Step 1 – Determine (C) consequence of hazard (impact)

Health & Safety		Environment & Heritage	Reputation
Substantial (5)			
Fatal Incident (Class 1)		Permanent widespread ecological damage	International negative media coverage. Loss of business from key sector.
Major (4)			
Permanent injury (Class 1)	Damage, which permanently alters a person's future (e.g. paraplegia, amputation of a limb).	Heavy ecological damage, costly restoration	Sustained national negative media coverage. Loss of long term key client.
Moderate (3)			
Lost time injury (Class 2)	Damage, which temporarily alters a person's future.	Major but recoverable ecological damage	Regional/short negative media coverage. Loss of Client / project.
Minor (2)			
Medical treatment (Class 2)	Damage, which temporarily inconveniences a person	Limited but medium term damage	Local negative media coverage. Site or project problem
Negligible (1)			
First Aid treatment (Class 3)	Actual injury which requires no treatment or simple first aid	Short term damage	Brief local negative media coverage.

Table 7.2:. Step 2 - Determine (P) probability of event occurring

Almost Certain (5)	Can be expected to occur 75% - 99%	Common / Frequent Ooccurrence	More than 1 event per month
Likely (4)	Will quite commonly occur 50% - 75%	Is known to occur or "It has happened regularly"	More than 1 event per year

Possible (3)	May occur occasionally 25% - 50%	Could occur or "I've heard of it happening"	1 event per 1 to 10 years
Unlikely (2)	Could infrequently occur 10% - 25%	Not likely to occur very often	1 event per 10 to 100 years
Rare (1)	May occur in exceptional circumstances 0% - 10%	- Conceivable but only in exceptional circumstances	Less than 1 event per 100 years

Table 7.3: Step 3 – Determine the Risk Level (R): multiply Consequence (C) by Probability (P)

Risk Assessment Matrix		Consequence (Impact)				
		Negligible (1)	Minor (2)	Moderate (3)	Major (4)	Substantial (5)
Probability (Likelihood)	Almost Certain (5)	Moderate (5)	High (10)	Very High (15)	Extreme (20)	Extreme (25)
	Likely (4)	Moderate (4)	High (8)	Very High (12)	Extreme (16)	Extreme (20)
	Possible (3)	Low (3)	Moderate (6)	High (9)	Very High (12)	Very High (15)
	Unlikely (2)	Low (2)	Moderate (4)	Moderate (6)	High (8)	High (10)
	Rare (1)	Low (1)	Low (2)	Low (3)	Moderate (4)	Moderate (5)

7

Table 7.4: Risk tolerance table

Risk tolerance (C × P = R)

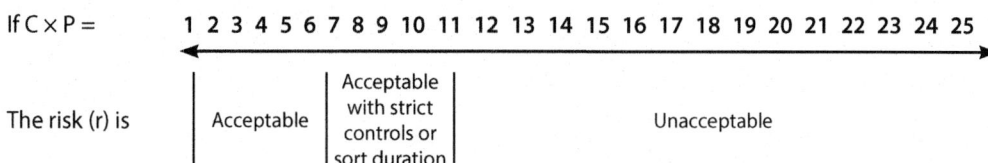

If C × P =   1 2 3 4 5 6 7 8 9 10 11 12 13 14 15 16 17 18 19 20 21 22 23 24 25

| The risk (r) is | Acceptable | Acceptable with strict controls or sort duration | Unacceptable |

Hierarchy of controls

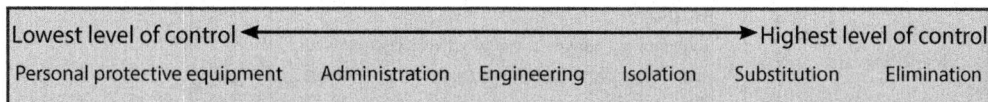

Lowest level of control ←→ Highest level of control

Personal protective equipment   Administration   Engineering   Isolation   Substitution   Elimination

Case study 7.4: Pyrotechnic displays

Most pyrotechnics present a fire hazard, as well as a risk of injury or damage to infrastructure. Controls that could be implemented include:

- ELIMINATION: Not using pyrotechnics. This is very effective but drastic. Is it really necessary or can something else be done?
- SUBSTITUTION: Using 'cold' pyrotechnics. These present no fire hazard as they rely on a cold chemical reaction to produce an effect.
- ISOLATION: Placing the pyrotechnics out of reach of the public and away from infrastructure or flammable materials.
- ENGINEERING: Using infrastructure (e.g. fencing) to prevent people from getting close to the display.
- ADMINISTRATION: Making it a requirement that only licensed pyrotechnicians can use displays (as is the case!)
- PERSONAL PROTECTIVE EQUIPMENT: Wearing a flame-retardant suit. This is not exactly practical!

Often a combination of controls is required. All hazards are tabled against the appropriate control measures, and the residual risk rating (the risk after controls are in place) is assessed. If it is still not at acceptable, more controls may be required. If no further controls can be implemented, the hazard may need to be eliminated altogether.

Potential safety and environmental hazards.	Risk rating			Control measures what steps are you taking to reduce either the likelihood or consequence of the risk	Residual risk rating			Person responsible to ensure method applied
	C	P	R		C	P	R	
Personal injury	4	3	12	Risk assessment performed prior to commencing work and review the Site OH&S Management Plan, Emergency Procedures and subcontractors' Safe Work Method Statements (SWMS)	3	2	6	Event Manager
Damage to surrounding infrastructure								Site Manager
Fire hazard				Display to adhere to national standards				Pyrotechnician
Misfire due to incorrect operation				Licensed pyrotechnician to operate display				
				Display location to be at safe distance from any flammable materials				
				Crowd management infrastructure to be in place to create safe exclusion zone around the display				
				Staff to be briefed about location and timing of display				
				Pyrotechnics to be kept in secure storage prior to and after display				

Table 7.5: Risk assessment – example for use of pyrotechnic display (hot sparklers).

See the sample form in Table 7.5. Use the same form and repeat the process for every hazard identified for your event and you are well underway to completing a risk assessment! This is a continuous and dynamic process; you should constantly revisit your risk assessment as your project evolves to ensure you capture any new hazards.

Crowd behaviour and event security

Security staff at events are critical to the protection of people and property, the maintenance of a safe and secure environment, the elimination of violence and anti-social behaviour, and the promotion of a safe event experience. These roles and responsibilities make event security a challenging and difficult task.

Crowd behaviour (and misbehaviour) at events can have enormous implications in terms of security management, the maintenance of control, and the risk of personal injury, loss of life, property damage and public disorder. Hence, security staff require the skills to control or manage crowd behaviour while at the same time, adopting a customer focus. In this regard, it is useful to distinguish between the concepts of 'crowd control' and 'crowd management'.

According to Getz (2012, p. 236), **crowd control** generally "*involves security and other measures that become necessary when there is a problem*". **Crowd management**, on the other hand, "*has to be integrated throughout the design process and management systems*" in order to facilitate a positive event experience and prevent problems from arising.

In terms of the event experience, what makes a crowd management approach superior to crowd control approach?

A key decision that potentially impacts on event safety, as well as other event outcomes, involves selection of an appropriate security company. The security industry is one in which the level of professionalism and customer focus may vary. Hence, it is important to select a company that is licensed, and only employs security staff who are licensed, fully qualified, hold other certifications such as first aid training, and capable of carrying out their role in a professional and dependable manner. Other important considerations include the number of security staff required and the extent to which the company and its staff have local knowledge and experience.

In terms of numbers, a general rule of thumb is one security guard per 100 attendees, however this number can vary depending on the size and type of event, as well as the area involved and the type of venue. Security needs at events in which alcohol is served may be greater than usual. In festive, high-energy situations, crowds may become more volatile and more difficult to manage. Fundamental to the expertise required by security staff is a basic understanding of crowd psychology and collective behaviour. This includes the ability to spot volatile situations quickly and take appropriate action.

Crowd psychology is a branch of social psychology concerned with the behaviours and thought processes of both the individual crowd members and the crowd as a separate entity. Collective behaviour is a key concept in sociology, and refers to social processes and events which do not reflect the existing social structure, but which emerge in a spontaneous way. This behaviour may take many forms but often violates societal norms and is driven by group dynamics, encouraging people to act in ways that they would consider unthinkable under normal circumstances. Both areas of enquiry examine similar phenomenon and often point to similar outcomes.

A key concept is the notion that the psychology of a crowd (or mob) differs from the psychology of individuals that are part of it and the psychologies of the individuals and the crowd interact. At a large event or whenever crowds form, the potential for anti-social behaviour exists and is heightened by the fact that the way in which a crowd acts may be heavily influenced by a perceived loss of responsibility amongst individual members of the crowd. The likely impact is influenced by the extent of group polarization in which likeminded people tend to reinforce one another's viewpoints. Group polarization tends to strengthen the opinions of individuals within the group. The degree to which the members of a crowd experience a perceived loss of responsibility, and an impression of universality of behaviour exists, also depends, at least partly, on the size of the crowd. With larger crowds, a greater impact could be anticipated.

? *Do you think that the influence of group behaviour on individual behaviour is likely to be greater for some individuals than for others? Why?*

Did you know? In sociology, the study of collective behaviour adopts a more positive perspective. Consistent with what may occur at many planned events, different types of crowds are identified that vary in terms of levels of interaction, emotional intensity, and levels of shared focus. Crowds may be divided into the following five categories:

■ *Casual crowds* refers to collections of individuals that have gathered temporarily in one location. There tends to be minimal interaction between crowd members and this is the type of crowd that could be expected amongst commuters at a train station or shoppers at a shopping centre.

■ *Conventional crowds* may refer to individuals who come together for certain types of planned events such as concerts, art shows and graduations. In this type of setting there is a degree of interaction as a result of their shared focus of attention and interest.

■ *Expressive crowds* are where people come together to release emotions. Examples include: celebration of a sporting or an election victory; mourning at a funeral.

■ *Acting crowds* are where there is high emotion, high energy and a high level of focus. An example is soccer hooliganism that may take place before, during and / or after the actual sporting event. Behaviour at these events may include rioting, violence and other forms of anti-social behaviour that can often have a significant impact on the external environment.

■ *Protest crowds*, unlike the previous four crowd types, have very clear direction, focus and leadership. There is also less variability in terms of the emotions of crowd members. For example, political protests and trade union demonstrations.

From an event security perspective, a key question relates to the extent to which the psychology of a crowd impacts on individual behaviour and the extent to which that influence may lead to anti-social behaviour. While opinions have varied over the last few decades, they may all provide insights into individual and crowd behaviour in an event situation.

? *What type of crowd generally exists at an international cricket match? What factors associated with that cricket match may impact on the type of crowd?*

There are three theories that explain extreme behaviour of crowds at events or in other collective situations. While these differ significantly, they all provide insights that can potentially inform event organisers about the security issues that may arise in an event context. They are:

■ *Contagion Theory* adopts an extremely negative view of crowd behaviour and, in fact, proposes that members of a crowd will often abandon all personal responsibility for their actions. According to this theory, crowds or mobs exert a hypnotic effect over crowd members and, as a consequence, they tend to identify with the mob leading them to engage in irrational and anonymous acts.

■ *Convergence Theory*, on the other hand, adopts the view that crowds are generally comprised of like-minded people with a shared purpose. Hence, crowd participation and behaviour express existing beliefs, opinions and sentiments, and are not necessarily irrational.

■ *Emergent-norm Theory* tends to adopt a view that could be regarded as a middle ground. According to this theory, crowd behaviour is representative of the values and beliefs of individual crowd members but is also shaped and influenced by the energy of the crowd and the emotions displayed within the crowd at a particular point in time.

While some of the theory that underpins our knowledge of crowd behaviour can be confusing and, at times, contradictory, an understanding of the various theories can provide insights that contribute to our capacity to address security issues in a range of different situations.

Key tips:

Continue to monitor and follow government advice in order to take appropriate action and make informed decisions about your events.

If you have to cancel your event make sure you are well prepared:

■ Contact your insurer to discuss the terms of your event cover.

■ Communicate with your stakeholders before you cancel or postpone your event.

■ Review the contract conditions to understand the impact of your cancellation.

■ Have a crisis communicating plan available to deal with cancellations.

■ Where possible consider delivering alternative solutions.

■ Manage your communications, and maintain engagement and trust with your audience.

Summary

In these litigious times, it is more important than ever for event managers to recognise and understand their legal obligations and be able to ensure compliance. There are a range of legal compliance issues that need to be addressed in the planning and conduct of events. Adherence to relevant legislation, regulative requirements, and the need to obtain appropriate licenses and permits, is essential for successful and sustainable operations in the events industry. And while relevant legislation and regulations vary from location to location around the world, legal compliance in the events industry generally involves a focus on:

■ Business registration, trade practices and taxes.

■ Employee rights, responsibilities and health and safety.

■ Event security, safety and licensing.

■ Compliance with regulations specific to certain event types.

Although there is broad acceptance for the need to proactively assess and manage the risks that exist at planned events, zero risk is not achievable. At the same time, every effort must be made to identify potential risks and maintain the capacity for immediate response to minimise their severity. The risk management process generally involves: identifying internal and external stakeholders; identifying the risks associated with running an event, as well as the causes; establishing controls for all risks and conducting a risk analysis; evaluating all risks and completing a risk management plan; implementation, documentation and communication of that plan to all stakeholders followed by on-going monitoring and review; and finally, immediate response to mitigate the severity of incidents as they occur.

Crowd behaviour at events can have major implications in terms of security, the maintenance of control, and the risk of personal injury, loss of life, property damage and public disorder. Hence, the key determinants of crowd behaviour need to be addressed so that a proactive approach to crowd management can be adopted. In this regard, a key concept relates to the influence of crowd behaviour on individual behaviour. Different types of crowds can be identified that vary in terms of levels of interaction, emotional intensity and levels of shared focus, and may be divided into the following categories: casual crowds; conventional crowds; expressive crowds; acting crowds; and protest crowds. Understanding the type of crowd that exists at a particular event provides clues in terms of how to address security and emergency management issues at that event.

7

Industry profile: Leo Gester, Risk management and safety expert, grant writer

Leo is an event producer and project specialist with over 11 years' experience managing different types of events. Examples include sporting events (Melbourne Cup Carnival, Australian Football League), music festivals (Beyond the Valley, Rainbow Serpent, Red Bull Music Festival), gala and themed events (Radio Awards), arts and cultural festivals (Virgin Australia Melbourne Fashion Festival, Dark Mofo, Melbourne Food and Wine Festival) to name a few. His expertise extends to managing corporate functions, brand activations, major exhibitions, but also smaller community events.

As an accredited Safety Officer Leo has an extensive track record managing staff and patron safety at events. During the pandemic Leo was an advocate of collaboration across industries to ensure events could continue to function under Covid safety plans – before Covid-safe plans were rolled out by the government. He has been actively collaborating and working with local councils in developing risk and safety plans, which he believes complement each other, but each has its own focal points.

Leo works closely with councils and funding bodies on grant applications and has been successful in winning over 30 grants totaling in excess of $450,000. As a grant writer, he has an extensive record in acquiring funds from private and public sectors. As a risk assessor Leo can prioritise risk and emergency plans which vary from minor to major events. He has well-developed problem-solving approaches and a strong focus on continuous improvement practices.

Key attributes and expertise

- Versatility and flexibility. Ability to work across sectors.
- Empathetic, active listener and curious
- Eye for detail, excellent written and verbal communication
- Committed to setting sustainable event goals
- Stakeholder management and knowledge exchange ability
- Dedicated to knowledge sharing and continuous improvement

When managing your event projects what are some key issues you come across?

It's not uncommon to encounter a box-ticking attitude to risk management. People can be reluctant to pay to develop adequate risk and safety planning and documentation, because they think 'what could possibly go wrong'? And depending on the risk profile of the event, the likelihood of disaster striking is often low. But that doesn't mean you shouldn't be prepared.

Regardless of the type of event, whether it's an outdoor wedding or a festival, a good event planner must strive to identify all risks involved. A key consideration is to plan and consult experts in risk and emergency planning that match your activities. Having a good understanding of the type of event and its objectives also assists in creating an effective emergency plan, while considering all stakeholder needs. Good knowledge in Covid-safety planning has also become essential, and the event manager should feel confident to carry out any emergency response plans. It's essential to brief all stakeholders on the plans in place, as well as the organisational structure of responsibilities, so there is awareness and a collaborative spirit to deal with issues should they arise. It's all good and well to have a plan, but if people aren't prepared to implement it when an emergency arises, it won't be much help.

What is the key advice to event planners when applying for council permits?

Don't use a cookie cutter approach. Some councils are far more demanding than others in the scope of information they require. It's easy to either provide too much information, which may lead to unnecessary questions, or not enough, which can delay your applications as you will be sent a RFI (Request for Further Information) and will go back to the bottom of the pile.

Don't forget that risks do not necessarily mean *risks of injury*. It can be financial risk, reputational risk, risk to the local amenity, etc. Councils have to balance the needs and wants of both commercial and residential stakeholders. Therefore demonstrating that you are addressing the various ways your event can have an impact is important. Noise management is essential, as is waste management, and controlling how patrons access and exit from your event. If people notify the council of excessive noise, leftover rubbish, or rowdy patrons turning business away from local shops, you may not get a permit again.

What are some commonly overlooked elements in risk management planning - when applying for grant applications?

Flow

Depending on the nature of the event, patron flow shows how the event planner has thought of entry into the event (ingress), internal flow, and exit (egress). Key considerations include scheduling of activities, site planning and appropriate distribution of gates and thoroughfares. This is important because, regardless of the number of expected patrons, whether it's 50 or over 10,000, choke points can appear and lead to crowd crush or damage to infrastructure in the event of an emergency.

An infamous example of crowd flow gone wrong is the 2016 Falls Festival crush when thousands of people tried to race from one stage to another at the same time. 80 people were injured and the organisers had to pay out $7M on top of hefty legal costs and facing an inquest. There were only two ways in or out of the tent, and while the exit widths and paths of travel were technically legal, their concentration at one end of the tent and the scheduling of acts led to this massive and sudden movement with devastating consequences.

Traffic and pedestrian management plan

Patrons remain the organiser's responsibility until they have left the *vicinity*, not just the *event site*. After a late night concert, it is not uncommon for patrons to wander off into the back streets and display anti-social behaviour (public urination, broken glass, shouting) – if you let them. An appropriate traffic and pedestrian management plan should be in place to ensure patrons arrive and leave safely, and without adversely impacting the local amenity. Event permits and licenses can quickly get cancelled when residents complain to authorities about the aftermath of an event.

This is often underestimated as planners spend so much time focusing on what happens during the event that they overlook what takes place outside of the event

7

site. Important factors include having good security and traffic management contractors, who proactively implement traffic and security plans developed collaboratively. Staggering egress (whereby people do not all leave at the same time) is the single most effective thing you can do to manage a crowd exiting an event, but it is not always easy. For instance, concert promoters always want the headliner to play last, and everyone sticks around for the headliner!

Fatigue management

Don't kill yourself working! Most grants require you to demonstrate an 'in-kind' component, which means something provided free of charge or at a discount. This could be free venue or equipment hire, consultancy or ancillary services, etc. But these are not always easy to get, so the most common thing people include is their own time (or their team's). It's not healthy to work around the clock for weeks and only get paid if the event goes well. It's also often not looked well upon by grant assessors, as the intention behind the grant is for you to produce a sustainable source of revenue while producing the intended outcome. It might seem like you're showing a willingness to make sacrifices to get the project up, but you're not doing yourself any favours.

What key advice would you give event planners when applying for council grants?

Make sure your risk management plan matches your activities. This is important so the assessor clearly understands you have the knowledge and confidence to implement the right measures to execute your event safely, and respond to emergencies adequately. Don't just use 'stock' standard plans, and remember there are interdependencies between risks. If it rains, your audience will need shelter: in a park or greenfield site this could be trees. But if there is also lightning, the last place you want to be is near a tree. What is your weather contingency? Can you direct your crowd somewhere else? Should you just cancel if a storm is forecast? And if so, do you have cancellation insurance?

Put thought into your event, show you know what you are doing –- or have consulted someone who does. Have a good eye for detail and understand chains of events, how one thing may lead to another. Good planning is about being pragmatic – don't hope for the best and plan for the worst.

Any final tips project managers?

Have an empathetic and collaborative mindset.

Events involve a lot of people that come together very quickly. As an event manager you have to negotiate around competing priorities and needs to achieve a shared outcome – but a lot of contractors and stakeholders don't see it this way. They sometimes want to get in, get their stuff done and get out, even if they get in the way of someone else. It's your job to make all the pieces of the puzzle come together neatly.

It's critical to understand people's needs, and know when to cater for them vs. when to put your foot down. But don't assume you know better than everyone else because you planned the whole event, some contractors have worked on more events than you ever will – because they constantly go from one to another day after day. So listen to people, make sure they understand you value their opinion, and when required, compromise – but constructively. It's a fine line, and it's not something you can learn in school. You just might have to make a few bad decisions before you understand how much rope to give people.

Have a sound budget plan

Make sure the budget is comprehensive (but have a contingency). Set your ticket price once you've factored in all costs, not before. It can be tempting to put the event on sale as early as possible to use the ticketing revenue to finalise your planning, but what happens if costs creep up and you suddenly find out that even if you sell out, you won't make any money?

There is always an element of financial risk in running an event, especially if it's not something you have executed already. But particularly when applying for grants, you should never budget based on a sell-out show. This will make your project look unviable, because if things don't go as well, you will be losing a lot. Depending on the scale and nature of the event, I usually budget for 30-70% attendance.

Finally, make sure your budget is transparent. You will spend a lot of time working on it so it will make sense to you, but not necessarily to someone else. Many grant assessors look at the budget first, and if it doesn't stack up or is too obtuse, they won't look at anything else. Break down your costs to highlight how you got there. For instance don't write 'Staff' and a figure attached to it, but provide notes to say "*XX* staff x *XX* hours at $*XX* p/h…" for each category of staff. It may seem obvious but a lot of people forget these details.

Be flexible and responsive.

It's OK for things to change. It is better to be responsive to changes of conditions adequately rather than stubbornly stick to the original plan which may be inadequate. Be ready to adapt to situations to negotiate the best outcome. Events are always about problem-solving and compromising. Consider everyone's priorities as they differ. Make sure everyone walks away happy. When it comes to risk management there is always someone who will be impacted by a particular measure and a chain of events. Be ready to acknowledge that and communicate the key compromises while upholding the standard that is required for the event to succeed.

7

Review questions

1. Although some of the details associated with liquor licencing vary from location to location around the world, can you identify the key issues and concerns that liquor licencing seeks to address?

2. There are three types of insurance policies that are relevant to different situations in which insurance cover is required. Describe three event-related situations in which each type of insurance policy applies.

3. With reference to the three elements of negligence, explain the actions that an event manager can take to mitigate the risk of a negligence claim at a local festival involving a range of physical activities.

4. When organising a major sporting event in which rivalry from opposing fans has been a traditional feature, what possible risks could be identified during the planning process? How could the event manager mitigate those risks?

5. Explain the key differences between crowd management and crowd control. With regard to the staging of an indoor music concert, which of these alternative approaches would you regard as the most appropriate?

6. Explain what you believe to be the most important knowledge, attitude, and skill requirements of security staff at a mega-sporting event?

7. With what sociologists describe as 'acting crowds' in which behaviour has, at times, involved rioting and violence, what actions should be considered during the planning and design stages to reduce the incidence of anti-social behaviour?

8. There are three theories that explain extreme behaviour of crowds at events or in other collective situations – contagion theory, convergence theory and emergent-norm theory. In reflecting on events that you have attended, which of these three theories would you regard as the most realistic?

9. A key element of the risk management process is the capacity for immediate response to minimise negative outcomes. What does this requirement imply for the personal attributes needed for security and emergency management staff?

10. What actions should be taken by event organisers to ensure that the risk management process is clearly understood by all event stakeholders?

Workshop activities

Scenario A

You have been approached to organise the annual graduation for your local university. There are 2000 graduates to consider with a number of indoor and outdoor restrictions and additional safety rules. In small groups discuss how you would reimagine this important event, so it can go ahead safely under the new restrictions.

Scenario B

You are working for a local council and an event organiser has approached you with an application for a local music festival. In a draft email, communicate all the relevant documentation that is required to complete and outline the key steps to the process.

Scenario C

You are planning a new festival to rejuvenate the local community. Create a communication plan with your stakeholders in order to be prepared should you need to cancel as a result of new restrictions. The communication plan should list these key points:

1. An overview of your planned event
2. A list of your key stakeholders
3. An email outlining your concern about an upcoming event disruption
4. A back up plan to be presented as an alternative solution.

Scenario D

As part of your risk management plan, you have been asked to design an emergency plan showing entry and exit points and clearly marking the car parking versus bus area. You can research local sites for existing plans and improve them. Alternatively, use design tools illustrate a traffic management/emergency plan for an existing major site of your choice.

References and further reading

Andersson, T. D., Getz, D., & Jutbring, H. (2020). Balancing value and risk within a city's event portfolio: an explorative study of DMO professionals' assessments. *International Journal of Event and Festival Management.* 11 (4), 413-432

Bassetti, C. (2016) A novel interdisciplinary approach to socio-technical complexity. In: Cecconi F. (ed) *New Frontiers in the Study of Social Phenomena.* Springer, Cham

Drury, J. (2020). Recent developments in the psychology of crowds and collective behaviour. *Current Opinion in Psychology*, 35, 12-16.

Feltmann, K., Gripenberg, J., & Elgán, T. H. (2020). Compliance to the alcohol law: overserving to obviously intoxicated visitors at music festivals. *International Journal of Environmental Research and Public Health*, 17(22), 8699.

Getz, D. (2012) *Event Studies: Theory, research and policy for planned events*, Routledge.

Interligi, L. (2010). Compliance culture: A conceptual framework. *Journal of Management & Organization*, 16(2), 235-249.

Lofland, J. (2017). *Protest: Studies of collective behaviour and social movements*. Routledge.

Ludvigsen, J. A. L., & Hayton, J. W. (2020). Toward COVID-19 secure events: Considerations for organizing the safe resumption of major sporting events. *Managing Sport and Leisure*, 1-11.

Mayer, M., & Cocco, A. R. (2021). Pandemic and sport: The challenges and implications of publicly financed sporting venues in an era of no fans. *Public Works Management & Policy*, 26(1), 26-33.

O'Toole, W., Luke, S., Brown, J., Tatrai, A., & Ashwin, P. (2020). *Crowd Management: Risk, security and health*. Oxford: Goodfellow Publishers.

Scott, C., & Radburn, M. (2020). Understanding crowd conflict: social context, psychology and policing. *Current Opinion in Psychology*, 35, 76-80.

Zhao, H., Thrash, T., Kapadia, M., Wolff, K., Hölscher, C., Helbing, D., & Schinazi, V. R. (2020). Assessing crowd management strategies for the 2010 Love Parade disaster using computer simulations and virtual reality. *Journal of the Royal Society Interface*, 17, 167: 20200116.

Ziakas, V., Antchak, V., & Getz, D. (2021). *Crisis Management and Recovery for Events Issues and Directions* Goodfellow Publishers.

Websites

www.apraamcos.com.au/

www.cvent.com/en/blog/events/event-postponement-and-cancellation-guide

www.melbourne.vic.gov.au/arts-and-culture/film-music-busking/filming-in-melbourne/filming-permits/

www.pavilionaustralia.com/

www.qmf.net.au/

www.visitscotland.org/events/advice-materials/health-safety

8 Hospitality and catering concepts

Learning objectives

On completion of this chapter, you will be able to:

➤ Explain various approaches to catering in the events industry

➤ Understand key issues associated with menu design

➤ Explain the various phases of catering operations

➤ Recognise the importance of sustainability in an event catering context

➤ Understand various approaches to sustainability in an event catering context

➤ Perform a hazard analysis to ensure food safety

➤ Provide an overview of approaches and processes associated with the elimination or reduction of food wastage

➤ Discuss procurement issues and challenges, as well as issues associated with the safe and secure storage of food

➤ Understand key principles of food and beverage matching.

Food is not only essential for our sustenance and survival but often defines a culture. It is in fact, a central feature of most cultures and lifestyles around the world. Cultural elements that can be expressed through the food that people eat, the way in which it is prepared, and the knowledge, skills and rituals that surround gastronomic traditions, are useful and effective ways of communicating and sustaining a national culture. As a result, food represents a particularly important element at cultural festivals and events.

? *What cultures that you are familiar with have recognisably different traditions in terms of the food that is eaten and how it is prepared and presented?*

Food is a key element in the successful staging of most festivals and events. It can represent an incredibly positive and engaging approach to enhancing and enriching an otherwise standard event. The broad array of food types, food presentations, and approaches to food service, can add colour and appeal, making the event appealing, memorable and significant.

What events have you recently attended in which food has added significantly to the colour, excitement, and impact of the event?

While the importance of event catering varies between events, there are few if any events that can afford to ignore the provision of some form of food or beverage. Even for events of relatively short duration or in which food and beverages are not a key focus, catering will generally need to be considered. In fact, even a two-hour meeting is likely to conclude with some food and/or beverages that facilitate social engagement, discussion, and perhaps the development of contacts. The impact of F&B service can be facilitated by event caterers through sound procurement practices, skilful and well-thought-out menu design, and creative catering practices.

The event catering process

The process of event catering varies depending on whether it is managed in-house or contracted out to external caterers. However, in general, event catering follows a three-phase process that commences with set-up, followed by the food and beverage (F&B) service, and finally, clean-up.

- **Set-up** involves getting the venue ready for F&B service. This may require the transportation of supplies to the venue. The venue may or may not have cooking facilities. If it does, other equipment, such as pots, pans and serving trays may need to be taken and unloaded at the venue, along with tables, chairs, and other furniture. Front of house set-up involves laying out tables and chairs according to a floor plan. For outdoor events, tents are generally divided into two staging areas, one for food service and the other, a temporary kitchen for cooking.

Case study 8.1: Setting up a food stall at a festival

The caterer would need to apply for a permit in order to participate at a festival. Consideration needs to be given on the lead planning time – is it three months or less? Can the caterer physically procure the food and recruit staff? What facilities are nearby? This information is usually obtained beforehand upon which permits are granted. Consider the layout of the site, water supply, proximity to the road and supply of electricity.

- **The service** involves a number of staff which generally includes:
  - ☐ Catering co-ordinator
  - ☐ Supervisor
  - ☐ Waiters
  - ☐ Stewards
  - ☐ Buffet attendants
  - ☐ Bartenders
  - ☐ Kitchen manager.
- **Clean-up** involves the cleaning of everything including equipment, and the packing and return of equipment and furniture. Supplies such as glassware, dishes and silver need to be thoroughly washed. All rented supplies need to be washed and returned, and the event venue restored to normal. It's often during clean-up that items can be damaged or lost, so care needs to be taken to avoid these problems.

Key questions

Some key questions to be considered in F&B provision are:

- Will F&B provision be a peripheral activity, or will it be a central feature and perhaps, an important income stream of the event?
- Should F&B be managed in-house, or should it be contracted to an external caterer or caterers?
- Should F&B service be developed in a manner that is consistent with the event theme, or should it be based on a standard F&B approach?
- Will alcohol be provided?
- How many catering staff are required?
- How can food safety be ensured?
- What should the menu look like?

8

- How can food wastage be eliminated or minimised?
- How will issues associated with COVID-19 be addressed?
- What other sustainability issues should be addressed?

Each of these questions will now be considered.

A central feature or a peripheral activity?

In view of its potential positive impact, a fair degree of planning and creativity must go into any event catering activity. Hence, unless client needs and preferences dictate otherwise, F&B should be treated with the high degree of importance it deserves. At the same time, there are a broad range of catering types that offer varying levels of sophistication. Different stakeholders will expect different levels and types of F&B service. For a mega or major sporting event for example, these catering types may include:

- VIP catering
- Staff catering
- Sponsor catering
- Competitor / athlete catering
- Fixed concessions
    - ☐ Fast food
    - ☐ Beverages
- Mobile concessions
    - ☐ Coffee carts
    - ☐ Hamburger / hot dog units
    - ☐ Ice-cream carts
- A combination

While VIP catering may involve the highest level of F&B service, hospitality and catering may also be a major part of the package that is offered to sponsors and their guest. On the other hand, competitors or athletes may have quite specific dietary requirements that relate to their sport.

How would you expect staff catering to vary from the catering that is provided to athletes or competitors?

In-house or outsourced?

For event organisers that offer the same or similar event on a regular or on-going basis, there may be a sound argument for managing the catering function in-house, particularly if the appropriate expertise exists within the event business. A key benefit of in-house catering is a deep knowledge of the event and the venue in which catering will take place.

Are you aware of any events in which catering is managed in-house? What is the style of catering provided?

However, for relatively large events, and particularly for outdoor events, catering is usually outsourced. This may involve outsourcing to one master caterer or perhaps, outsourcing to several smaller caterers.

In what circumstances do you think an event would benefit by contracting out to several caterers?

Selection of the most appropriate caterer is an important decision but as with most decisions that involve the selection of suppliers, evaluating the potential for development of a sound, long-term relationship is the most important consideration. The expertise and style of the event caterer needs to be consistent with the size and nature of the event, the profile, and culinary preferences of attendees, as well as the needs and preferences of other participants. However, the basis for a sound, ongoing business partnership also needs to exist between the event caterer and event organiser. From a cost management perspective, key issues include:

- What payment terms and conditions can be negotiated?
- What does the per capita expenditure (ie. cost per attendee) look like?
- Are deposits or upfront fees required?
- Will the event caterer take responsibility for breakages and losses?
- Who is going to be responsible for permits and licences, including liquor licenses?

What items could be considered when seeking to reduce the cost of event catering? In what circumstances could cost be a particularly important concern?

Themed or standard?

A strong and unique theme allows an event to stand out amongst current, emerging, and potential competitors. However, for that theme to have maximum impact, it needs to be supported and reinforced by all other elements of the event, including F&B. When a theme can be reinforced, and in the absence of other priorities, event catering should be consistent with, and support, the theme.

If the event theme relates to a nationality or culture, a consistent F&B approach will be relatively straightforward. Even with an historical theme, there may be approaches to catering that can be utilised to create the appropriate ambiance. In some circumstances, the use of food colours may be another way of providing support to an event theme.

Some events adopt a historical theme. How might aspects of catering be planned and designed for an event with a medieval theme?

Responsible service of alcohol

For a large proportion of events, alcohol service is available and can range from sipping wine as part of an outdoor picnic, drinking beer or wine as part of the networking process at a business event, tasting a range of wines at a wine and food festival, to much heavier consumption of alcohol at a New Year's Eve party. However, from a legal perspective all of these events are treated in the same way.

Responsible Service of Alcohol provisions are established in several countries, primarily to reduce the risks associated with excessive consumption of alcohol. Several events, including major sporting events, have been cancelled as a result of violence or other anti-social behaviour accompanying intoxication amongst attendees. Injuries due to broken glass from bottles or glasses may be another risk associated with alcohol consumption at events. Responsible Service of Alcohol generally involves:

- Ensuring that there is no under-age drinking. The drinking age varies in different parts of the world.
- Preventing disruptive, violent, or intoxicated behaviour
- Refusal of service to intoxicated individuals
- Other measures to ensure that all patrons, guests, and staff are treated with respect.

Event security also has an important and obvious role when the consumption of alcohol is part of the event.

Explain the benefits and risks associated with the service of alcohol at festivals and events. When might it be advisable to withhold the service of alcohol?

Catering staff numbers

The number of staff that are required will obviously vary depending on the type of event and the level of F&B service. In general, the more sophisticated the F&B service, the lower the ratio of staff to clients. While actual numbers may vary, the following ratios provide a guide:

- Silver service: 1 to 10
- 5-star service: 1 to between 20 and 30
- Standard catering: 1 to between 40 and 50

As well as the type of F&B service being offered, the physical dimensions of the venue also need to be considered when determining staff numbers.

How can food safety be ensured?

Food safety is clearly an important aspect of any event. In the absence of any problems, efforts to ensure food safety may go unnoticed. The outcomes associated with the provision of contaminated food can be disastrous.

Raw, partially or fully cooked food may become contaminated at a range of points during all phases of getting food from the farm to the consumer. Food safety planning involves identifying all critical control points (CCPs) at all stages in the production, distribution, and service of food. Identifying these critical points and taking appropriate action is essential.

A CCP is any stage or step in the process of getting food to event participants where the food may become contaminated or corrupted in some way. Hence, a CCP also represents a point at which preventive measures should be applied to eliminate or at the very least, minimise a food safety hazard. Bacterial growth, chemical contamination, or any other forms of adulteration of food are hazards that must be identified and addressed.

At what stage or stages is the risk of food contamination the greatest?

One systematic plan that can be implemented to ensure food safety is referred to as Hazard Analysis and Critical Control Point (HACCP). HACCP generally involves the following 7 step process:

1. **Conduct a hazard analysis**. Due consideration must be given to all possible food hazards. These could relate to:

   ☐ Ingredients utilised in the preparation of food

   ☐ Staff involved at any point with the provision of food

   ☐ Equipment that is used in the provision of food

☐ Chemicals that may come in contact with food

☐ The various processes involved in getting food to event participants.

The need for each hazard to be addressed in the HACCP plan must be determined. As with any risk management process, both the likelihood and severity of the risk must be evaluated as part of this process.

2. **Identify all CCPs.** This involves identifying any point at which a food hazard may exist and hence, any point at which that hazard can be completely eliminated or at the very least, reduced to a safe level.

3. **Set critical limits.** To be effective, these must be observable and measurable limits that when achieved, eliminate or at least, control the hazard.

4. **Establish a monitoring system.** This system must provide the means to ensure that critical limits are achieved.

5. **Establish corrective actions** that must be taken if and when a critical limit is not achieved.

6. **Establish verification procedures.** These are ongoing procedures that ensure that the HACCP plan is working.

7. **Establish recordkeeping procedures.** This is an extremely important step in the HACCP process. If anything goes wrong, it allows for an examination of the whole process to identify how the problem occurred and how it can be eliminated in the future. Recordkeeping involves:

☐ A summary of the hazard analysis

☐ The full HACCP plan

☐ Supporting documents that have been used to determine:
   ◆ CCPs
   ◆ Critical limits
   ◆ Procedures

☐ Records that have been created during the plan operation, including:
   ◆ Monitoring
   ◆ Corrective action
   ◆ Verification records.

The role of procurement in food safety

The process of procuring or purchasing food for a festival or event can have major implications in terms of food safety. Key actions are:

■ Ensure that selection of a food supplier is based on performance in terms of food quality and safety, and not on financial considerations.

■ Seek out food with minimal packaging and recyclable materials.

- Packaging needs to be food-safe and capable of holding the food without breaking or leaking, particularly while in transit.
- Demonstrate a clear preference for local products that have a good safety record.
- Conduct the research required to find out about the best, most reputable suppliers and the most favourable deals that can be negotiated.
- Ensure that all food items are stored safely and securely prior to delivery and consumption.

How would you go about the conduct of research to identify the best or most appropriate supplier? What are the key characteristics you would be looking for?

Case study 8.2: Preparing meals for athletes

Scenario: You have been approached by a major football club to prepare balanced meals for athletes during a sporting carnival. The information given to the caterer is the number of athletes (40), three meals per day over 5 days. The brief requests the caterer to include equal number of vegetarian and meat options. Access is via the oval with water supply and electricity. In this case the caterer would need 4 staff per day to help with food preparation and adopting the silver service service as mentioned above.

Event menu guidelines

Development of a creative and attractive menu selection is an essential element of event catering. Poor menu design can detract significantly from the perceived quality of F&B service. In particular, it is important to provide menu choices that are clear and unambiguous, but without overwhelming attendees with a huge menu that seeks to embrace too much variety.

Some more specific guidelines for menu development include:

1. Commence with a sound understanding of the profile of event participants. This includes a knowledge of demographic issues such as age and region but more importantly, a knowledge of their food preferences. While that doesn't leave out the possibility of providing a menu selection that takes event attendees beyond their comfort zones, these decisions need to be made with an awareness of current preferences.

2. Provide an appropriate range of choices and try to anticipate any special needs or dietary requirements. As already indicated don't overdo the number of menu choices.

3. As much as possible, incorporate locally sourced foods and clearly communicate this on the menu. Also include seasonal foods and make sure that all food is as fresh and nutritious as possible.

4. Be aware of ethnic or regional tastes that may be relevant given the profile of event attendees. This may be particularly important when considering spicy or peppery food items.

5. Ensure that the provision of food and beverages integrates well with the overall event schedule.

6. Provide an appropriate setting including ample space and comfortable furniture. The room and furniture may vary depending on the event objectives. For example, at business events where the development of contacts represents an important outcome, a larger space with less furniture may be required, allowing people to move around and network.

7. Finish off with an attractive presentation that adds some colour and flair to the F&B service.

Menu styles

When styling the menu consider the category and the event it fits in:

- Cocktail style luncheons, canapes on arrival and dinners
- Stand up dinner style events (plates can be served otherwise remain at food stations)
- Buffet style or sit-down menu.

Case study 8.3: Menu styling for a cultural wedding

Yo India is a food truck business offering Indian food experiences for a range of private and public events. It has been globally recognised as one of the top 80 food trucks around the world and carries numerous local awards. Yo India delivers a variety themed events including weddings with couples from diverse backgrounds. This is how the owner, Conan, approached the menu styling of a Sri Lankan wedding considering cultural influences.

Image 8.1: Yo India food truck

Understand your clients.
In this case, the bride was Sri Lankan and the groom was Australian. So the first thing is to understand their own vision for the wedding. Is it going to be casual? Or very traditional? As in a lot of South-Asian families, the parents also have a large say in the food due to relatives and community attending the event – so I also had to understand the dynamics of the family, and if there are any cultural or religious restrictions.

Understanding budget limitations
Key consideration is to check if there is a budget. Some cultures are hesitant to openly share the budget, therefore being discreet is important. Be transparent. Let them know of menu costs. If they have preferences then you can give an indication of initial cost and together work out a plan that fits the client budget.

Understand the type of guests attending
What is the demographic of the people attending? As the bride was from Sri Lanka and the groom from Australia, Conan had to think of a menu that would be able to respect the bride's culture but also ensure that it would cater to local taste and trends.

Flow of event
Understanding how the event will be delivered. How many people are attending? What is the wedding day schedule? Where is the venue? The flow of the event plays a large role in the menu design especially if there are any time restrictions due to the venue. Time is a critical factor. Casual cocktail style events are becoming very popular but the traditional set-menu is always there, yet it requires more time.

Selecting the menu
The couple decided on a casual cocktail style with roving canapes and mains. This allowed everyone to mingle and respected the limited time that was allocated by the venue. The dessert would simply be the wedding cake. All the dishes respected the bride's Sri-Lankan roots with a touch of Melbourne. For the starters, the couple chose popular foods such as vegetarian samosas, paneer skewers, tandoori chicken sliders and Sri Lankan style tacos. For mains the couple chose chili jam chicken, coconut lamb curry & chickpea masala.

Service design according to the space
As a food truck business, Yo India has no permanent base. The truck is a moveable business and fits in with the client specification and given space. Therefore it's important to get a sense of place before determining how the service will be delivered. This can be decided once an initial inspection has been conducted. The team subsequently works out the design of service and particularly how the space is divided and which waiting staff are responsible for each section.

8

> **Did you know?** Food is key element in many cultures. Sometimes key decisions take place over social food experiences.

Alternative F&B presentations

As with menu selection, the approach taken to presentation can add to the appeal of the F&B service. Some alternative F&B presentations include:

- **Family style** which generally involves F&B service with platters of food set in the middle of tables. Diners are then able to serve themselves, selecting the type and volume of food they require.

- **Food stations** which adopt a cafeteria-style approach. Tables are staffed and generally feature different aspects of the menu.

- **French service** which adds a degree of flair to the F&B service. Here, flambé dishes or other dishes where preparation is completed at the table, adds some dramatic presentation to the dish.

What factors would you consider when deciding on the F&B presentation to be used at a business conference?

Food wastage

Food wastage occurs in an event context whenever processed, partially processed, or unprocessed foods, destined for consumption by event participants, are not, in fact, consumed. It may occur at any stage of the food chain. This is a major issue in terms of environmental sustainability.

The production of food has a massive impact on the planet, with a greater environmental impact than any other human activity. While food is an obvious necessity for human existence, it is grown at an incredible environmental cost. And about one third of that food is wasted. That loss occurs while, at the same time, more than 10% of the world's population is starving. This represents a tragic loss of land, water, and other resources as well as an enormous cost in terms of climate change, making food wastage perhaps the world's dumbest problem, occurring, as it does, at the intersection between social justice and climate change. While in general, one third of the world's food that is produced for consumption is wasted, the percentage may be closer to 40% in many developed countries. It has been estimated that more than 795 million people are starving, yet they could all be fed if less than half of the wasted food could be diverted to them.

From a climate change perspective, food wastage accounts for 8% of global emissions. If we were talking about a nation's global emissions, food wastage world come in at third, behind China and the United States. It is for these reasons that food wastage has become a key challenge that parts of the events industry are now seeking to address. Several food festivals around the world are therefore adopting a clear focus that addresses the problem of food wastage.

'Feeding the 5000' seeks to highlight what it refers to as 'the global food wastage scandal'. The events champion delicious food offerings as a way of highlighting the problem of food wastage and catalysing a global movement. Over 50 'Feeding the 5000' events have been staged around the world. At these events, delicious communal feasts are served up to 5000 people. Food for the event is made up entirely from food that would have otherwise gone to waste. The event itself brings together a broad coalition of different groups and organisations that are seeking to address the food wastage crisis, highlight the problem and extend its profile from a political perspective, and encourage and inspire new local initiatives.

In recognition of the fact that a key reason for food wastage is the 'Fear Of Running Out', a number of venues in the United Kingdom and Ireland have launched the #FORO initiative. This initiative aims to help venues, caterers, event organisers, event attendees, and other event participants, to reduce levels of food wastage.

In addition to the 'Fear Of Running Out', what factors do you think lead to food wastage at events?

The MICE industry is still a huge contributor to food wastage. In the meetings and events sector of the United States alone, approximately $21 billion worth of food is wasted, generally as a result of 'the Fear of Running Out'. Wastage also occurs as a result of poor planning and lower than anticipated levels of attendance. Most of the food that remains uneaten is still safe and nutritious.

Several other initiatives focus on the donation of food to shelters and community food banks, as a way of addressing the problem. In this way, food wastage is reduced by donating food that is prepared for an event but not eaten.

In the United States, a national, non-profit, New York-based organisation called ReFED, 'Rethink Food wastage through Economics and Data' utilises a broad range of evidence-based solutions to address food wastage.

ReFED estimate that through an annual investment of $14 billion over a 10-year period, it's possible to reduce food wastage by an incredible 45 million tons per year. That reduction represents a net annual benefit of approximately $73 billion. That represents an unbelievable five-to-one return, once again highlighting the fact that there is no trade-off between sustainability and long-term economic benefits, particularly in terms of reducing food wastage. Over a 10-year period, it is anticipated that the ReFED initiative can create more than 51,000 jobs.

In combatting and hopefully reducing food wastage, key questions that should be asked of event caterers are:

■ How is your F&B being managed once it has been prepared and delivered?

■ Will food that is left over, either at back of house or front of house, be used in a different meal?

■ Will food that is left over be donated or simply dumped?

■ Are food scraps being saved in the kitchens for re-use or compost?

Food audits should also become a regular part of the event catering process. Questions that should be asked as part of a food audit include:

■ How much uneaten food was left in the back of house?

■ How much uneaten food was left in the front of house?

■ Can the variety of food that is produced be reduced while, at the same time, providing a large enough range to satisfy dietary requirements and dietary preferences?

■ What special meals are ordered in advance but, for some reason, never picked up?

■ What happens with extra meals when attendance at events is lower than anticipated?

Issues associated with minimising food wastage need to be taken seriously and should be considered at planning and design stages. Addressing these issues not only tackles key problems associated with social justice and climate change but also offers the potential for long-term economic benefits.

> **Consider this:** There is the potential for huge cost savings through the reduction of food wastage at events. Why do you think there are not more event organisers seeking to take advantage of these potential savings?

Covid-safe event catering

The need for a Covid-safe environment leads to a broad range of considerations including:

- Issues associated with density;
- Physical distancing during the preparation of food in the back of house;
- Physical distancing during the provision and consumption of food in the front of house;
- Regular deep cleaning throughout all parts of the venue including kitchens;
- Personal hygiene: the provision of sanitiser dispensers and the utilisation of appropriate signage;
- Tracing which can utilise both digital and manual approaches;
- Staff training in all aspects of Covid-safe practices;
- Monitoring to ensure Covid-safe practices are carried out effectively;
- Consultation with all event participants to improve awareness and gain feedback;
- Ongoing incident management to address problems and achieve continuous improvement.

Several aspects of what were initially regarded as Covid-safe will become accepted approaches to event catering over the long-term.

Designing food experiences

An event manager needs to give due consideration to the type of experience provided. This means close consultation with the client to understand the main event goals. For example, if you are delivering a food service for a professional conference organiser (PCO) try to understand what the conference is all about. Does the PCO wish to encourage networking as part of the conference? If so, the menu design needs to allow for networking to take place, therefore it's an important discussion to have beforehand. A cocktail style evening and/or extra time allowance for a pre-dinner canape style may facilitate networking over a strict sit-down dinner.

Pairing food and wine

Event mangers do not always happen to be experts in food and wine pairing. There are experts who can assist with the choice of beverage according to the menu design. Consult them when designing themed food experiences to ensure memorable moments. Some basic principles to follow in food and wine pairing are outlined in this video: https://youtu. be/xuQo41ljHoY

Summary

Food is central to most cultures and is an essential feature of most planned events. Selection of food types, food presentations, and approaches to food service, can represent a creative and colourful way of making an event appealing and memorable. And while the importance of event catering varies, even for events of relatively short duration or in which food is not a key focus, catering in some form will need to be considered.

Catering at an event can be a peripheral activity designed primarily to provide sustenance, or a central feature and perhaps, an important income stream. It can be managed in-house or contracted to external caterers. Another important consideration relates to whether or not the F&B service should be designed in a manner that supports and reinforces the event theme. In many cases, the utilisation of catering to support the theme is relatively straightforward and adds significantly to the impact of the event.

A key consideration at several events relates to whether or not alcohol service is provided and how associated risks can be avoided. Regardless of the event, Responsible Service of Alcohol provisions must be adhered to. Another consideration relates to the number of catering staff required and this clearly depends on the level of service to be offered.

Food safety needs to be given adequate attention and can be addressed by following HACCP which generally involves:

- Conducting a hazard analysis
- Identifying all CCPs and setting critical limits
- Establishing a monitoring system
- Establishing corrective actions
- Establishing verification and recordkeeping procedures.

The minimisation of food wastage is a key sustainability issue that must be addressed. One third of the world's food is wasted while, at the same time, more than 10% of the world's population are starving. They could all be fed if less than half of the wasted food could be diverted to them. From a climate change perspective, food wastage accounts for 8% of global emissions and it is for these reasons that food wastage has become a key challenge that parts of the events industry are now seeking to address.

Approaches to minimising food wastage can vary but include donating to shelters and similar facilities, establishing food audits, or simply rethinking the amount and variety of food provided – directly tackling the usual response to 'the Fear Of running Out'.

The need for a Covid-safe environment gives rise to further considerations, aspects of which will become accepted approaches to event catering over the long-term. These include issues associated with density, physical distancing at back and front of house, regular deep cleaning, personal hygiene, tracing, staff training, monitoring to ensure compliance and effectiveness, and on-going incident management.

Industry profile: Conan Gomes, Event catering expert

Conan is an expert in catering for various styles of events. From private functions such as weddings and engagements, corporate functions and birthdays to public events such as community and music festivals, sporting events (minor, major), Conan is flexible enough to adapt his skills and business delivery to any event where food is required. Conan is owner of Yo India, rated by Lonely Planet as one of the best 80 food trucks globally. He works closely with local businesses to source ingredients and ensure sustainable and ethical food practices.

Skills and strengths

- Expertise in food concepts
- Menu styling and costing
- Food safety and handling
- Sourcing local food ingredients
- Application and permits
- Experiential food expert
- Stakeholder management
- Delivery of food experiences at all types of events

What are some key considerations with catering styles?

- First thing needed to be known is the type of event catering, number of people, location and timing. Once this is established, then the menu and service style can be designed according to what guests would like.

- Discuss all the requirements as a team and work with guests to choose the menu. Guests may have their own preferred providers however most likely may follow the event manager's suggestions in the delivery of an exceptional experience and based on a trustworthy relationship and sound advice.

- Timing is key: how does the catering expert ensure the fastest service?

- What are the formalities of the event and does it affect the menu? For example, are there any preferred snacks? Heavy meals? A combination?

- Number of people that can be served and the style of service. The fastest style is the one where guests pick up from the food truck with a limited menu. This can be done for guests of up to 200 people in a single event. Whereas, a buffet and cocktail style event can cater up to 300.

What are some considerations in your business?

Food service

Key things are how to conduct the food service and the staff requirements. For example, in public events customers come and order, pay and collect their food. In private functions, caterers may need to hire staff as the guest experiences are different.

- A table service involves waiters so it's advisable to train and brief staff beforehand.

- A cocktail style suggests waiters go around with platters. Brief the staff in the direction so all guests have a fair opportunity of being served.

- The service may be a combination of cocktail style and table service therefore flexibility is key.

Catering planning and operations

Space and layout

It is important to have an inspection of the site in order to evaluate the equipment requirements, entry and exit points. If space is limited, then as a caterer I am limited in the type of food option/menu I can offer especially for large scale events.

Casual staff recruitment

On very busy events I usually have a maximum of 5 people working in the kitchen. Additional waiters are required depending on the type of event. Sometimes waiters are not required if guests pick up the food from the food truck.

Food supply and storage

All food is cooked and plated in the food truck. No external kitchen is used. All food is stored in the truck and sourced fresh on the day.

Procurement issues and challenges

Supplier shortages or mistaken delivery on the day of event means I have to rush to find from somewhere else, often at a more inflated price. For large public events, sometimes it's hard to estimate how busy it gets. If it's busier than expected, running out of food means closing service so I can go to buy more food then prepare it.

Food and beverage matching

I encourage event caterers to seek food and beverage matching advice from wine connoisseurs. Matching local food with local wine is advisable in order to show support to local communities. This also provides opportunities for new collaboration especially when the local winery may also be a venue. Private functions may consider acknowledging the winemaker and any local food producers to educate guests on their community support efforts.

Health and safety

Being health conscious is important. Clients may ask for food experiences without prior knowledge of a healthy and balanced diet. As a qualified food professional, I share my knowledge in food trends and balanced food options, and this is a good way to build a trusting relationship with a client who hasn't the relevant expertise. It is important to convey trust in food handling and safety. As a caterer, make sure there are safe storage options during private events. I see it as my responsibility to educate the client on why it's important to cater for the right amount of people.

Forecasting guest numbers

If participating at repeated festivals, you can forecast the number of guests based on previous years. It is important to follow the trends and conduct research in consumer behaviour. At private events we always prepare extra food options due to the possibility of extra patrons attending the event.

Any final tips for event caterers?

Be flexible and prepare to cope with unexpected changes. For example, weather unpredictability may lead to extra food due to patrons not attending a public festival. As a meal provider, be prepared to deal with unexpected changes and plan to adapt to these changes. This may include setting up relationships with partners who are able to accept your extra food at short notice. An event caterer must be flexible, and this will create a distinctive advantage to your catering business over other suppliers who are not adaptable to unforeseen changes.

8

Review questions

1. The effort and resources devoted to event catering tends to vary significantly between events. Explain the factors that need to be considered when deciding how much time and other resources should be devoted to the planning, design, and implementation of event catering.

2. Several events have a unique event theme that may be supported and reinforced by appropriate F&B service. Using examples, explain how the type of food, the menu selection, the presentation of food, and the manner in which food is provided, can be planned, and designed creatively to support various event themes.

3. Event organisers need to decide whether the F&B service will be managed in-house or contracted out to external caterers. What are the key factors that need to be considered when making this decision? If contracting out to external caterers, what factors should be considered in the selection of appropriate caterers?

4. The service and consumption of alcohol at festivals and events brings with it some significant risks. What actions would you take and what processes would you put in place to mitigate those risks?

5. Food may become contaminated with bacteria at any point during all phases from procurement to consumption by attendees. Are there other food hazards that need to be considered? Explain the process that you would go through to identify and address all potential food hazards.

6. The purchasing of food for a festival or event can have major implications in terms of food safety. Discuss guidelines that need to be followed when purchasing food for consumption by event attendees.

7. Food wastage at events has become an important issue in recent decades. Discuss the impact of food wastage in terms of environmental sustainability. Explain the various approaches that can be taken in order to eliminate or at least, reduce food wastage at events.

8. Focusing in particular on the MICE sector, what guidelines can be developed for event caterers to ensure that food wastage is minimised? How can 'the Fear Of Running Out' be offset or overcome?

9. What are the key issues that need to be considered when conducting a food audit for an event?

10. How are issues associated with Covid-19 and the potential spread of other viruses likely to impact on event catering? What would you envisage as the most likely long-term impact?

Workshop activities

Scenario A

You have been approached to design a menu for a wedding of mixed culture. Decide on the cultural backgrounds of the bride and groom and consider the guest demographic. What menu style will you recommend to the couple?

Scenario B

You have been approached by a professional conference organiser to design the menu for a full day conference (9-5pm followed by a gala dinner 7.30-10.30pm). Based on 100 delegates, decide on what menu items and catering style you will offer. Decide on the number of staff required to help deliver the catering in order for the event to go smoothly. Decide on the set up of the food and beverage stations. (Use butchers' paper or digital shapes to show the layout). Breakdown of the event as follows:

- Registrations open at 8 am for a 9 am conference start
- Morning tea 10.30-11 am
- Lunch break 12.30 -1.30pm
- Afternoon tea 3-3.30pm
- Gala dinner starts at 7.30 with canapes starting at 6.30pm. Gala event includes a sit down 3 course meal and concludes at 10pm.

Scenario C

You have been approached to design a different style graduation event as a result of the pandemic. The brief includes a picnic style event including formal presentations. The event must include separate marquees for food and beverages to follow Covid-safe practices. Design the evening event starting at 5pm and concluding at 8.30 pm and design a food service experience that promises a memorable evening for graduands and guests. Share your findings in class and exchange best practices for the future of themed events.

8

References and further reading

Çagri, S., Mehmet, P., Mehmet, S., & Mustafa, Ç. (2017). A green model for the catering industry under demand uncertainty. *Journal of Cleaner Production*, 167, 459-472.

Derqui, B., Fayos, T., & Fernandez, V. (2016). Towards a more sustainable food supply chain: opening up invisible waste in food service. *Sustainability*, 8(7), 693.

Figueiredo, B., Larsen, H. P., & Bean, J. (2021). The cosmopolitan servicescape. *Journal of Retailing*, 97(2), 267-287.

Filimonau, V., Nghiem, V. N., & Wang, L. E. (2021). Food waste management in ethnic food restaurants. *International Journal of Hospitality Management*, 92, 102731.

Hennchen, B. (2019). Knowing the kitchen: Applying practice theory to issues of food waste in the food service sector. *Journal of Cleaner Production*, 225, 675-683.

Oldfield, T.L., White, E., & Holden, N.M. (2016). An environmental analysis of options for utilising wasted food and food residue. *Journal of Environmental Management*, 183(3), 826-835.

Slorach, P.C., Jeswani, H.K., Cuéllar-Franca, R., & Azapagic, A. (2019). Environmental and economic implications of recovering resources from food waste in a circular economy. *Science of The Total Environment*, 693.

Tuomi, A., & Tussyadiah, I. P. (2020). Building the sociomateriality of food service. *International Journal of Hospitality Management*, 89, 102553.

Websites

www.eventbrite.com/blog/event-catering-ideas-tips-ds00/

fingerfoodpeople.com.au/

www.socialtables.com/blog/event-planning/budget-friendly-catering-ideas/

yoindia.com.au/

bubblefood.com/case-studies/

Videos

youtu.be/dJfy-Ji8UMY – Pairing wine with food

youtu.be/xuQo41ljHoY – Six basic rules for pairing food with wine pairing

youtu.be/NIhN0Sy9lxY – Wedding catering trends for 2020

9 Stakeholder engagement and leadership

Learning objectives

On completion of this chapter, you will be able to:

➤ Understand the roles played by the broad range of internal and external stakeholders that exist in an events context

➤ Discuss issues associated with power and influence and explain the key sources

➤ Appreciate the value of a systematic approach to stakeholder analysis

➤ Provide an overview of the various approaches to engaging, communicating, liaising, and negotiating with event stakeholders

➤ Recognise the importance of networking and explain the associated skills and techniques

➤ Discuss the skills and techniques required for the development of sustainable, ongoing stakeholder relationships

➤ Understand the benefits of leveraging stakeholder relationships via co-branding activities.

An essential element of an event manager's job involves the development of sustainable working relationships with a broad range of stakeholders. Event stakeholders include all of the organisations and individuals who have an interest in the staging of an event and may have some impact on event outcomes. These stakeholders may be internal or external to the event business and while the importance and influence of stakeholders varies significantly, it is essential for event managers to have a sound knowledge of their interests, needs, and potential impact. So too is the capacity of event managers to effectively, engage, communicate, and negotiate with all key stakeholders.

Which internal and external stakeholders do you believe have the greatest potential impact on event outcomes?

Internal stakeholders

The event business itself and the event managers are the first and most obvious internal stakeholders. Other internal stakeholders include:

- Employees of the event business. They may be employed on a full-time, part-time, or casual basis.
- Volunteers that regularly take part in the broad range of volunteer tasks for one or more of the events that are staged by the event business.
- Contractors and consultants that are engaged on a regular or semi-regular basis to carry out specialist tasks for the event business.

These internal stakeholders are essential to the planning, design and staging of events and have a major impact on event outcomes. While employees, contractors and consultants are paid for their services, volunteers generally become involved as a result of a passion for, or interest in, the type of event being staged.

External stakeholders

External stakeholders are outside the event business but still have an impact on outcomes and an interest in the staging of the event. They include:

- Sponsors who provide cash or other resources that support the staging of events. The level of sponsorship varies, as does the profile or other benefits that are provided by the event business to the sponsor in return.
- The media, stakeholders that may have a positive or negative impact on the running of an event and so must be given a relatively high priority.
- Event attendees or the customers of the event business that pay for the experience that they gain from attending the event. They include:
  - ☐ The spectators at a sporting event
  - ☐ The audience at a music or entertainment event
  - ☐ The guests at a business event.
- The event product which includes:
  - ☐ The athletes or competitors at a sporting event

☐ The artists or performers at a music or entertainment event

☐ The speakers or presenters at a business event.

▪ The host community, which includes the residents in the immediate area surrounding the venue and the businesses that operate in that location. Their impact may be positive or negative but their views, needs and desires need to be taken into account.

▪ Event suppliers that specialise in the provision of event-related equipment, supplies, and technology.

▪ Venue providers, both in-door and outdoor.

▪ Government departments and agencies at all levels, local, state and federal.

▪ Emergency services: police, fire, ambulance, SES.

▪ Transport providers.

▪ Competing events, which generally have a potentially negative impact.

▪ And even the general public needs to be considered.

The potential impact of the abovementioned external stakeholders varies considerably. However, event managers need to be cognisant of that potential impact, as well as their needs and interests, and respond accordingly. Key factors that need to be considered are:

▪ The type of stakeholder

▪ Stakeholder expectations, particularly with regard to their need for event-related information and ongoing communication.

▪ Existing and emerging relationships between various stakeholders.

▪ The level of influence that stakeholders have, both in terms of direct influence over the event or event business, and in terms of influence over other stakeholders.

☐ Or conversely, their level of dependence.

▪ Cultural issues, particularly when operating in an international context.

▪ The capacity to engage with particular stakeholders, and any associated barriers or limitations.

▪ The legitimacy of particular stakeholders.

▪ Their knowledge and understanding of event-related issues.

All of these factors may impact on the priority that is given to various event stakeholders, as well as the manner in which they are engaged and managed. The capacity to effectively engage with stakeholders will also be determined by issues associated with power and influence.

9

? *Which external stakeholders would you give the highest priority? Why?*

Leadership and power

Leadership is required from event managers in terms of leading and managing employees and volunteers, but also in terms of influencing the other internal and external stakeholders that were identified earlier.

In an events context, key leadership roles include:

- The maintenance of high levels of energy, focus and motivation amongst employers, volunteers, and contractors. This generally involves:
  - ☐ Creating a vibrant, achievement-orientated work environment.
  - ☐ Maintaining a collaborative, team environment
  - ☐ Creating an environment that fosters continuous learning and personal development
  - ☐ Demonstrating high levels of energy and passion
  - ☐ Communicating a clear and inspiring vision for the future.
- Recognising, appreciating, and rewarding effort, particularly the effort and creativity that stimulates organisational performance and ultimately, enhances event outcomes. It involves:
  - ☐ Providing timely and positive feedback
  - ☐ Demonstrating trust through delegation of tasks and responsibility
  - ☐ Providing public recognition for outstanding performance.
- Being decisive and making sound, sometimes bold, decisions. Key determinants of effective decision making include:
  - ☐ Recognising and minimising decision biases
  - ☐ Coping with low probability events where there is little if any guidance from previous decisions
  - ☐ Understanding risk, how to assess it, respond to it, and communicate its significance to others
  - ☐ Gaining support and commitment for implementation.

The ability to carry out these leadership roles generally requires the power and ability to influence others. This capacity for leadership and influence is greater when a manager can effectively draw upon several power bases.

? *In a leadership role, what are the key benefits of being decisive? Can you think of any potential problems associated with an over-emphasis on decisiveness?*

Power and influence

The terms power and influence are often used interchangeably. However, power refers to access to resources and the potential or capacity to gain co-operation. Influence refers to the processes by which power is exercised. An understanding of these concepts is important from both the perspective of the power and influence that stakeholders have in terms of shaping event outcomes and also in terms of the influence that event managers have over the behaviour and contributions of event stakeholders.

Several studies have researched the sources or bases of power that individuals rely upon to influence the actions and attitudes of others. One of the earliest and most influential of these was carried out by social psychologists John French and, Bertram Raven. They identified six bases of power, divided into two groups, positional, and personal. The six bases are as follows:

Positional power bases

Legitimate power relates to an individual's power derived by virtue of a formal relationship or their title or position in an organisation. For example, the title sponsor for an event derives legitimate power from their formal relationship with the event and the event organisation. However, the nature of the contractual relationship provides for rights and responsibilities in both directions and hence, power is shared between the event organisation and the title sponsor.

Reward power is, in general, still derived from a formal position or relationship which provides the means to offer various rewards. That power to offer reward provides the capacity to influence others. For example, an event organiser has the power to give food and beverage (F&B) service providers rewards by selecting them to cater for their events. In so doing they can stipulate a range of requirements, influencing the type of service that is provided.

Can you think of any situations in which an event stakeholder can utilise reward power to influence an event organiser?

Coercive power is the power to remove rewards or punish as a result of a formal relationship or position. Hence, in the same way that event organisers can reward contractors through the ongoing development of contractual arrangements, they can remove those arrangements as a result of non-compliance with the needs or requirements of the event organiser.

Informational power is the power that comes from access to valuable information. This may result from someone's formal position or through existing contacts, relationships, and networks. For example, event stakeholders that have access to competitor information through their personal networks, may be willing to share that information. As a result, they have a degree of power over the event organiser. Developing a sound relationship with these stakeholders becomes more important as a result of their informational power.

Personal power bases

Expert power is the power derived from someone's personal expertise, their skills and knowledge. It could be expected that virtually all event contractors have a degree of expert power and hence, the development of sound working relationships with these stakeholders is also important.

Referent power is the personal power that comes from someone's personality and perceived attractiveness. To some extent, referent power can be fostered or developed by anyone and is a key element in the development and maintenance of useful contacts and networks.

Consider this: People often say that 'information is power'. What are the implications in terms of the ongoing development of contacts and networks and the type of contacts that tend to be the most valuable?

Stakeholder analysis

In order to gain a better understanding of various stakeholders and how they can be effectively engaged and managed, it may be useful to discover more about them through a systematic stakeholder analysis.

In an event context, stakeholder analysis is a systematic process that involves acquiring and analysing information about the broad array of internal and external stakeholders that event managers deal with. Here, the key purposes are: first, to determine whose needs and interests should be given priority when initiating, planning, implementing and staging events; and second, to determine what approaches should be taken in engaging and working with, various stakeholders and stakeholder groups.

Over recent decades, the diversity of stakeholders involved with events has expanded significantly, leading to greater levels of complexity and a greater need to understand their interests and objectives, and to develop strategies for effective communication and engagement. Stakeholder characteristics that need to be identified, and examined include:

- Whether they adopt a positive or negative attitude towards staging the event
- Their knowledge and understanding of the event and related issues
- Current and potential alliances with other stakeholders
- Their capacity to influence event outcomes
- The methods they are likely to employ in influencing event outcomes
- Their level of interest in the event
- Ways in which effective engagement can be achieved.

? *How would you try to engage and manage the host community when they have negative perceptions and attitudes about the running of the event?*

A systematic and well developed stakeholder analysis can be effectively utilised in a number of ways. It can be used primarily to identify the key actors but also to:

- Assess their interests, alliances, potential alliances, and importance with regard to the running of the event
- Facilitate effective interaction with key stakeholders and stakeholder groups
- Reduce opposition that may arise as a result of misunderstandings
- Increase support and commitment to the successful staging of the event
- Increase the probability of positive outcomes and overall event success.

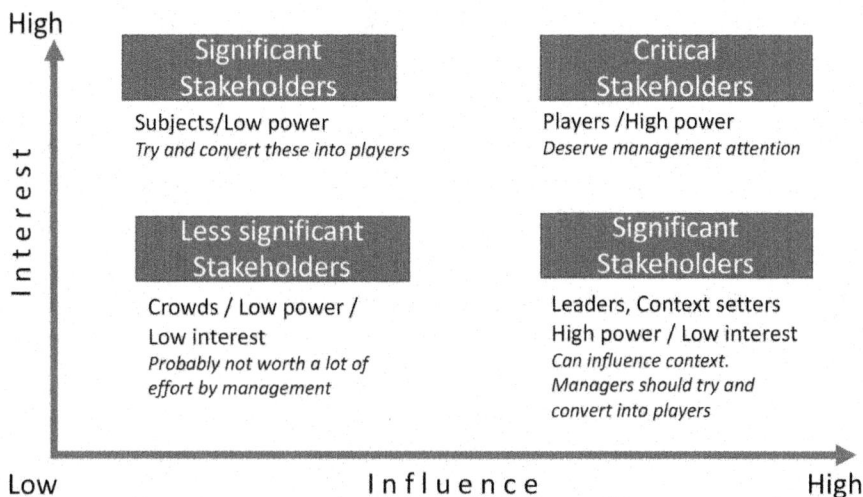

Figure 9.1: Stakeholder Power versus Interest grid. Source: Ackermann and Eden (2011)

A useful approach to stakeholder analysis involves the development of an **Influence versus Interest Grid.** This grid can be used to:

■ Prioritise and engage various event stakeholders

■ Monitor stakeholder relationships, particularly in terms of the actual and potential development of alliances and coalitions

The *horizontal (influence) axis* indicates the event stakeholder's capacity to influence event outcomes. This may be based on capacity to:

■ Exert power over others

■ Provide / withhold resources

■ Access information, etc.

The *vertical (interest) axis* indicates how important or significant aspects of the event or event outcomes are to the stakeholder. This interest may be:

■ Financial

■ Political

■ Social or cultural

■ A combination.

Event stakeholders are positioned on the grid so that comparisons can be made in terms of their relative influence and interest.

■ *Players*: stakeholders in the top right-hand quadrant (high interest and influence) are obviously the most critical in terms of event outcomes.

■ *Leaders / Context Setters*: Stakeholders in the bottom right-hand quadrant (high influence / low interest) may be regarded as very important as they may be persuaded to support other stakeholders with a higher interest in the event.

■ *Subjects*: Stakeholders in the top left-hand quadrant (high interest / low influence) can also be regarded as very important to event outcomes as they may attempt to form alliances with more powerful stakeholders.

Developing a sound understanding of where event stakeholders are located on the grid relative to each other allows patterns of influence between stakeholders to emerge and be understood. This is key to developing effective stakeholder management strategies, particularly in terms of:

■ Prioritising the various event stakeholders

■ Engaging key stakeholders

■ Monitoring stakeholder relationships in terms of actual and potential alliances and coalitions.

Working with internal stakeholders

The need to effectively engage with internal stakeholders, particularly employees and volunteers, is fairly obvious. Success in the conduct and management of any major human endeavour is unlikely in the absence of capable and highly motivated people and this is particularly true in the events industry. While the old adage that 'people are an organisation's most important resource' can be legitimately applied to virtually any organisation, it is even more relevant in the case of event management.

Events are services or perhaps more precisely, 'service experiences' and while the quality of tangible products can be improved, worked on, and tested well before a customer ever sees or purchases them, the quality of a service is only ever tested at the 'moment of truth'. Hence service quality, and in this case, event quality, depends critically on the ability of employees and volunteers to respond in the right way at the right time. Event success is largely the result of whether or not employees and volunteers are up for the challenge.

In what ways do you think that the management of volunteers should differ from the management of employees?

Event employees and volunteers have a vested interest in event success, and it is human nature for people to want to be associated with successful outcomes. A successful event is generally a satisfying and motivational experience for both employees and volunteers and is likely to result in the continued staging of the event in the future.

However, the motivations, needs and interests of employees on the one hand, and volunteers on the other, are quite different. Employees may be motivated by an on-going need for job security, career progression, salary, and other job-related benefits. The motivations of volunteers are more complex and more diverse. They don't earn a salary and hence, their motivations are not financial, certainly not in the short term. They are likely to have a strong interest in the event itself and a desire to be associated with it in any way possible. Of course for some, volunteering may represent a first step to establishing a career in events.

Other internal stakeholders, the event organisation, the event managers, as well as contractors and consultants, also have an obvious and significant impact on event outcomes. As with employees and volunteers, they all have a vested interest in event success.

Working with sponsors

When considering external stakeholders, sponsors are, for the obvious financial reasons, amongst the most important. Over recent decades, event sponsorship has expanded rapidly, primarily as a result of:

■ Growth in the popularity of various events and festivals;

■ Growth in the perceived effectiveness of sponsorship as a means of enhancing brand awareness;

■ The high cost of more traditional approaches to enhancing brand awareness.

There are several types of event sponsorship. These include:

■ *Financial* in which cash is provided to support the staging of an event;

■ *Value in kind* sponsorship in which other resources, generally consistent with what the sponsor is known for, are provided to support the staging of an event;

■ *Sponsorship packages*, generally designed by the sponsor to meet a range of event needs in a manner that reflects the sponsor's preferences;

■ *Tailor-made sponsorship packages*, generally designed in a manner that meets the unique needs of particular events;

■ *Naming rights* or *Title sponsorship* in which the sponsor that contributes the most to an event, receives a higher profile than other sponsors.

Regardless of the type of sponsorship, significant mutual benefits arise. From the sponsors perspective, these benefits include:

■ Enhancing the organisation's image;

■ Promoting brand awareness;

■ Demonstrating product features;

■ Promoting brand image;

■ Integrating with, and supporting, other marketing activities;

■ Providing employees and clients with access to key elements of the event and enhancing client relationships.

At the same time, there are obvious and significant sponsorship benefits from the perspective of event organisers. These include:

■ The provision of cash, products and perhaps, services from the sponsor;

■ The development of broader, more comprehensive, and beneficial business relationships and partnerships;

■ The opportunity for various types of event leveraging.

Here, *event leveraging* is an important concept to understand. While event sponsors provide funds, products, services and perhaps, other benefits that facilitate the staging of an event, this may only be the starting point. Significantly more may be spent by the sponsor on other promotional activity to maximise the direct marketing benefits associated with the event. This additional investment helps to communicate the link between the brand and the event to the consumer. It is generally referred to as 'activating' or 'leveraging' the event sponsorship.

Can you think of any examples of event leveraging that may apply to sporting events?

These leveraging activities generally fall outside the initial sponsorship agreement that is developed between the sponsor and the organiser. However, they are generally encouraged by event organisers. Event leveraging is an investment that continues to raise the profile of both the sponsor and the event and can be viewed as a useful extension of the initial sponsorship partnership.

A key determinant of success when developing relationships with sponsors, involves achieving the right 'fit' between the sponsor and the event. In fact, fit is a critical element of the sponsorship relationship from the perspectives of both the sponsoring organisation and the event organisers. It makes sense for a sponsor to select an event with the same characteristics as their target market. Furthermore, the type of event should fit with the sponsoring organisation's values and image.

Key issues or questions that need to be considered in the formation of sponsorship arrangements and development of sponsorship policies are:

- To what extent do the event organisers and other existing event stakeholders want to encourage commercial sponsorship?
- Are there certain categories of companies that would be regarded as unsuitable sponsors?
- Are there certain types of sponsorship activities that would be regarded as unsuitable?

In terms of the implementation of sponsorship agreements, it is important that the needs, interests, and objectives of the sponsor are considered, understood, and addressed. Key issues can include:

- The possibility of ambush marketing by non-sponsoring organisations;
- The potential for disagreement as a result of incompatibility between one or more of the sponsors;

■ The effective and appropriate use of title sponsorships;

■ Dissatisfaction as a result of perceived inequity amongst sponsors

■ The appropriate utilisation of sponsor logos.

Working with other external stakeholders

Over recent decades, the importance and impact of **the media** has, for several events, grown significantly. At the same time, the virtual audience has become substantially greater than the live audience. Hence, effectively engaging the media and perhaps regarding the media as an event partner have become important considerations. The impact of the media may be enormous, and this impact cannot be ignored. Hence, every opportunity should be taken to maximise engagement with the media.

? *What approaches do you think would be the most effective in maximising engagement with the media?*

The views of **host communities** should be considered and addressed as early as possible when initiating and planning events. The problems that have been experienced by several major events can be traced back to a failure on the part of event organisers to address host community concerns during the event planning process.

Every effort should be made to ensure that events are consistent with, and support, community objectives. Furthermore, as well as ensuring that they don't cause harm, annoyance, or inconvenience to members of the host community, events should:

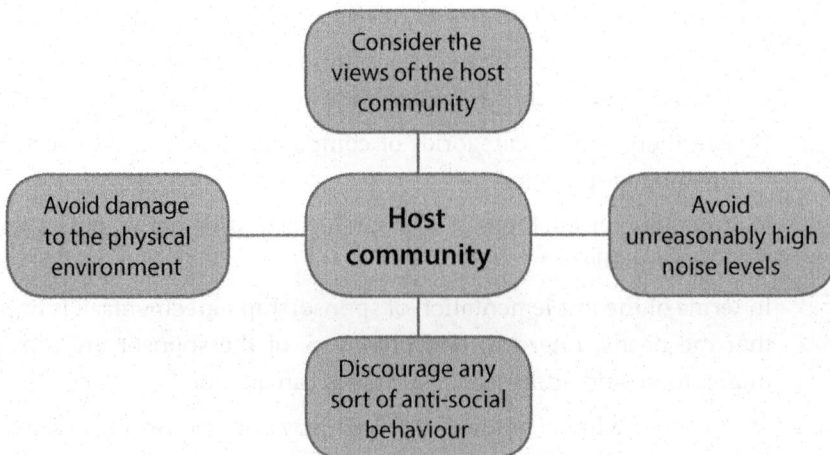

Figure 9.2: Host community needs must be considered during the event planning process

The necessity to address the needs and wants of **event attendees** is obvious and, in this regard, the first step involves establishing a customer value proposition. Here, a realistic understanding of the needs, interests, and motivations of the audience, the spectators, or in the case of corporate events, the clients, is essential. Understanding the changing needs of attendees and maintaining the capacity to meet those needs is essential for event success.

In order to get the most out of the **event product,** their needs and interests should also be considered and addressed. The event product includes:

■ The performers, musicians, and entertainers at music and entertainment events;

■ The athletes and competitors at sports events;

■ The speakers or presenters at business or corporate events.

What 'needs' and 'wants' should be addressed for athletes at a sporting event?

The development of sound working relationships with **event suppliers** can often reduce problems associated with the procurement of appropriate supplies and may also reduce supply costs. And over recent decades, event technology has become an important change agent within the events industry, significantly impacting key aspects of the event management process.

When considering which event stakeholders should be given priority, a broad range of factors need to be considered. Importantly though, stakeholders that have the greatest impact on the event experience of attendees should be given a high priority. Several other primary stakeholders including, for example, local government, must also be given high priority because without their support, staging the event may not be possible.

9

Networking and social capital

Networking and the development of useful contacts is essential in any business context, but perhaps even more essential in the events industry. Here, the key concept that needs to be considered is the development of *social capital*.

Social capital is a key concept in sociology. It refers to the value of, or resources available through, personal and business networks. The central notion associated with the concept of social capital is that personal and business networks have real value. From a business perspective, contacts and networks may facilitate the completion of tasks, the achievement of goals, and the creation of value through cooperative and collaborative effort. From a more personal perspective, they may provide opportunities for social interaction and emotional support.

Hence, social capital may be regarded as the collective value of all the people we know, all personal and business networks. It is the reciprocity that arises from these networks, the things that we do for each other, that is the essence of social capital. It is developed through the maintenance of networks and, as well as the mutual benefits that come with reciprocity, there are a wide variety of benefits that may be generated as a result of:

■ Greater levels of trust;

■ The generation of information and ideas;

■ Opportunities for business development and innovation;

■ The development of cooperation, collaboration, and goodwill.

Networks may be divided into two types:

■ **Bonding networks** that connect people who are similar; this is *particularised* (in-group) reciprocity, or

■ **Bridging networks** that connect a range of diverse individuals; this is *generalised* reciprocity.

It is important to understand that both types of networks are useful and may be developed and maintained through the staging of planned events.

The power of social capital resides in networks of relationships and access to social capital depends on:

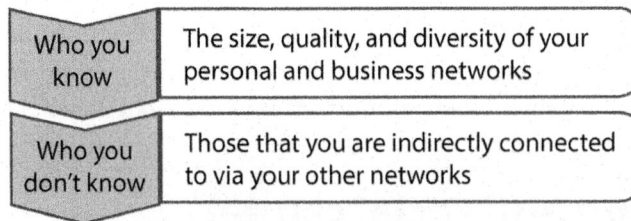

Who you know	The size, quality, and diversity of your personal and business networks
Who you don't know	Those that you are indirectly connected to via your other networks

Figure 9.3: Dependency factors relating to social capital

When considering the beneficial impact of social capital derived through the staging of events, particularly business events, a key issue is the effectiveness of face-to-face communication when compared with that of alternative communication channels. Historically, meetings involving face-to-face communication have over the centuries, continued to play an important role in most societies, and for good reason. Recent studies have indicated that the increasing reliance on electronic communication has led to the existence of less empathy amongst many people.

Less empathy implies a reduced capacity to understand and share the feelings of others and a key problem is that, as empathy wanes, so does trust. The need for trust is important in any business relationship.

? *What strategies can be initiated to address reduced levels of trust that tend to result from reliance on electronic forms of communication?*

It is necessary to recognise that the importance of face-to-face communication, as well as the emphasis on personal relationships and trust, varies between cultures. In several Eastern cultures, particularly in China, the development of trust and sound personal relationships is an essential prerequisite to the development of a workable business relationship. This reality may not be recognised by Western businesses seeking to develop contractual relationships in the East. Unless ample time and energy is devoted to face-to-face communication and interaction, to banquets and other forms of social engagement, to the development of trust and sound personal relationships, business relationships are likely to suffer. In Eastern cultures, trust, personal contacts and relationships, and what is often referred to as *guanxi*, is far more important than contractual relationships.

Consider this: what communication tools will you use to deliver key messages to stakeholders? Examples of communication tools are given in Figure 9.4.

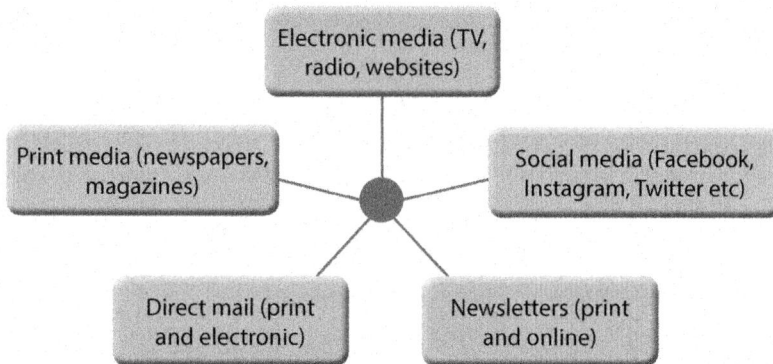

Figure 9.4: Communication tools for stakeholder management

Guanxi is a term that is used throughout Asia, but particularly in China, to describe networks that are utilised primarily for business and other instrumental purposes. They are developed and sustained through:

- Various form of social interaction in a business or personal context
- Wining, dining, and the conduct of dinners and banquets
- Mutual gift giving
- Other forms of reciprocity involving favours and other benefits.

The utilisation of guanxi in China and other parts of Asia highlights major differences between Eastern and Western cultures and between Eastern and Western approaches to the development of contacts and networks. Incredible importance is given to face-to-face communication and interaction in Asia when compared with Western approaches. And while guanxi is a term that is generally under-appreciated and misunderstood in the West, understanding its importance, and appreciating the value of personal and business relationships, is a vital pre-requisite to carrying on any form of business in most parts of Asia.

As discussed however, the development of useful networks and contacts and hence, the creation of social capital is an essential element of doing business, particularly in the events industry, in Western, as well as Eastern, cultures.

Case study 9.1: Aardklop National Arts Festival, Potchefstroom, South Africa.

Source: Van Niekerk and Gertz (2019)

The Aardklop National Arts Festival is one of the five big arts festivals in South Africa which offers a variety of Afrikaans productions in both performing and visual arts. The festival was established in 1998 to mainly serve the broader arts community in the northern half of South Africa and is hosted in Potchefstroom. Over the years the festival experienced changes which were influenced by a number of stakeholders. Some of these included groups of people who tried to influence the direction of the festival. In continuing operations, the festival succeeded in strengthening the social connection among the community. The different (internal and external) stakeholders associated with this festival are:

Internal stakeholders	External stakeholders
Board of Directors	Sponsors
Permanent staff	Local government
Temporary staff	Emergency services
Volunteers	Directors and producers from production companies
	Participants: artists, singers, musicians, dancers, performers
	Other service providers: electricians, cleaning services, etc
	Stall holders/exhibitors
	Local businesses and local community
	Festival goers/attendees/supporters

Figure 9.5: Internal and external stakeholders Aardklop national arts festival.

Each event may attract different stakeholders. When considering the internal and external stakeholders of the Aardklop national arts festival their position on the stakeholder grid may appear as below:

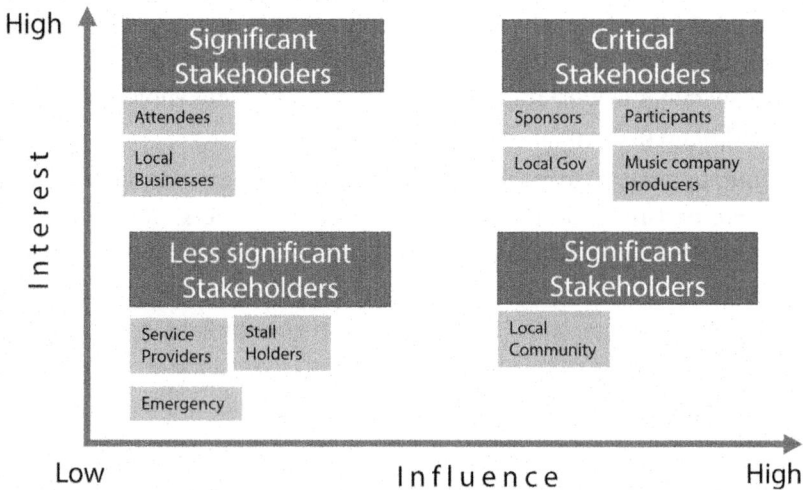

Figure 9.6: Stakeholder interest versus influence for the Aardklop national arts festival.

Key considerations:

- Within the power versus influence grid, each stakeholder will have a different place. Some will always be important, but some might or might not be influential depending on the type of event. In most events the music directors might not have so much influence but in a national arts festival, the key music directors will have a massive impact.
- Local businesses won't have much influence on the event, however their interest is not super low or super high. They will sit in the edge of the grid. They need the extra local activity or simply like to be involved.
- The local community might have a big influence on the outcome if they have a negative view of the event. The organisers need to work closely with the local community, get them involved and get their feedback.

Did you know? One of the biggest challenges with festivals is acquiring sponsors and government support. While these two stakeholders represent different interests, they are both significant contributors to festivals.

Summary

Key event outcomes may be heavily impacted by the event manager's capacity to effectively engage, communicate, and negotiate with a broad range of internal and external event stakeholders. Hence, the development of sustainable working relationships with key stakeholders is an essential part of an event manager's job.

Internal stakeholders include: the event business and its managers; full-time, part-time, and casual employees; volunteers; contractors and consultants. External stakeholders include: sponsors; the media; attendees; the event product; the host community; suppliers and technology providers; venue providers; local, state and federal government agencies; emergency services; transport providers; competing events; and the general public.

The potential impact of the different stakeholders varies considerably. Event managers need to be cognisant of their potential impact, as well as their needs and interests, and respond accordingly. Particularly in terms of leading and managing employees and volunteers, but also in terms of influencing the other stakeholders, leadership skills are a key requirement of event managers. In an events context, key leadership roles include:

■ The maintenance of high levels of energy, focus and motivation amongst employers, volunteers, and contractors;

■ Recognising, appreciating, and rewarding effort;

■ Being decisive and making sound, sometimes bold, decisions.

The ability to carry out these leadership roles generally requires the power and ability to influence others. This may involve the utilisation of some or all of the six power bases which include: legitimate power; reward power; coercive power; informational power; expert power; and referent power.

A better understanding of various stakeholders and how they can be effectively managed, can be gained through systematic stakeholder analysis. One approach to stakeholder analysis involves the development of an Influence versus Interest Grid which can be used to:

■ Understand patterns of influence between stakeholders;

■ Develop effective stakeholder management strategies;

■ Prioritise the various event stakeholders;

■ Engage key stakeholders;

■ Monitor stakeholder relationships in terms of actual and potential alliances and coalitions.

Engaging and working effectively with internal stakeholders generally involves understanding their needs, interests and motivations, and responding accordingly. Engaging and working effectively with external stakeholders also involves the development of a sound understanding of their needs, interests, and objectives, as well as their potential impact. For sponsors in particular, workable management strategies must be formulated and may involve strategies aimed at event leveraging and a closer partnership between the sponsor and the event organiser. For these strategies to be effective, a sponsorship agreement should be underpinned by a sound fit between the sponsoring organisation and the event organiser. Sound working relationships must also be developed with the media, the host community, event attendees, the event product, event suppliers, and other external stakeholders.

The development of social capital through networking and reciprocity brings with it a wide range of benefits, as a result of: greater levels of trust; the generation of information and ideas; opportunities for business development and innovation; and the growth of collaboration and goodwill. The creation of social capital is an essential element of doing business, particularly in the events industry, in Western, as well as Eastern, cultures.

Industry profile: Grant Gray, Stakeholder relationship management and business development expert

Grant Gray is a strategic leader specialising in managing stakeholders and driving partnerships across a broad hotel and hospitality sector. His partnerships range across the broader corporate, meeting & event and entertainment sector. When managing partnership strategy plans, Grant looks to utilise creative thinking and innovation as key principles in order to drive overall business performance. As a strategic thinker, he prioritises stakeholder interests and supports organisational objectives while striving for excellence in business development.

9

One of his key strengths is managing contracts and providing service solutions to different stakeholder groups such as: local government, community, corporate, business, education, health, and industry clients. To achieve continuous improvement he holds regular stakeholder meetings internally and externally, refining objectives and key performance indicators to support change. Through team collaboration and leadership, Grant strives for ongoing improvement in organisations. By analysing markets and stakeholder interests, he develops collaborative activities that aim for positive change, common goals and the effective implementation of strategic plans.

Expertise:

- Stakeholder and relationship management
- Development and implantation of sales and Marketing strategies.
- Team development and leadership
- Strategic leader and creative thinker
- Identifying, analysing and capitalizing on emerging hospitality trends

What are some key steps an event manager should follow to engage and manage stakeholder interests?

First step is identifying the individual needs and requirements of each stakeholder. There are individual needs and priorities, therefore it's important for the event manager (EM) to pay attention to the detail that may make a difference in the negotiation. For example, a key consideration is to understand what are the key drivers that the stakeholder is looking to achieve from the event. Understanding what is important to them is a strong starting point to building a long term business relationship.

Can you give us some stakeholder examples and the type of relationships you build?

As an event manager, it is not only important to carry out the event for the client but also to understand the liaison and the communication lines you will have during planning, execution and evaluation phases. For private events, as an example, you may have direct communication with the bride and groom, whereas with corporate events, your line of communication may be via the executive assistant (EA), whilst the real client is the company director. In this case the EM needs to respect the liaison reporting line and build the relationship with the EA, understanding what components of the event are important to them and those important for the principal owner of the event. Ultimately, if the EA is not happy with communication and gaining acknowledgment that you are meeting both levels of expectations, you may lose the business. It is therefore important to ask the right questions and build the relationship as a key to completely understanding the clients' goals and objectives.

What are some key attributes when dealing with stakeholders?

Ability to build rapport in formal and non formal situations. Sometimes you may get key information from clients by phone or over a coffee, which is crucial in delivering the expected client experience. In addition, EMs should try and feel relaxed and allow for open conversation to happen. Above all, clients are human and it is the one way we can create connections and establish new relationships. One key consideration is to be an active listener and ask open ended questions. Make sure the client feels at ease to talk to you at all times. Responding in a timely manner to enquiries will also ensure the EM's credibility and reliability. Speed to action in the initial stages of attending to a lead more often than not is key to winning the business.

How can a manager increase stakeholder (eg sponsor) value during an event?

One key element in creating and building value for stakeholders is understanding the core required outcome, goals and objectives of each stakeholder, as these vary from event to event and person to person. EMs need to be able to provide pertinent ideas to improve the perceived outcome for each stakeholder. An example is to give key advice and solutions to enhance the ultimate event experience. Stakeholders have different priorities so this means EMs need to think strategically and creatively and allow for the exchange (co-creation) to happen. Stakeholders may have high influence with little event experience; therefore, EMs should ensure events run smoothly while building stakeholder reputation through their event expertise.

When managing event sales contracts, what challenges do you mostly face?

As an EM you need to make sure you have the key components and the finer details in the contract. A good eye for detail, will ensure there are minimal mistakes later. Some key detail to include consists of:

Well structured cancellation terms : This will ensure that if the client requires to cancel the event, you have structure in place to protect the business and any potential loss of revenue, set out over a period of time. An example could be: free cancellation 120 days prior to the event; return of 50% of the charges from 120 to 90 days, 25% of the charges 90 to 60 days prior and 0% of the charges for cancellation in less than 60 days. Even with this written into the contract, this can be challenging, especially if a client looks to negotiate different terms to the ones signed due to cancelling an event. It is up to the EM's expertise to manage the client relationship to uphold the agreed terms and come up with strategies that ensure the terms are met.

Attrition clauses: This allows for your clients to have a structured approach to consolidation on final numbers for their events. An attrition clause thus allows the client to contractually reduce their attendee numbers by a certain percentage over time, if required. Attrition is an important factor for consideration, therefore it would be noted in the sales contract and consideration needs to be given for such changes. An example can include allowing an attrition rate of up 10% attendee reduction at 90 days prior to the event and potentially a further 10% 60 days prior. The venue may have a policy and procedure in place to accommodate for the scale of reduction.

Clients challenging the negotiating terms: This is a real challenge and EMs need to be prepared to handle these situations. One should hold firm to contractual terms as much as possible, as that is why they are built into the contract and agreed upon. It is also important that the client is made well aware of the contractual terms upon agreement, to avoid any potential issues.

9

Contracts are binding: In addition, it is advisable for the contract to be sent to a legal team to make sure all clauses are covered, written correctly and provide the venue adequate cover. There are a variety of clauses that may or may not be required, but each venue should have a well prepared and legally reviewed contract template.

Review questions

1. Event employees and volunteers are key internal stakeholders. Explain how their motivations are likely to differ and discuss the implications of those differences in terms of influencing and managing them.

2. In view of their ongoing impact, event sponsors are amongst the most important of all external stakeholders. Describe the approach that you as an event manager would adopt in the development of a sponsorship agreement for a sporting event, and discuss the key outcomes that you would endeavour to achieve.

3. Power bases may be either positional or personal. Which set of bases would you regard as the most effective over the longer-term? Why?

4. Developing sound fit is an essential element of a workable sponsorship arrangement. Using examples, explain the factors that determine sponsorship fit. Can it change overtime and if so, how can it be monitored?

5. Reliance on electronic communication tends to imply reduced levels of trust. This has obvious implications in a Covid-19 situation. What strategies can be developed to address this over the longer term?

6. Host communities have the potential to enhance or limit event outcomes depending on attitudes to the event. What strategies can be put in place during the planning process to ensure that a positive relationship is developed and maintained with the host community?

7. Ambush marketing by non-sponsoring organisations can cause irreparable damage to existing sponsorship agreements. What strategies can be put in place to minimise the threat of ambush marketing?

8. From the perspective of a sponsor, a key benefit of sponsorship is the promotion of brand awareness. What can be done at a major sporting event to support and facilitate brand awareness for a title sponsor?

Workshop activities

Scenario A

You are a media representative and have been assigned the task to promote a new sporting event that will take place in your main city, which will increase tourism activity in your destination.

a. Identify the internal and external stakeholders that are involved in this event.

b. Brainstorm opportunities for each stakeholder that will benefit from the promotion of the sporting event.

c. Design an 'interest' versus 'power' grid that identifies the key players that can influence the success of the sporting event and improve the image of the destination. Explain your reasoning.

Scenario B

You have just secured a key sponsor for your 2-day conference. Undertaking the role of a sales event manager, draft a contract between the conference owner (e.g. an industry association) and the sponsor (e.g. a private business) that outlines the terms and conditions of the agreement.

Scenario C

You have just been given the permit to organise an arts/music festival that will rejuvenate your local community. Your task is as follows:

a. Analyse the needs of your host community.

b. Develop a plan on how to implement your festival with the least disruption to your host community.

c. In a pitch presentation, invite key representatives from the host community to provide feedback on your festival plan.

d. Considering feedback from the key community representatives, revise your plan and execute the live event accordingly.

Scenario D

You are a professional conference organiser and have just undertaken the responsibility for organising a virtual conference.

1. Identify the key business relationships that will affect the success of the online event.

2. Develop a stakeholder engagement plan on how to successfully manage engagement throughout the event planning process.

9

Scenario E

Your local council has launched a campaign to attract new events as strategies to boost business activity. As an event manager you undertake this opportunity and wish to invite key stakeholders to be part of this venture.

a. Decide on the type of event you wish to deliver.

b. Decide who your key internal and externals stakeholders are.

c. Develop key messages for identify the relevant communication tools to deliver the message accordingly.

References and further reading

Ackermann, F., & Eden, C. (2011). Strategic management of stakeholders: Theory and practice. *Long Range Planning*, 44(3), 179-196.

Antchak, V., Ziakas, V., & Getz, D. (2019). *Event Portfolio Management*, Goodfellow Publishers.

Chi, C. G. Q., Ouyang, Z., & Xu, X. (2018). Changing perceptions and reasoning process: Comparison of residents' pre-and post-event attitudes. *Annals of Tourism Research*, 70, 39-53.

Fotiadis, A., Xie, L., Li, Y., & Huan, T. C. T. (2016). Attracting athletes to small-scale sports events using motivational decision-making factors. *Journal of Business Research*, 69(11), 5467-5472.

Frawley, S. (2015). Organizational power and the management of a mega-event: The case of Sydney 2000. *Event Management*, 19(2), 247-260.

French, J. & Raven, B. (1959). The bases of social power. In *Studies in Social Power*, D. Cartwright, Ed., pp. 150-167. Ann Arbor, MI: Institute for Social Research.

Jordan, T., Gibson, F., Stinnett, B., & Howard, D. (2019). Stakeholder engagement in event planning: A case study of one rural community's process. *Event Management*, 23(1), 61-74.

Merrilees, B., Getz, D., & O'Brien, D. (2005). Marketing stakeholder analysis: Branding the Brisbane goodwill games. *European Journal of Marketing*, 39(9/10), 1060-1077

Morgan, A., Taylor, T., & Adair, D. (2020). Sport event sponsorship management from the sponsee's perspective. *Sport Management Review*, 23(5), 838-851.

Van Niekerk, M., & Getz, D. (2019). *Event Stakeholders*, Goodfellow Publishers.

Websites

www.sa-venues.com/events/northwest/aardklop-national-arts-festival/

www.projectmanager.com/stakeholder-management

Videos

https://youtu.be/kmduwJRDhkE – Tips on how to engage stakeholders

https://youtu.be/1_U6JUxIEnc – Engaging and managing stakeholders

10 Finding and motivating talent

Learning objectives

On completion of this chapter, you will be able to:

➤ Appreciate the importance of acquiring talented employees and volunteers

➤ Discuss employee and volunteer recruitment strategies

➤ Appreciate the importance of a systematic approaches to induction and training

➤ Provide an overview of the various approaches to the empowerment of event employees and volunteers

➤ Understand the key differences between the motivations of employees and volunteers

➤ Discuss key human resource management issues in an event industry context

➤ Appreciate the difference between volunteerism and exploitation

➤ Explain the key principles associated with the promotion of employee well-being.

Finding the best talent, and keeping them motivated and productive, are essential elements in establishing and maintaining a competitive advantage. The capacity of an event enterprise to consistently stage successful events, and consistently provide attendees with positive and memorable experiences, is generally a reflection of the quality of their employees and volunteers. Over the longer term, concerted efforts to acquire and motivate the best talent available can lead to greater levels of organisational creativity and innovation, as well as long term survival in a dynamic, turbulent, and uncertain industry environment. Furthermore, a talented and productive workforce is generally one in which individual employees and volunteers can thrive and grow, promoting empowerment and well-being.

? *What approach to human resource management is likely to facilitate the empowerment of event employees and volunteers?*

Employee and volunteer recruitment strategies

Acquiring the best talent is more important for events than for most industries. Success in the staging of an event can only ever be achieved at the so-called 'moment of truth' and is facilitated at that time by the efforts and expertise of event employees and volunteers. Most successful event enterprises are constantly on the look-out for outstanding talent that can take their events from good to exceptional. However, there are obvious differences between the recruitment of employees, people that are seeking full or part-time employment in the events industry, and that of volunteers, whose relationship with the events organisation is more flexible, more open-ended, and probably more short term.

Employee recruitment

When forecasting future staff needs, the experience gained from previous events and other staffing needs provides the most reliable basis. In addition, however, there are a range of more sophisticated techniques, including trend projection and multiple regression that can be incorporated into the process. When considering supply issues, both the internal labour supply, that is, current employees and volunteers that are used on a regular basis, as well as the external labour supply, needs to be considered.

? *What would you regard as key benefits of being able to recruit volunteers as permanent employees?*

Event employees want to be proud of the organisation they work for and hence, the best way to ensure the capacity of an event enterprise to attract talented employees is through successful employer branding, or in other words, becoming an 'employer of choice'. Employer branding can be regarded as the way in which an organisation is able to proactively influence and manage the perceptions of job seekers, potential employees, and other key stakeholders, about its reputation as an employer. It can be expensive and time consuming but in a highly competitive labour market, is well worth the investment.

> **?** *What would you regard as the key attributes of the type of employer that you would like to work for?*

Possible approaches that can be adopted to employer branding include:

- Developing and maintaining a positive, productive, and motivational work environment.
- Rewarding and compensating employees appropriately.
- Developing and implementing appropriate human resource management policies, particularly in terms of career progression, training and development, and equal employment opportunity.
- Developing and maintaining a reputation as a progressive employer, particularly in terms of business ethics, social responsibility, and sustainability.
- Maintaining ongoing, positive employee engagement with a focus on employee health, safety, and well-being.

Other approaches that can be utilised to operationalise and enhance the effectiveness of employee recruitment include:

- Social recruiting or the utilisation of a broad range of social networks to find and attract potential employees.
- The volunteers that have been utilised for a number of events may also be a potential source of new employees.
- Proactive recruitment strategies in which, rather than waiting for prospective employees to apply, talent is sourced directly from external talent pools such as LinkedIn.
- All of these approaches acknowledge the fact that the best talent is less likely to be looking for a new job and hence, the emphasis needs to be on actively seeking and finding talent rather than passively waiting for talent to respond to advertisements. This should be an on-going process.

Recruitment of employees may also be facilitated through:

- The use of data driven metrics to facilitate a better understanding of how well current recruitment strategies are working and how they can be improved.
- The use of applicant tracking software aimed at making the recruitment process more systematic, more data driven, and more structured.

10

Did you know? Motivating volunteers is important in order to secure engagement throughout the event. Ensure little touch points such as checking in how they are going, providing food, frequent breaks and ensuring their wellbeing. Failure to maintain volunteer motivation may result in quitting. Read about volunteer dropout rates at the 2016 Rio games: www.independent.co.uk/sport/olympics/rio-2016-thousands-olympic-volunteers-quit-over-long-hours-and-lack-food-a7194776.html

Selection

While the selection process for event volunteers is relatively straight forward, involving the development of a match between the characteristics of prospective volunteers and event needs, the selection process for event employees is, and should be, far more involved. The selection of event employees is an important investment decision that requires adequate time, consideration, and effort. When selecting the most appropriate candidate, the final decision should be based on:

■ The candidate's cognitive and thinking ability, their affective ability or emotional intelligence, and their behavioural qualities.

■ Their motivation to learn, to acquire knowledge and expertise, to effectively handle their emotions, and to maximise performance through the demonstration of appropriate behaviours.

■ The extent to which their personal characteristics can match or perhaps enhance, the organisation's culture

An array of techniques and methods are available when making selection decisions. These include a range of different types of interviews, the conduct of reference checks, consideration of other information including applications and resumes, and a range of employment tests.

Have you recently been for a job interview? If so, what were your impressions of the interview process?

In traditional interviews, interviewees are generally asked a range of questions that may relate to:

■ Previous relevant experience

■ The applicant's skills, knowledge, and attitudes

■ How the applicant would handle various job-related situations

■ How they would cope with various job-related problems and difficulties

■ What they currently know about key aspects of the industry, the organisation, and the job

While traditional interviews involve one interviewee and generally, one or more interviewers, they can also take the form of group interviews.

Have you ever taken part in a group interview? What would you regard as the advantages and disadvantages of a group interview?

A type of interview sometimes used to test an applicant's capacity to work in high pressure, stressful environments is a stress interview. The use of stress interviews is often criticised for ethical reasons but may be appropriate when the demands of the work environment are likely to require a psychological profile that can handle stressful, high-pressure situations. The tone and content of questions are generally designed to put applicants under extreme pressure to test their ability to respond appropriately, think on their feet, and stay calm.

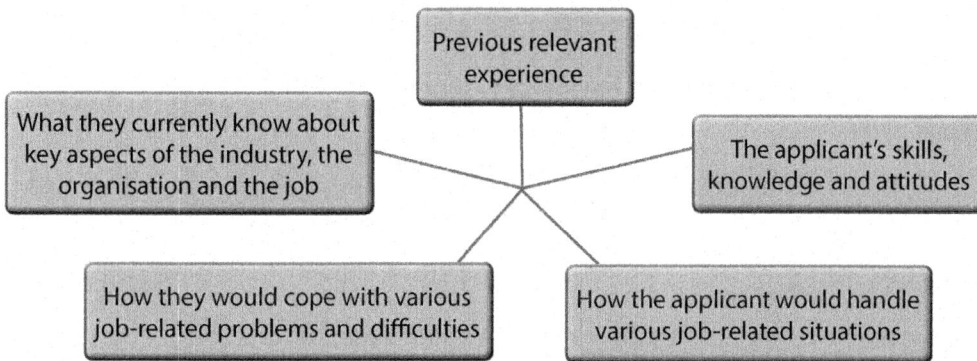

Previous relevant experience

What they currently know about key aspects of the industry, the organisation and the job

The applicant's skills, knowledge and attitudes

How they would cope with various job-related problems and difficulties

How the applicant would handle various job-related situations

Figure 10.1: Interview related questions

Can you think of situations in which a stress interview may be appropriate for a job in the events industry?

Group interviews in which a group of applicants are all interviewed at the one time, are sometimes used to:

Observe and test how candidates interact and communicate in a situation that simulates a real work environment

Test how applicants cope in a highly competitive environment

Provide a basis for comparisons between candidates

Observe and identify dominant and passive personalities

10

Figure 10.2: Group interview considerations

Induction

Induction is the process of introducing new employees and volunteers to the event enterprise and the tasks associated with carrying out their role. It includes all of the efforts required to receive and welcome employees and volunteers, making them feel comfortable with their new role, and providing them with the information that allows them to get started. A key objective of the induction process is to provide focus and direction to new employees and volunteers, introducing them to the organisation, to the values and culture of the organisation, to their supervisor and co-workers, and to their jobs.

If carried out effectively, induction facilitates a better understanding of organisational expectations and has the potential to transform average on-the-job performance into exceptional performance.

What information would you regard as the most important when starting a new job?

While induction that is required for both employees and volunteers, their induction needs differ. The induction needs of employees are generally more long term, more focused on organisational issues, and more comprehensive.

> **Did you know?** Technology can assist in managing engagement and increasing participation by large numbers of volunteers. One key feature is the setup of communication and registration systems. Data can be used to allocate roles according to availability, skills and volunteer expertise. See examples at: www.rosterfy.com

Employee induction

Employees generally want to feel proud of the organisation that they work for and hence, employee induction needs to reinforce the view that the new employee has made the right decision to join the organisation. They need to feel welcome, appreciated, and inspired to commence work in their new role.

They need to be introduced to other staff and provided with a broad range of documentation and information including:

- A welcome message from management
- Health and Safety information
- An overview of the new role

- Employment contracts and associated documentation
- Employment policies and practices
- Access to computer
- Access to corporate information, training programs, etc.
- Organisational structure, maps, and staff profiles
- Key aspects of the organisation's history
- The organisation's vision, values, mission statement, and strategic plan
- Links to work team information and access to social media

The induction program doesn't have to be completed in one day and in fact, given the amount of information to be provided, is probably more effective when completed over a few days. And as well as the focus on formal introductions and documentation, it should also encourage less formal engagement and communication.

Volunteer induction

Despite the fact that the relationship between the volunteer and the event enterprise is less formal and less direct than for employees, an induction that welcomes them to their new role and provides information that informs and motivates is still essential. Event volunteers need to be introduced to all employees and other volunteers with whom they will be having ongoing interaction.

Information that needs to be provided to event volunteers, and from volunteers, as part of the induction process includes:

- Human Resource Management documentation and other requirements including next of kin contacts, etc.
- Health and Safety requirements
- Any workplace risks and hazards
- Medical history of the volunteer
- Organisational policies and procedures
- Site specific information including evacuation procedures

Another important aspect of the induction process involves providing the volunteer with the opportunity to ask questions and seek any other relevant information. Every effort should made to ensure that the new volunteer feels welcome, informed, motivated, and ready to start.

10

Workplace health and safety

As well as simply representing a legal obligation and an inescapable responsibility that all event organisations have toward their employees and volunteers, workplace health and safety can be regarded as a major organisational investment in the physical and mental health, and potential productivity, of their human resources. Hence, health and safety policies can go well beyond avoiding injury or illness, and include things like the provision of gym memberships, medical services, and a range of work sponsored activities.

Another key element of workplace health and safety involves measure to combat and eliminate workplace bullying. Workplace bulling includes sexual harassment which, in view of the ethical, social, legal, and organisational implications, must be effectively addressed and eliminated. An awareness of health and safety issues and development of a culture that values health and safety will generally lead to higher levels of productivity and employee welfare.

What would you regard as key organisational benefits of reducing or eliminating workplace bullying?

Training and development

Sound and well-thought-out training programs need to be established for event volunteers to ensure that they have the required knowledge and skills, as well as the confidence, to carry out their roles effectively. They also represent a useful means of engaging volunteers, increasing their attachment to the event enterprise, and enhancing their motivation and well-being.

For event employees, training and development can be more long term, more comprehensive, and more closely tied to the strategic direction of the event enterprise. A range of motivational benefits can be gained through the provision of training and development, as well as greater levels of knowledge, skills, and expertise. It enhances expectations about one's capacity to complete tasks successfully, work productively, and gain associated organisational rewards, while at the same time, it provides an important intrinsic motivator. Most people have an intrinsic need or desire for their lives to be a learning experience or a growth experience. Rather than being regarded as a cost therefore, training and development initiatives should be regarded as important on-going initiatives with the potential to significantly enhance employee motivation. In the case of event volunteers, tasks can be organised in a manner that they too are seen as learning opportunities.

The motivation and well-being of employees and volunteers

As discussed earlier, what motivates employees is likely to be different from what motivates volunteers. Yet the same principle can be more broadly applied. All individuals are different and what motivates, inspires, and elicits maximum effort from one person may have little, if any, impact when applied to someone else. The assumption that all people are similar or perhaps, the same as oneself, is a common mistake.

People are, in fact, different and the most basic difference in terms of incentives that may be useful in motivating individuals relates to those that are extrinsic and those that are intrinsic.

- **Extrinsic** incentives include money, quantifiable employee benefits, promotion, and career progression.
- **Intrinsic** motivation comes from a deep interest in the work itself, a passion for what is being achieved, and perhaps a need for self-fulfilment, challenge, responsibility, and autonomy.

For event employees, the emphasis may be on extrinsic motivation but is more likely to be a combination of extrinsic and intrinsic motivation. However, for event volunteers, the emphasis can be assumed to be clearly on intrinsic motivation, highlighting the need for different approaches, or at least a different emphasis, in the management and motivation of employees and volunteers.

Despite differences between what motivates employees and volunteers, there are some factors that are common to both. Everyone, including employee and volunteers, is:

- Inspired and motivated by great leaders that demonstrate vision, integrity, trust in their people, as well as a sincere desire to enhance their well-being.
- Motivated through working in a vibrant and productive team environment. Teams provide synergistic benefits in that the team productivity can be greater than what could be expected through simple aggregation of individual performances, but more importantly, teams have the power to provide a work environment that can be incredibly motivational, inspirational, and creative.
- Motivated by a productive and healthy organisational culture. Here, key outcomes include enhanced levels of creativity and greater levels of personal well-being.

10

Leadership and culture

Leadership and culture are two sides of the same coin and in fact, a leader's most important challenge involves creating and sustaining a healthy and productive organisational culture (Schein & Schein, 2016). In the events industry, this involves a clear and observable focus on the design and conduct of financially viable events that are successful, impactful, and memorable but, at the same time, inspire positive social change and demonstrate environmental responsibility.

Great leadership and a healthy, productive culture, inspires employees and volunteers, enhances motivation and well-being, and is likely to lead to high levels of creativity and innovation, and the staging of exceptional events. A key element of great leadership involves demonstrating trust in employees and volunteers. In fact, the desire to be trusted is basic to human nature and hence, trust. Motivation, and well-being are closely intertwined. And while trust can be communicated verbally, actions clearly speak louder than words. In a work context, perhaps the most effective way to demonstrate trust is to delegate responsibility and important tasks. Delegation can be not only a highly effective intrinsic motivator but also an effective way to expedite the completion of a range of tasks. The need to delegate applies to volunteers as well as employees. Given that event volunteers are generally motivated by intrinsic incentives, providing them with appropriate levels of responsibility and allowing the completion of responsible tasks can also generate higher levels of motivation, commitment and productivity.

As an employee, what would you regard as the key benefits of delegation?

Working in a dynamic team environment can be a motivational experience for employees and volunteers but it is important that the creation of team spirit and the team development process, and the design of jobs are influenced and managed strategically in a positive, well-thought-out manner. With regard to job design, jobs can be enriched through an increase in the extent to which they involve planning and evaluation functions, providing individuals with greater levels of autonomy, challenge, and control.

While the creating and sustaining a healthy and productive organisational culture is a leader's key responsibility, it is a complex and often difficult challenge. Key characteristics of a positive culture include:

- **Clear and observable core values** that provide focus, purpose, and direction, and generally emphasise financial, social, and environmental sustainability. The welfare of employees and volunteers, and respect for event attendees and the host community are key elements of social responsibility.

- ▮ Frequent and effective communication throughout the event organisation and amongst employees and volunteers. And often the most effective communication is the informal communication that needs to be encouraged and nurtured by the enterprise's leadership.

- ▮ Growth and development opportunities for the organisation's workforce. This is important for volunteers as well as for full and part-time employees. In fact, the provision of these opportunities for volunteers is what clearly distinguishes volunteerism from exploitation.

- ▮ Teamwork and collaboration as a key element in all efforts that are directed toward the staging of exceptional events.

- ▮ The provision of incentives and rewards that focus on contributing to the core values of the event enterprise, achieving positive event outcomes, and working effectively and collaboratively as a team member.

Event organisations that exhibit healthy and productive cultures are generally the enterprises that design and stage exceptional and memorable events.

Case study 10.1: Managing volunteers at the Super Bowl

The Super Bowl is held annually in February in the USA. Typically, the magnitude of this event requires around 10,000 volunteers. In order to recruit and motivate this talent, Rosterfy (volunteer management software) helped organisers schedule interviews and selection which varied from an initial 35,000 participants down to the final number of successful volunteers. To engage volunteers Rosterfy assisted with maintaining consistent communication of the planning of the event. Like every other stakeholder, volunteers would like to know what is happening in all phases of event planning. Therefore, Bennett Merriman, CEO Rosterfy, ensured that the platform secured a database of information that helped manage consistent communication and made volunteers feel included in the workforce journey. Training programs were developed as videos in a fun and interactive way.

Bennett Merriman

https://www.rosterfy.com/blog/rosterfy-signs-sixth-consecutive-super-bowl

10

Summary

Finding, empowering, and motivating talent is an essential element in the development of a sustainable competitive advantage. Hence, the recruitment of talented employees and volunteers should be a proactive, on-going process involving considerable attention and effort. When considering ways of attracting talent, employer branding is possibly the most effective approach and generally involves:

■ Developing and maintaining a positive, productive, and motivational work environment.

■ Rewarding and compensating employees appropriately.

■ Developing and implementing appropriate human resource management policies.

■ Developing and maintaining a reputation as a progressive employer.

■ Maintaining ongoing, positive employee engagement with a focus on employee health, safety, and well-being.

Given that volunteers are more likely to be attracted to the event itself, rather than the event enterprise, volunteer recruitment strategies need to focus more on the event brand than the employer brand. However, in view of the transient nature of many volunteers, the emphasis should be on developing a pool of potential volunteers. Volunteer recruitment strategies will vary depending upon the event. However, this process can be followed:

■ Identify likely volunteer expectations and motivations.

■ Identify event needs.

■ Quantify event needs in terms of the volunteer numbers.

■ Develop a set of volunteer requirements in terms of knowledge, skills, attitudes, and talents.

■ Identify where potential volunteers may be targeted.

■ Develop a communication and recruitment strategy.

■ Utilise word-of-mouth strategies involving current volunteers.

■ Commence the selection process.

When selecting the most appropriate candidate, an array of techniques and methods can be utilised, but the final decision should be based on:

■ Cognitive and thinking ability, emotional intelligence, and behavioural qualities.

- Motivation to learn, acquire knowledge and expertise, and achieve high levels of performance.
- The extent to which there is a match with the organisation's culture

Induction is a useful way of providing employees and volunteers with focus and direction. Employee induction needs to reinforce the view that the new employee has made the right decision to join the organisation. They also need to feel welcome, appreciated, and inspired to commence work in their new role. Hence, they need to be introduced to other staff and provided with a broad range of documentation and information that, amongst other things, includes:

- Health and Safety information
- An overview of the new role
- Employment contracts and associated documentation
- Employment policies and practices
- Organisational structure, maps, staff profiles and key aspects of the organisation's history
- The organisation's vision, values, mission statement, and strategic plan
- Links to work team information and access to social media

Although the relationship between volunteer and event enterprise is somewhat looser than for employees, an induction that welcomes them to their new role and provides information that informs and motivates is still essential. They need to be introduced to all employees and other volunteers with whom they'll be having ongoing interaction.

There are a number of key Human Resource Management policies that need to be developed and adhered to. These include policies related to workplace health and safety, workplace bullying, and sexual harassment. Sound training and development programs should also be established. These have the benefit of providing employees and volunteers with the knowledge, skills, and competence to effectively complete tasks but just as importantly, they act as an intrinsic motivator.

Other human resource policies that create a healthier, more productive workplace include the establishment of appropriate reward systems, the maintenance of on-going engagement with employees and volunteers, and the creation of a heathy workplace culture, consistent with high levels of social and environmental responsibility.

There are clear and obvious differences between the motivation of employees and volunteers. For event employees, the emphasis may be on extrinsic motivators such as money and career progression, but it is more likely to

10

be a combination of extrinsic and intrinsic motivation. However, for event volunteers, the emphasis is likely to be on intrinsic motivators such as a passion for, and interest in the events and associated tasks. Despite these differences, there are some factors that are common to both. Everyone is likely to be:

- Inspired and motivated by great leaders.
- Motivated through working in a vibrant and productive team environment.
- Motivated by a productive and healthy organisational culture.

There is a clear link between leadership and organisational culture. Key characteristics of a positive culture include:

- Clear and observable core values.
- Frequent and effective communication throughout the event organisation and amongst employees and volunteers.
- Growth and development opportunities for volunteers and employees.
- Teamwork and collaboration as a key element in the staging of all events.
- The provision of appropriate incentives and rewards.

A healthy and productive culture goes a long way to ensuring positive organisational outcomes.

Industry profile: Annmaree Angelico, Expert in human resource management and safety

With over 27 years' experience in managing small to large scale events, Annmaree is an expert in the events and entertainment spaces. She is an expert in the emergency planning for large scale events with a focus on production and logistics for music festivals, major sporting and corporate events held in stadiums, convention centres and outdoor spaces. At the 2018 Commonwealth Games, in addition to safety and risk management programs, she developed and implemented procedures and training programs for stakeholders. Her passion and expertise lie in business, emergency, safety and risk management while ensuring safety protocols are met within the respective departments she works.

During the pandemic, Annmaree shifted her mindset from the private business sector to working for the government. Her goal is to extend her talent and safety expertise during the 2023 Women's FIFA World cup and 2032 Brisbane Olympic Games.

Skills and Expertise

- Staff recruitment mentoring, training and induction programs
- Risk and emergency planning across stakeholders
- Strategic financial and business management
- Project management and logistics
- Development of protocols and auditing tools
- Leading and managing teams
- Contract management

What are some key considerations during talent recruitment?

Lead time in recruitment

One of the major challenges in large scale events is the lead time for planning and resource management. For example, at the 2018 Commonwealth Games, I had just over a year to plan and formulate a team of 80 people in various roles; 70 of which were assigned to teams which also required specialist qualifications as staff were undertaking additional roles such as 'emergency wardens'. Whilst we had in excess of a year to plan, it wasn't possible to recruit all staff on a full time basis, only those in key senior roles and administrative support. A total of 551 shifts equating to 10,871 man hours were delivered, this achievement was primarily due to the time spent in recruiting the right team members, in coaching individuals, encouraging inclusivity amongst the team, the induction and training sessions, and management making themselves available to team members who required additional support or guidance.

Hiring from diverse backgrounds

Recruiting candidates from diverse backgrounds is also important. In line with company values that endorse values of diversity and equality, teams need to achieve gender and cultural balance. As part of our recruitment strategy 10% of the workforce consisted of indigenous groups. It was important that the team could come together as one diverse cultural group and share our values.

Understanding diverse contractors

Contractors come from a variety of backgrounds, each employed to deliver a particular service or function within the event delivery process. Whilst the contractor employers have a legal obligation to induct their employees, it is imperative that the event owner also conducts inductions as per local legislative and WorkSafe requirements. It's important for a company to meet its legal duty to provide induction and training, where required, to all stakeholders in what the company stands for, with clear guidelines on expectations in delivering the event.

10

Importance of providing customised training and staff induction programs

Each event has its own staff requirements and, in my events, managing risk and safety is paramount. Accordingly, I develop customised programs to induct staff, contractors and volunteers with detailed information that guides them in understanding key event requirements in addition to our company's methodologies and policies. To ensure that these are fully understood, specific inductions are prepared and delivered multiple times across several team members. Multiple delivery allows smaller teams to ask questions and be more actively involved in the induction session.

The production schedules and different shifts that may impact on the induction process; it may not always be possible to deliver inductions face to face, so consider delivering online inductions that test the inductee's knowledge of what the induction contains. Also, contractors on site may be casuals with limited English language skills. Therefore, it may be prudent to provide induction material in different languages.

Engage high level stakeholders to assist with training

In training it is advisable to engage staff with the various high level stakeholders in order to fully understand and adhere to the stringent governance and compliance requirements. It is important for all talent to understand the role of the multiple local, state and international stakeholders involved in the event. Stakeholders can also join in the delivery of induction and training programs thus ensuring talent can deliver exceptional service and event outcomes.

Can you give an example of key information to be included in induction programs?

As many team members may never have heard of your organisation, it is important to go back to basics such as including information about the company, and its culture. The culture lets you know the type of company it is and what it stands for. The culture of an organisation is also identified by its policies, code of conduct, worker support including wellbeing and safe work practices. Without these key principles, staff (full time, casual and contractors) and volunteers are not able to understand the way of delivery. Provide an induction pack with detailed venue information such as: floor plans, venue contacts and emergency management plans. Also include:

- What the company policies are (including social media, confidentiality, acceptable behaviours, incident management).
- Roles and responsibilities.
- Team member expectations which is important for staff safety but also highlights consideration of the patrons, athletes, delegates, officials and volunteers.
- Accreditation processes and uniform standards.
- Employer, staff, contractor and volunteer safety and wellbeing responsibilities under the applicable legislation and long shift hours.
- Accident and incident management and reporting including first aid; infection prevention (such as COVID-19); special circumstances such as an act of terrorism;

alcohol and other drugs; amenities; bushfires and air quality; electrical safety; food safety; hazardous substances; LPG safety – forklifts (outdoor events); manual handling; personal protective equipment; risk principles including hazard identifications; site specific rules (e.g. emergency procedures, parking, smoking); vehicles and plant; visitor access; weather conditions; working at heights.

What are some key personality traits and attributes that talent needs to possess?

- Resilience.
- A willingness to delve into the unknown.
- Flexiblity and adaptability because events get moved, cancelled, rescheduled.
- Awareness of how their personal actions may affect others in the workplace.
- A willingness to be mentored by senior staff.

Any final tips when leading teams of staff, contractors and volunteers?

Businesses have suffered during the pandemic with staff wellbeing issues. Provide key advice on how to manage healthy teams and maintain a special focus on staff safety and wellbeing. Whilst employers have an obligation to providing a safe working environment, all staff have an obligation for their own wellbeing. Stress can have a major impact on our wellbeing. Some things you can do to reduce work stress:

- "It's okay to say no".
- Try not to take work home.
- Take regular breaks.
- Take a break from technology.
- Arrange flexible working times if possible.
- Set realistic and achievable work goals.

Review questions

1. Event volunteers may often feel that they can contribute more than their volunteering opportunity allows. In what ways can an event organisation empower volunteers in a manner that enhances their contributions to the successful staging of events and promotes well-being?

2. When someone seeks out a role as an event volunteer, they usually expect to gain useful experience and be able to, in some way, contribute to successful event outcomes. Hence, there should be mutual benefits for the volunteer and the event organiser. Unfortunately though, some event volunteering experiences tend to be characterised by exploitation rather than mutual benefits. What processes can be put in place to ensure that the volunteering experience is a positive one?

10

3. In terms of providing new employees with focus and direction, an effective induction process is essential. What do you regard as the key characteristics of effective induction?

4. Event employees and volunteers have different needs and different reasons for being involved with events. Outline the key differences and how those differences can be addressed in motivational and leadership strategies that are applied to employees and volunteers.

5. In any work-related situation, people like to feel that they are trusted. Using examples, explain how an employer can demonstrate trust and how that can contribute to higher levels of motivation.

6. The way in which a job is designed can significantly impact on motivation and job satisfaction. Explain the key elements of an events job that require attention during the design process.

7. Using event industry examples, explain the importance of organizational culture and the link between leadership and culture and describe the type of organisational culture that is likely to be associated with the design and staging of exceptional events.

Workshop activities

Scenario A

Your task is to recruit 50 casual staff for a local festival or conference of your choice.

1 Develop a position description including the level of responsibility required for paid staff.

2 Prepare interview questions that assess motivational factors for their choice to engage with your event.

3 Design an induction program that includes key information about the event and the systems and processes in place that ensure ongoing communication about the event.

4 As part of induction, develop a half day training session for each of the positions of: a) Meet and greet; b) Covid vaccination check; c) Bag check; d) Managing a volunteer stand.

Scenario B

You have been assigned the role of Volunteer Management for a large international event of your choice.

1 Prepare an induction brief to volunteers with all the relevant information about the event.

2   Design a volunteer agreement showing a flexible arrangement and reflecting meaningful responsibilities.

3   Design interactive and fun video activities that will engage volunteers in a team spirit, as this may reduce the possibility of dropout rates.

4   Develop a sample roster schedule for the duration of the event that ensures frequent breaks and meal areas for the volunteers, without reducing the supply of workforce.

Further reading

Cain, L., Orlowski, M., & Kitterlin-Lynch, M. (2021). A holistic investigation of special event volunteer motivation. *Event Management*, 25(5), 473-487.

Engelhardt, L., & Olberding, J. C. (2016). Managing and Motivating Event Volunteers. In *Social Enterprise and Special Events* (pp. 79-100). Routledge.

Gambrel, P. A., & Cianci, R. (2003). Maslow's hierarchy of needs: Does it apply in a collectivist culture. *Journal of Applied Management and Entrepreneurship*, 8(2), 143.

Giudici, M., & Filimonau, V. (2019). Exploring the linkages between managerial leadership, communication, and teamwork in successful event delivery. *Tourism Management Perspectives*, 32.

Hackman, J. R., & Oldham, G. R. (1975). Development of the job diagnostic survey. *Journal of Applied Psychology*, 60(2), 159.

Muskat, B., & Mair, J. (2020). Knowledge sharing and power in the event workforce. *Event Management*, 24(5), 597-609.

Qi, H., Smith, K.A., & Yeoman, I. (2019). An exploratory study of volunteer motivation at conferences: a case study of the First World Conference on Tourism for Development. *Asia Pacific Journal of Tourism Research*, 24(6), 574-583.

Schein, E.H. & Schein, P. (2016). *Organizational Culture and Leadership*, 5th Ed., Jossey-Basss.

Wrathall, J., & Gee, A. (2011). Event Management Theory and Practice. McGraw-Hill.

Zievinger, D., & Swint, F. (2018). Retention of festival volunteers: Management practices and volunteer motivation. *Research in Hospitality Management*, 8(2), 107-114.

10

Websites

monacosound.com.au/

www.rosterfy.com/the-engaged-volunteer-podcast

www.visitscotland.org/events/advice-materials/event-volunteering

11 Sustainability, evaluation and industry trends

Learning objectives

On completion of this chapter, you will be able to:

➤ Explain the importance of event sustainability

➤ Discuss the business case for sustainability

➤ Recognise the scope of event sustainability and the three pillars of sustainability

➤ Discuss imperatives for reducing the carbon footprint associated with all stages of the conduct of planned events

➤ Explain current industry trends, recognising the potential of planned events to initiate real change in all aspects of sustainability

➤ Examine practices in all areas associated with sustainability and explain current industry trends that move beyond sustainability to a focus on regeneration.

Sustainability has been defined as *"the process of living within the limits of available physical, natural, and social resources in ways that allow the living systems in which humans are embedded to thrive in perpetuity"* (Sustain SU, 2010). Hence, in terms of environmental sustainability, there needs to be a focus on the use of renewable rather than non-renewable resources. And even with renewable resources, there needs to be a focus on avoiding over-utilisation and wastage. Sustainability is about more than just 'being green'. It is about doing things efficiently and effectively, being innovative and creating a positive impact, achieving excellence, and leaving lasting legacies.

With the same focus on the longer term, sustainable development can be defined as development that meets the needs of the present without compromising the ability of future generations to meet their own needs. With the world's population increasing at an incredible rate, the challenges associated with sustainable development have become enormous. Increases in population naturally lead to increases in energy usage, and adding to that dilemma is the fact that increases in per capita income accelerate energy usage even further. According to the worldometer the current growth in population is approximately 81 million people per year and the fact that the world's two most populated nations, China, and India, are amongst the fastest growing economies, makes that dilemma an even bigger one. The key implications of a wealthier, more populated world are that the world's natural resources are being used up at a far greater rate than the rate at which they can be regenerated. For several years, the carrying capacity of our global ecosystem has been greatly exceeded.

The importance of sustainability

According to the Events Industry Council, sustainability for events means, *"taking action towards preserving our natural environment; promoting a healthy, inclusive society; and supporting a thriving economy"*. Serious attempts at the application of sustainability concepts to mega events can be traced back to at least the early 1990s with the planning and staging of the Barcelona 1992 Olympics. Although sustainability has been taken seriously in the events industry for at least the last three decades, we still have a worsening outlook in terms of climate change, which is highlighted by changes to the way in which it has been framed over the last decade, moving from a 'climate risk' to a 'climate crisis' (Coles, 2021).

At the same time, extreme inequalities exist in the distribution of wealth and natural resources. Large parts of the world are experiencing extreme poverty and roughly 800 million people are starving. And while food production comes at enormous cost in terms of energy usage and climate change, at least a third of the food is wasted. If 40% of that wasted food could be redirected to the starving millions, the problem of world starvation would be solved, making food wastage not only one of our biggest sustainability problems but one of the world's dumbest problems.

The events industry is responsible for a significant proportion of food wastage. Most event managers and event caterers have experienced FORO, (Fear Of Running Out). This drives event caterers and managers to over-cater, and waste one of the world's most valuable resources.

11

? *What strategies could be developed to reduce or offset food wastage at events?*

While we often hear about the climate change 'debate' there is no real debate. Significant levels of global warming have been recorded for at least the last century, with temperatures now 1° Celsius above pre-industrial levels and increasing at a rate of 0.2°C every decade. 1° C may not seem like much but it has already led to significant problems including sea level rises, species extinction, and extreme weather events. Scientists urge for efforts to keep the temperature increase below 1.5°C and indicate that rises greater than 2°C above pre-industrial levels would be disastrous.

In addition, multiple studies that have been published in peer-reviewed journal articles clearly indicate that at least 98% of actively publishing scientists agree that global warming is the result of human activity. Planned events are one category of human activity that leads to global warming. Furthermore, global warming will continue well after the causes are brought under control, perhaps by as much as 50 years. Scientists warn that there is a 'tipping point', a point of no return, which may be rapidly approaching. Immediate action is now required.

Did you know? Scotland is positioning itself as a conference destination having hosted the global conference on climate change, featuring a two week schedule including 50 events and focusing on finance, energy, nature, youth and empowerment. In view of the immediate action required by global leaders in the fight against climate change, the destination presented key sustainability initiatives required for event planning. One key consideration was the need for global collaboration to achieve a net zero economy. The United Nations (UN) climate change conference was held in November 2021 in Glasgow, Scotland and set out to unite the world in the battle against climate change. The key goals at the summit included:

- Secure global net zero by mid century
- Protect communities and natural habitat
- Mobilise finance for climate change
- Collaborate to deliver on goals

For more on the COP26 goals visit https://ukcop26.org/cop26-goals/

? *While there are compelling reasons for event sustainability, does the development of comprehensive sustainability policies and practices make good business sense? Why?*

The business case for sustainability

While the case for sustainability is compelling in terms of human life on our planet, there is also a business case for sustainability. Yet sometimes in the mistaken belief that the costs outweigh the benefits, environmental and social concerns are ignored or neglected. However, the costs are often short-term while the benefits are often long-term and hence, the real trade-off is not between profits and sustainability but between the short-term and the long-term. In a culture and a time in history in which 'time is money', the short-term often wins out. This is particularly the case when event managers are presented with an extraordinary array of competing demands:

- Market
- Environmental
- Social
- Economic
- Technological.

And all of the associated changes and impacts need to be recognised, addressed, and managed.

But the reality is that the benefits associated with the development of a good track record in terms of social and environmental issues more than pays off financially. The most obvious benefits are:

- Avoiding legal issues and associated costs through compliance with relevant regulations and legislation;
- Reducing the cost of wastage;
- Increasing revenue as a result of greater levels of customer (or event attendee) acceptance and loyalty;
- Becoming an employer of choice and gaining greater levels of acceptance, loyalty, and commitment from employees and volunteers;
- Developing a more positive reputation amongst a broad range of stakeholders;
- Developing a more enlightened vision of the future.

The last of these benefits may take time, and may only occur after sustainability efforts have become embedded within the business, but may also be referred to as enlightened self-interest. These embedded sustainability efforts have a clear, positive, and lasting impact on the business performance of all enterprises including event companies. By embedding

11

sustainability efforts into their events, sustainable event enterprises seek to create value for all stakeholders, including:

- Employees and volunteers
- Event attendees
- Shareholders and investors
- Event suppliers
- Host communities
- Civil society
- The planet.

? *In what ways do you think employees and volunteers may benefit from working for an event enterprise with embedded sustainability practices?*

Porter and Kramer (2011) refer to this approach as the creation of shared value. They argue that enterprises can generate economic value by identifying and addressing social problems that intersect with their business. Examples of this intersection between social and business issues include:

- Positive environmental impacts
- Energy use
- Water use
- Supplier access and viability
- Employee and volunteer skills
- Employee and volunteer safety, and mental and physical health.

Much of the strategic value of sustainability stems from the fact that, in practice, the development of sound sustainability policies and practices implies a need for ongoing engagement and communication with a broad range of stakeholders. This involves not only educating stakeholders but, given that we operate in a rapidly changing, competitive environment, learning from them as well. Hence, through ongoing engagement, liaison, and discussion with key stakeholders, as well as continuous, often incremental, adjustments to business and sustainability practices, event enterprises put themselves in a better position to predict, anticipate, and respond to:

- Economic and financial imperatives
- Social issues and concerns
- Environmental needs
- Regulatory and legislative changes.

What would you regard as the most important benefits of ongoing engagement and communication with event stakeholders? Which stakeholders would you regard as the most important? Why?

Staying in touch in this manner facilitates achievement of the key objectives of any enterprise, that is, to effectively stage planned events that are:

- On time
- On budget,
- To standards consistent with the needs and interests of key stakeholders.

A failure to develop and maintain stakeholder engagement can lead to:

- Increased levels of conflict
- Reduced levels of stakeholder cooperation.

This can seriously disrupt the ability of an events enterprise to stage planned events on time, on budget, and to specified standards. In fact, effective and ongoing stakeholder engagement and communication goes much further than a demonstration of Corporate Social Responsibility. It can be regarded as another example of enlightened self-interest.

It can also be viewed in terms of sound risk management. With globalisation, and particularly with international events, supply chains may extend around the world, leading to vulnerability in terms of:

- Climate change
- Natural disasters
- Food scarcity
- Poor labour conditions.

In fact, the value at stake as a result of sustainability issues could be immense. Climate change alone presents major risks that can significantly impact the operations, revenues, and expenditures of event enterprises around the globe. And unlike traditional forms of business risk, the risks that are associated with social and environmental concerns are often hidden in the short-term, but become obvious in the long-term.

Risk management in these circumstances requires a focus on the long-term, making investment decisions today that involve:

- Long-term capacity building
- The development of adaptive strategies

11

Case study 11.1: Edinburgh Festivals

The 'Festival City 2030 Vision' is Edinburgh's plan to focus on sustainability principles shared by key players of the industry. These principles showcase the city as a leader and innovator in responsible festival design and delivery. The festival environmental policy highlights stakeholder collaboration as key focus when embedding sustainability principles and encourages event attendees to consider environmental issues. The policy sets out clear goals for reducing the waste, energy and managing resources in sustainable ways. For more visit www.edinburghfestivalcity.com/about/vision

? *Explain the importance of risk management in the current environment. What are the likely outcomes from ignoring the levels of risk associated with events?*

Investments in sustainability can also be a driving force for innovation. Rethinking, reimagining and redesigning events to meet social and environmental imperatives can create a broad array of new opportunities. The current trend in virtual events and hybrid strategies is just one example. The traditional view that there is a trade-off between sustainability efforts and financial performance is simply wrong. There is no trade-off. Or if there is, it is between the long-term and the short-term. Long-term financial benefits accrue as a result of the development of an enhanced reputation leading to a competitive advantage, and significant cost savings through:

■ Sustainability-related operational efficiencies

■ More efficient transport and logistics

■ The minimisation of waste

■ More sustainable use of energy and water.

Some organisers may be sceptical about customer interest in sustainability, particularly in terms of willingness-to-pay. However, most commentators point to a clear shift in attitudes amongst attendees, that began decades ago. They now have clear expectations that highlight a need for greater levels of social awareness, and of integrity and transparency. Coupled with greater choice of alternative events, these expectations should not be ignored. And a good track record for social and environmental responsibility can:

■ Increase employee and volunteer loyalty

■ Improve efficiency and productivity

■ Facilitate the recruitment of high calibre employees and volunteers

■ Enhance levels of employee retention and morale.

Over recent decades, a different type of employee and volunteer appears to be emerging. In general, they are more focused on:

■ Values, purpose, and work-life balance

■ Environmental and social issues and concerns

■ Working in a progressive organisation

■ Being part of a positive and progressive culture

In what ways do you think that the attitudes and expectations of today's event employees and volunteers differ from those of the past?

The three pillars of sustainability

There are three pillars of sustainability that intersect and overlap. These are also called event impacts and compose the triple bottom line of events.

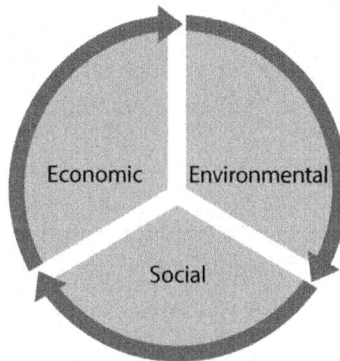

Figure 11.1: Triple bottom line event impacts

1. **Economic sustainability** focuses on corporate profitability, job creation, economic growth, and full employment. Events that are popular, that provide employment opportunities and memorable experiences, and are managed efficiently, contribute to economic sustainability.

2. **Environmental sustainability** focuses on the well-being of our physical environment. The emphasis is on sustaining and restoring nature, protecting our planet, reducing stressors such as greenhouse gas emissions, and maintaining water and air quality. As the quality of the environment is inextricably linked with health, efforts to preserve nature will benefit people as well. And because natural resources foster economic development, a close link also exists between environmental and economic sustainability. Both social and economic systems exist within a physical environment and depend upon that environment.

11

3. **Social sustainability** focuses on human health and well-being, social justice, education, corporate social responsibility, employee security, and employee health and safety. As discussed, human health goes hand in hand with environmental well-being. And issues such as employee security go hand in hand with economic well-being. Events can contribute to social sustainability through education, through raising awareness of social issues, through appropriate treatment of employees and volunteers, and through providing memorable event experiences that contribute to the mental health of event attendees.

The three pillars overlap and are inextricably linked. It may be argued however, that given the fact that economic and social systems exist within the physical environment, environmental sustainability, and efforts to reduce an event's carbon footprint are of utmost concern.

Reducing the carbon footprint

Strategies can be developed at all stages of event planning, design, and management to reduce an event's carbon footprint. The focus of these strategies can be on several key elements of the event including these.

Venue and accommodation

The choice of venue is one of the first and most important decisions that an event organiser will make. A key consideration should be the transport options that are available as a result of the venue's location. The closer the venue is to public transport, the better. Accommodation should preferably be either at the venue or if not, within walking distance. Clearly, the use of motor vehicles to travel from accommodation to the venue should be avoided. Other strategies should include:

- Selecting a venue that has developed a reputation for sustainability, and has sought and achieved recognised, sustainability certification.
- The venue's sustainability, waste, energy and water management practices should minimise any negative impact on the environment.
- Its sustainability policies and initiatives should include the use of eco-friendly materials and minimise the use of energy and other resources.

Transport

A key requirement at any event involves getting attendees, VIPs, and other participants to and from, and around the venue. It also involves the transport of supplies, creating the potential for significant carbon emissions.

Considerable carbon emission reductions can be achieved by selecting a venue close to public transport. Further reductions can be achieved by:

- Encouraging **active travel** which includes walking and cycling. The provision of relevant information aimed at helping attendees to plan their journey may facilitate a greater uptake of active transport options.
- Encouraging the use of **public transport** through the provision of maps, timetables, and other information as part of the marketing process.
- Discouraging the use of **private vehicles** by limiting the availability of car parking and encouraging car share.

Consider this: A recent example of innovative sustainability initiatives at event venues is urban beekeeping. This has become an interesting feature of several green venues in cities around the world, including Paris, London, Toronto, San Francisco, Melbourne, New York, and Hong Kong. This sustainable use of venue rooftops leads to the production of a delicious honey that benefits the local community, involves less food miles, is unique to each site, and helps to green the surrounding location.

Hospitality and event catering

The provision of some type of food and beverage (F&B) service is a key element at most planned events. However, this comes at an enormous environmental cost and hence, every effort should be made to provide food in the most sustainable manner possible. Key strategies include:

- Minimising food wastage. Avoid the temptation to over-order as a result of a fear of running out. Every effort should be made to accurately forecast food and beverage needs and order accordingly. If food is left over, every effort should be made to either donate or compost.
- Where possible and appropriate, integrate cooking into the event and in doing so, source food in a manner that demonstrates a clear preference for organic, seasonal, regional, and Fairtrade foods and beverages.
- Utilise eco-friendly catering materials, avoid single-use plastics, and avoid other single-use products such as plates, cups, and utensils.
- Whenever possible, source food locally to reduce the need for transportation and to support local producers.
- Develop a menu that includes vegetarian and vegan options. This expands the diversity of food options but more importantly, reduces reliance on meat products, lowering the negative environmental impact associated with meat production.

11

■ Contract eco-friendly event caterers that comply with sound sustainability policies and practices, demonstrate a preference for organic food, and have developed a reputation as a green caterer.

Energy usage and climate-compensation initiatives

Energy usage must be considered when selecting a venue, accommodation and suppliers. These choices should demonstrate a preference for energy generated from renewable sources. Regardless of the source, energy usage must be minimised in all areas including heating, cooling, and lighting.

Given the difficulties that are often associated with completely avoiding the negative impact of energy usage, climate-compensation initiatives, including forestry, should be considered as one way of offsetting that impact. Strategies aimed at reducing carbon emissions must precede climate-compensation initiatives. Alternatives, including online events, hybrid strategies, or the staging of smaller local events, should be considered.

Water usage

Water is a scarce and valuable resource that should be used in a responsible and sustainable manner and protected from pollution and contamination. Strategies aimed at the responsible and sustainable use of water include:

■ Identifying and minimising unintended water loss.

■ Regularly servicing appliances and equipment to avoid water loss, pollution, or contamination.

■ Implementing water saving techniques.

■ Keeping water clean and utilising eco-friendly cleaning materials.

Waste management

From the planning through to the staging and closure of events, there needs to be a clear focus on the minimisation or avoidance of rubbish and waste. Proper waste management and disposal involves:

■ Reducing the amount of potential waste that is utilised at the event and comes to the event. Preferably, attendees should bring nothing to the event that won't be either consumed or returned home with them.

■ Reuse of event-related materials at future events or by someone else.

■ Repair of event-related material that is broken or damaged.

■ Recycling of waste. Anything that is not reused or repaired should be recyclable.

Procurement of materials and use of resources

Sustainability considerations should be an integral feature of all aspects of procurement, including the selection of sustainable, eco-friendly products and services. Sustainability certification is provided by a range of bodies around the world to set standards and facilitate the procurement of sustainable products and organic food. In Australia for example:

■ FSC (Forest Stewardship Council) certification establishes standards for responsible and sustainable forest management. For more visit www.au.fsc.org/en-au/for-business/fsc-certification

■ ACO (Australian Certified Organic) certification sets standards that are consistent with national and international production standards, for all sectors of the organic industry. For more visit www.aco.net.au

Communication and documentation

Communication and documentation should be provided to inform all event stakeholders about sustainability policies, procedures, and initiatives. In this regard, Pre- and Post-event sustainability reports provide stakeholders with relevant information as well as establishing a firm basis for continuous improvement. In this way, successful, on-going communication leads to greater levels of trust and credibility.

Consider this: The Gold Coast Convention and Exhibition Centre (GCCEC) in Australia has a checklist that assists event managers in planning green events. This provides instructions on the use of simple eco-friendly practices to assist in carbon savings for all minor and major events. By adopting key sustainable initiatives, companies enhance their brand reputation while contributing to delivering sustainable events. Download your green event checklist here: www.gccec.com.au/green-event-checklist.html

Gaining an understanding of 'circular economy' principles is central to the notion of regeneration. It revokes the myth that sustainability or regenerative efforts come at a cost. In fact, the application of 'circular economy' principles on a global scale would abate several billion tonnes of pollution each year and potentially lead to enormous economic benefits. However, abandoning the 'linear economy' approach and embracing 'circular economy' concepts and principles will never happen in the absence of a concerted, holistic approach by governments around the world. It must be backed by eco-friendly and innovation-friendly government policies that recognise the longer-term benefits to community and industry, and don't pander to short-term vested interests.

11

Image 11.1: Photo courtesy of Lightsoak Photography.

Reimagining sustainability

Despite concerted sustainability efforts over recent decades by a range of industries including the events industry, scientist warn that we currently face a climate change crisis. According to several scientific reports we now have perhaps a decade to reverse current trends. A recent report by the Intergovernmental Panel on Climate Change (IPCC) states:

> *"It is unequivocal that human influence has warmed the atmosphere, ocean and land. Widespread and rapid changes in the atmosphere, ocean, cryosphere and biosphere have occurred."*

Gaining an understanding of 'circular economy' principles is central to the notion of regeneration. It revokes the myth that sustainability or regenerative efforts come at a cost. In fact, the application of 'circular economy' principles on a global scale would abate several billion tonnes of pollution each year and potentially lead to enormous economic benefits. However, abandoning the 'linear economy' approach and embracing 'circular economy' concepts and principles will never happen without a concerted, holistic approach by governments globally. It must be backed by innovation-friendly, government policies that recognise the longer-term benefits to community and industry, and don't bow to short-term vested interests.

Social issues and impacts

Further to environmental impacts a number of studies have focused on economic and social measurements however these frameworks still remain unclear (Mair *et al.*, 2021). Specifically, Mair *et al.* (2021) suggests that these frameworks no longer answer bigger research problems and do not consider social issues, therefore, new frameworks are required to answer the bigger problem utilising critical and interdisciplinary approaches Stakeholder views are important, especially when designing frameworks to measure local festivals (Van Niekerk & Getz, 2019).

Ongoing issues in communities such as marginalisation and inclusivity are valid reasons to continue research in measuring impacts. General issues such as human justice and inclusivity in events need to be prioritised within new sustainability frameworks. Events can therefore brand places as authentic communities where identities can rejuvenate and inclusivity can be celebrated (Ooi & Stöber, 2010). It is important therefore to continue research to uncover the deeper issues at local communities.

Case study 11.2: Relay for Nature

Relay for Nature is a sustainability project that involves technology and local fisherman in the collection of ocean plastic. As people want to be involved with sustainable projects globally, they can sponsor fishermen in this innovative project. Key stakeholders involve the fishermen, who collect the plastic, and the NGO (nongovernoment organisation) or research departments that manage the operations.

For more visit www.theoceanrace.com/en/news/12926_Relay4Nature-meets-an-innovative-project-that-is-helping-to-clean-the-ocean.html

ISO 20121

ISO (International Standards Organisation) in consultation with the events industry, in 2012 developed *ISO 20121: Event Sustainability Management Systems*. This standard guides event organisations in creating a management framework to ensure sustainability is embedded into the full event planning lifecycle and that knowledge is kept within the organisation, rather than lost, which is often a challenge with the 'gig economy' nature of events recruitment. The system approach steps through aspects such as stakeholder engagement, leadership commitment, issues identification, policies, objectives, operational control and continual improvement.

11

There are various institutes offering sustainability training however the Institute for Sustainable Events (ISE) offers self-paced training to event practitioners specifically in implementing ISO 20121. For more visit www. ise.world.

The ISO20121 standard started in London but has since been taken up by countries across the globe. ISO20121 asks event practitioners to:

- Identify potential areas of concern in their events and their event management operations
- Develop a sustainability policy that provides an outline of their commitment to sustainability
- Develop clear, specific, and measurable objectives and targets that underpin their sustainability policy
- Provide staff training in relevant areas of sustainability
- Engage with event suppliers on issues related to sustainability and develop a sustainability communications plan
- Monitor sustainability outcomes, measure their success, and develop, audit, and review appropriate sustainability documentation

For more visit iso.org

Event evaluation frameworks

Event evaluation frameworks assist in measuring the triple bottom line impacts which include: economic, social and environmental impacts. As event organisers seek to evaluate event experiences, it is key to utilise frameworks and evaluate against sustainability goals. Getz (2018a) provides frameworks that guide event evaluators in their assessment of various aspects of events such as organisations, staff, attendee experience or event quality.

The process of evaluation may include formative and summative strategies. Formative strategies include ongoing monitoring in order to address problems that arise in the process that can also be adapted. For example, in event planning when issues arise during the program development event managers can make changes and adapt the program to ensure issues are addressed throughout the process of event planning. Summative evaluation assesses event success at the end of the event and evaluates outcomes and impacts. These may include consequences or long-term impacts to the local residents or stakeholders.

For local events, planning qualitative and quantitative instruments may be sufficient to inform operational improvements. However, to solve more complex issues at policy level, these instruments may not be sufficient. Theoretical models and processes are required to answer complex program and political questions that arise especially with the planning of major or mega events. A sample of instruments that measure the TBL of community events can be found by Schlenker, K., Foley, C., & Getz, D. (2010) in their Encore festival and event evaluation kit on ResearchGate. Refer to the reference.

Planning an event evaluation

Getz (2018a) highlights the key stages when planning an event evaluation.

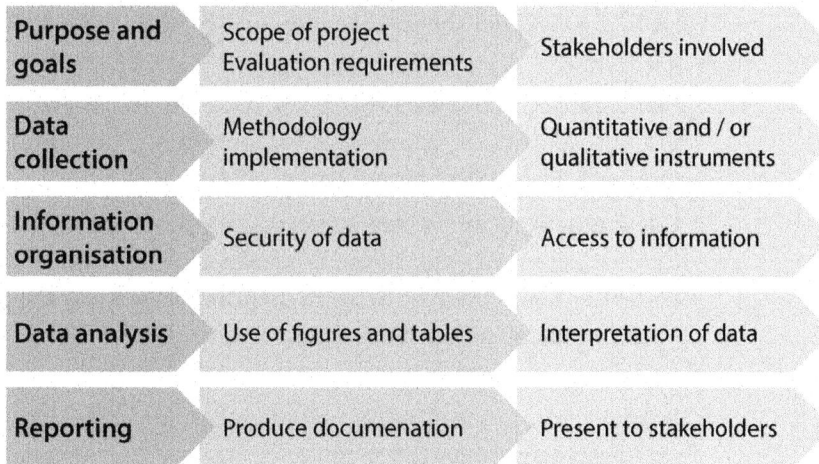

Figure 11.3: The five key stages are of planning an event evaluation.

Furthermore, Getz (2018a) highlights the key contents of an evaluation report which include:

1. **Executive summary:** all the key points demonstrating findings.
2. **Introduction:** background and aim of evaluation. What the key problem is; why evaluation is important and what is to be evaluated and who is involved.
3. **Evaluation plan:** what tools and instruments are used for the evaluation.
4. **Summary of results:** analysis of quantitative and qualitative data. Identification of patterns.
5. **Interpretation of results:** what the data means for the different stakeholders and the future planning of events.
6. **Conclusions:** key learnings that arise from the evaluation process.

Adapting to event industry trends

Dr Miguel Moital, event expert and principal academic in event management explains why event practitioners need to pay attention to prominent trends of society. As an academic, Miguel felt he had to follow the trends in order to positively influence change to his students. His personal experience during the pandemic led Miguel to upgrade his home office with a state-of-the-art home studio.

The set-up took one year, as it involved a great amount of learning, designing and implementing. Miguel's advice is to take small steps so initially begin with this key equipment: laptop or PC, teleprompter, microphone, one camera and a monitor.

According to Miguel the five benefits for having a state-of-the-art home studio include:

1. **Stand rather than sit** as this gives different energy when delivering virtual experiences. You have a lot more body freedom and can talk more naturally with others when standing.

2. **Use animations and visualisations.** This helps with the flow of educational activities – so, no more screen sharing. Miguel uses a lot of animations, and because he has a dedicated laptop for the powerpoint, he doesn't need to touch the slides. This allows for greater flexibility.

3. **Ensure creativity.** Miguel enjoys greater flexibility in producing learning experiences. No two seminars are the same. He says: "I constantly try to produce different flows. I can swiftly move from camera 1 to camera 2, or from computer 1 to computer 2, or even bring in picture in picture where two video inputs show on the screen."

4. **Engage with the audience.** Miguel has a reduced sense of separation between himself and audience, as the settings allow him to look at the camera. Teleprompters can make you feel more connected to the audience.

5. **Have fun delivering sessions.** You can feel more energetic and convey a different level of energy and emotion. With the home studio Miguel never gets bored during session delivery. He can always introduce variation and activities and bring flow in the seminar. It's important to enjoy the virtual teaching experience.

Image 11.2: Set up of a state-of-the-art home studio by Dr Miguel Moital

For more on setting up a home studio visit https://youtu.be/xY99Q2noQ44.

Case study 11.3: White Knight Events delivering green events

White Knight Events specialises in corporate events and the not-for-profit sector. In a local fundraising event, whilst sustainability was not the main objective, both Almila, Company Director, and her client, agreed this was an important component for a meaningful event. White Knight Events hired all furniture and sourced all food and alcohol from local suppliers, including individual catering boxes (using recycled materials and eco cutlery) from a local social enterprise. They asked the local community for donations of specific household decorations that could be repurposed and included a named, reusable, insulated cup per guest that was taken home as their gift.

Image 11.3: Photo courtesy of White Knight Events.

11

Additionally, the company created bathroom baskets with toilet paper, soap, hand sanitiser, and tissues so guests could use the public toilets and even the venue was selected because of its proximity to a train station, encouraging guests to think about ways they could reduce the impact of their commute. This event was a success with all guests appreciating the effort made to be greener. Often, it's about educating clients on ways events can be sustainable while producing events that are just as good, if not better. Guests generally feel better attending events where the environment has been considered and efforts have been made to reduce environmental impacts. This way of thinking is something Almila encourages all specialists to consider into their day to day operations.

For more visit: www.wkevents.co

Summary

Described as *"the process of living within the limits of available physical, natural, and social resources in ways that allow the living systems in which humans are embedded to thrive in perpetuity"*, sustainability is primarily concerned with doing things efficiently and effectively, being innovative and creating a positive impact, and leaving lasting legacies. Sustainable development can be defined as development that meets the needs of the present without compromising the ability of future generations to meet their own needs. However, as the world has become wealthier and more populated, sustainability and sustainable development become more difficult to achieve.

The application of sustainability concepts to planned events can be traced back at least the last three decades. Yet we still have rampant pollution, species extinction, imminent biodiversity collapse, rising sea levels, and a climate change crisis. At the same time, at least a third of the world's food is wasted while almost 800 million of the world's population are starving, a problem that could be solved by redirecting less than 40% of that waste.

Multiple studies confirm the view that global warming is the result of human activity, which includes planned events. There is clearly a business case for sustainability. There is no real trade-off between profits and sustainability and the most obvious benefits include:

- Avoiding legal issues and associated costs
- Reducing the cost of wastage
- Increasing revenue as a result of customer acceptance and loyalty
- Becoming an employer of choice

■ Developing a more positive reputation amongst stakeholders

■ Developing a more enlightened vision of the future.

A balanced approach to sustainability involves recognising three pillars – environmental, social, and economic sustainability. In terms of environmental sustainability and reducing the carbon footprint of events, clear policies and practices can be identified for all key stakeholders but particularly for organisers, caterers, and venue managers, primarily in the areas of transport, food and beverages, venue and accommodation, energy and water management, waste management, and procurement. But while sustainable policies aim at a net zero impact on the environment, a new regenerative approach is required which involves moving away from the 'linear economy' to the 'circular economy' approach.

A number of evaluation frameworks are used across industry sectors to measure the triple bottom line impact of events. As the industry moves forward, these frameworks need to be revisited and adapted to the ongoing changes and trends. The key message is that the industry is ready for reinvention, which has already been demonstrated by the expansion of online and hybrid strategies and the use of innovative technologies.

Industry profile: Meegan Jones, Event sustainability expert

Meegan is an expert on event sustainability, ranging from small scale to large scale events. She is globally known for her expertise and receives invitations to speak at industry and academic conferences on the topic of sustainability. Her work across many destinations around the world, along with participating in industry working groups, has meant that she has created global partnerships with other events professionals who share her passion for ensuring events are delivered with key sustainable practices. Meegan believes the concept of sustainability is accessible to all events professionals and needs to be embedded into everyday practice.

Skills and expertise

■ Sustainability expert through career experience

■ Management from community to mega events

■ Communication and information campaign management

11

- Sustainability project and stakeholder planning
- Development of sustainability strategies and operational plans
- Identification, prioritsation of issues and designing customised solutions

What traits and attributes do event managers need when considering sustainability?

Sustainability is not an add-on exercise. When it comes to sustainability, the devil is in the detail. Event organisers should seek advice from sustainability experts, but the best approach is professional development. You can't know all the answers but get to the point where you know all the questions, and then know where to look to get help. Event managers are naturally detail-oriented and problem solvers so we're already halfway to success.

Given the topic is so broad, what are some key questions to ask?

When starting out on the sustainability journey, I suggest you start with the five big main topics, and then dive down into them depending on the context of your event. They are 1) purchasing, 2) waste (these two could be combined into one 'circularity', 3) climate impact, 4) inclusion, and 5) engagement. Ask where materials are coming from, what they're made of, who made them, what the climate impact is. Once in your possession, what is the onwards responsible journey from them? Diversity, equity and inclusion should be considered across everything from purchasing to staffing to attendee experience. And the biggest one – how to use your event platform for good – engagement with workers, suppliers, volunteers, athletes, musicians, and importantly, attendees and the local community.

What is your recommended strategic approach to event sustainability?

A first step is looking from organisational point, what your principles and values are, and work out your strategic framework. Find the big heartfelt issues that you want to embed into your approach. Key questions to consider:

- What do you stand for?
- Is there a chance to do good in the world?
- What do you and stakeholders care about?
- Can you create a bold vision?

What is your operational approach?

The devil is in the detail, always. Planning is king. Awareness and buy-in by all the people involved is paramount. Even if you know the answer, involve those who are responsible for execution, in co-creating the solution with you, that way you've got their buy-in. We all know in the heat of the moment and high stakes of a live event, people revert to the easiest path. You need foresight to build the easiest path to be the most sustainable path.

How can you best prioritise sustainability issues?

First, identify issues and prioritise which you want to work on. Cast wide to understand the top sustainability issues for the event type. Create a shopping list of potential typical sustainability issues. Run a workshop with your team and prioritise the sustainability issues that are relevant in your event, that together you can work on.

Expand on the discussion of issues and then narrow down the issues. Use 'decision filters' such: How relevant is the issue? What do stakeholders care about or expect us to act on? How big is the issue compared to others? What improvement can we get compared to the relative effort? Is the issue important given the event setting or context? What is best practice in the industry? How can we be an innovator or leader?

What are some key recommendations when dealing with sustainability issues?

Deal with issues in collaboration with your stakeholders. To achieve best sustainability practices, embed key terms into contracts. *Create a project plan.* Draw on good organising skills – work out any timelines doing budgets and who is responsible and build a collaborative approach. Be flexible and reactive as circumstances change.

How can you engage your audience in sustainability practices?

Look at where the touch points are and insert the key messages: from when audiences get invited to when they experience the event. Set the scene with an invitation as part of a 'welcoming process'. Offer festival goers onsite experiences with all the touch points from food to audio visual. A manager needs to look at the personality of the event but not go too far. Set the right tone at the right amount so you don't over do it. For example, if your event is in sport, prioritise sport then sustainability.

How can we harness sustainability values into audiences?

Event audiences can get into the psyche of the event and identify with what it stands for, but this needs to be done strategically and carefully. An event sets peoples' psyche up to be receptive to that transformative experience where they can harness energy and get a sense of community for whatever topic you care about. Design the experience in a way so that audiences interact and become part of the sustainable solution.

What are the key steps to developing a sustainability plan?

As an event manager wishing to undertake sustainability practices in events you need a plan! Creating a Sustainability Action Plan will help guide you. Here are the essential ingredients:

1. *Vision.* Set your ultimate positive outcome/s.
2. *Values.* What are the key principles and values that support the way you work?
3. *Materiality assessment.* Identify what sustainability issues are 'material' – important to you, stakeholders, the community and the planet.

11

4. *Goals, objectives and targets*. Set ambitions and measurable indicators of good performance.

5. *Policy*. Wrap it all up in a policy – this is what you will and won't do.

6. *Actions*. Create key action points to address sustainability issues. Dig as deep into various functional areas of the event as you need to.

7. *Delegation*. Assign responsibility for taking action and meeting objectives.

8. *Compliance*. Remember to include all relevant points in contracts and agreements.

9. *Monitoring*. Include how you will monitor progress, success and take 'real time' action for immediate improvements.

Any final tips?

I recommend on-going learning and cross collaboration with practitioners from other disciplines. I learnt lessons from hundreds of events over the past 20 years, and bring my knowledge into an online course which can build essential practical knowledge for event managers in sustainability management.

For more visit https://www.ise.world/

A final word and reflection by Peter Jones, International event expert and consultant

Peter Jones specialises in the delivery of public and corporate events. Whilst he is based in Melbourne, his events occur all around Australia and he is a key driver for international events. According to Peter, the ongoing pandemic presents challenges but also opportunities to reshape our industry. Events are going through transformation and there is acceptance that world has been changed forever. The requirement for full vaccination to enter major events sets the scene for new safety practices and site design requirements. The turn of public events suggests creative thinking and innovative solutions are important in the transition to the new normality. The current trends on experiential marketing and hybrid conferences also indicate new skills are required, and courses must be revamped to reflect revised industry needs.

Skills and expertise

- End to end event delivery
- Specialist in major public and corporate events
- Design and theming concepts for corporate organisations
- Managing large complex event operations
- Engaging and managing business relationships
- Arranging contractual stakeholder agreements
- Stakeholder engagement and management

How have events adapted so far in the new normal?

Events have become hybrid, as for many they offer a viable solution. We see AV companies investing a lot of money in technology. Some events have been able to adapt to digital platforms, but others cannot get the same outcome. For example, fundraising events are pretty much based on the human connection and understanding of what the charity is all about. It requires a lot of creative thinking to achieve the same goal if it becomes a virtual event. Mass public gatherings will be based on full vaccination of patrons.

What changes have you seen that affected the delivery of events?

New delivery models have surfaced, such as hybrid events, which will be around for a while. Business events need to happen, so event managers need to be ready and adapt them online or adopting a hybrid model. If people cannot attend an event, they will be able to enter via Virtual Reality systems.

- Contact tracing will be here forever. It's a bit like security measures which were introduced 10 years ago as a result of terrorism attacks. We still live with those and they are a good thing. Contact tracing will become part of events, and safety for all patrons will become a priority.

What are your thoughts on adapting to a new reality?

Our industry is fragmented in terms of the different sectors. However, one positive thing out of Covid is that it's made us become proactive. We don't wait until the last minute to see what happens. We come up with solutions and work closely with our clients to make sure their event happens. We pose the questions: what do we need to do to achieve your event goal? Now, what will happen if we go into lockdown? These thoughts did not exist two years ago. We have created flexible and creative thinking along the way.

11

How do you monitor current event trends?

I work closely with associations (Meetings Events Australia, Victoria Tourism Industry Council, Business Events Council of Australia, Exhibitions and Events Australia and with government. As an event manager you can't sit there and do nothing. Together we have a voice, so we know what is going on and we make sure we are heard. Due to the uncertainty, it is important to monitor timeframes and adapt accordingly. Event managers should always reach out to their collaborators if unsure. It's important to be part of an association and maintain connections, as associations are the first point of call when something collapses. We have learnt that our industry is vulnerable but together we can share knowledge, focus and adjust to the new reality.

How do you ensure business innovation?

It is important to be proactive and have innovating thinking for the future of events. Work with stakeholder groups as collaboration is really important. As humans will always need to connect, events will always be here. It is just a matter of flexibility and adaptability. Having support network groups will help guide you in the next phase of event leadership.

Another key consideration is to reflect on our industry and continue the discussions with all stakeholders. Receiving insight and ideas is important and it helps develop creative thinking. Now more than ever we need a united voice in industry to continue to deliver the magic of what our events are all about.

Ongoing training is also important and developing meaningful relationships with all stakeholders a priority. If there is one thing that came out of the pandemic it is the need to look after our people. Together we can achieve change and make sure our industry is rejuvenated with positive outcomes for all stakeholders. Develop communication plans and campaigns that will help deliver key messages to influential stakeholders such as government and councils.

What are the key learnings from the industry changes?

- One key learning is to appreciate the economic value our industry offers to society. As the event industry is slowly recovering, one certainty is the number of people it employs. Events offer social benefits, and they reach every aspect of our lives. We need to view events with a society lens and appreciate what they offer.

- As our industry is slowly recovering, having a united voice is important in dealing with sudden closures and new restrictions. Each stakeholder brings a different skillset therefore operators should consider collaboration in their delivery efforts.

- There is no doubt it's been a hard journey particularly for the smaller operators. To lose good staff due to the pandemic has been the hardest thing to deal with after developing meaningful relations. As there is currently a skill shortage, strategies are required to hire staff with the revised skillset in the new normal.

- Events are currently delivered in hybrid models, so technology remains important. Flexibility and safety comprise an important skillset to have in our industry. Being able to understand event safety requirements and adapt to sudden changes remains key for operators. Event courses need to be adapted and meet new industry requirements.

Review questions

1 Discuss the scale and significance of the problem of food wastage at planned events, identify key causes of food wastage, and explain strategies that could be applied by event organisers, venue managers, and event caterers to reduce or eliminate food wastage.

2 Identify and discuss the benefits of embedded sustainability for an event business, for attendees, employees and volunteers, as well as other key stakeholders.

3 Explain the three pillars of sustainability and how they relate to each other.

4 Identify and examine the steps that can be taken at all stages of the planning and management process to reduce an event's carbon footprint.

5 Compare and contrast a sustainable approach with a regenerative one. Which is the most relevant in the current environment? Why?

6 Discuss the concept of a 'circular economy' and explain how it differs from the concept of a 'linear economy'. Provide examples of how 'circular economy' concepts can be applied to the MICE industry and explain the likely event outcomes.

Workshop activities

Scenario A

You have been hired as a sustainability consultant for a festival of your choice. Your task is to outline the importance of environmental issues and provide advice on how to improve sustainability practices.

1. List the stakeholders that need to collaborate in a call to action campaign targeted at the respective festival audiences. Raise awareness of the sustainability initiatives undertaken at the festival.

2. Build an educational component into the festival program.

3. Develop a sustainable toolkit including useful resources on being green during the festival (this could be designed as a website or an app).

11

4. Develop policies in relation to a) waste management; b) energy use; c) travel to and from the festival; d) water; and e) procurement/local food and catering supplies

Scenario B

You have been hired to develop a sustainability plan for a new festival. Review the steps to developing a plan by industry expert, Meegan Jones, and develop one for an event of your choice. Key criteria for inclusion:

1. Vision.
2. Values.
3. Materiality assessment.
4. Goals, objectives and targets.
5. Policy.
6. Actions.
7. Delegation.
8. Compliance.
9. Monitoring.

Scenario C

You have been assigned the task of organising an event evaluation plan. Consider the scope of the event and its main aims, and develop appropriate measurements (qualitative and quantitative) for assessing the attendee experience and the success of the event against organisational goals and objectives. What key recommendations are there for future event improvements?

References

Andersson, T. D., Jutbring, H., & Lundberg, E. (2013). When a music festival goes veggie: Communication and environmental impacts of an innovative food strategy. *International Journal of Event and Festival Management*, 4(3).

Beard, C., & Russ, W. (2017). Event evaluation and design: Human experience mapping. *Event Management*, 21(3), 365-374.

Bigwood, G. (2020). The Regenerative Revolution: A new paradigm for event management. The IMEX Group. www.imexexhibitions.com/the-regenerative-revolution (visited 22 November 2021)

Bladen, C., Kennell, J., Abson, E., & Wilde, N. (2017). Event impacts, sustainability and legacy. In *Events Management* (pp. 372-400). Routledge.

Brown, S., Getz, D., Pettersson, R., & Wallstam, M. (2015). Event evaluation: Definitions, concepts and a state of the art review. *International Journal of Event and Festival Management*, 6(2).

Coles, T. (2021). Tourism, Brexit and the climate crisis: on intersecting crises and their effects. *Journal of Sustainable Tourism,*29(9), 1529-1546.

Collins, A., & Cooper, C. (2017). Measuring and managing the environmental impact of festivals: The contribution of the Ecological Footprint. *Journal of Sustainable Tourism*, 25(1), 148-162.

Getz, D. (2018a). *Event Evaluation Theory and methods for event management and tourism*. Oxford: Goodfellow Publishers.

Getz, D. (2018b). *Event Impact Assessment*. Oxford: Goodfellow Publishers

IPCC (2013) Climate Change 2013: The Physical Science Basis. Contribution of Working Group I to the Fifth Assessment Report of the Intergovernmental Panel on Climate Change [Stocker, T.F., D. Qin, G.-K. Plattner, M. Tignor, S.K. Allen, J. Boschung, A. Nauels, Y. Xia, V. Bex and P.M. Midgley (eds.)]. Cambridge University Press, Cambridge, UK and New York, NY, USA, 1535 pp.

Jones, M. (2017). *Sustainable Event Management: A practical guide*, 3rd edn. Routledge.

Mair, J., & Smith, A. (2021). Events and sustainability: why making events more sustainable is not enough. *Journal of Sustainable Tourism, 29*(11-12), 1739-1755.

Mair, J., & Laing, J. H. (2013). Encouraging pro-environmental behaviour: The role of sustainability-focused events. *Journal of Sustainable Tourism, 21*(8), 1113-1128. https://doi.org/10.1080/09669582.2012.756494

Mair, J., Chien, P. M., Kelly, S. J., & Derrington, S. (2021). Social impacts of mega-events: A systematic narrative review and research agenda. *Journal of Sustainable Tourism*, 1-22. doi:10.1080/09669582.2020.1870989

McHugh, L. H., Lemos, M. C., & Morrison, T. H. (2021). Risk? Crisis? Emergency? Implications of the new climate emergency framing for governance and policy. *Wiley Interdisciplinary Reviews: Climate Change*, e736.

Morseletto, P. (2020). Targets for a circular economy. *Resources, Conservation and Recycling*, 153, 104553.

Ooi, C.-S., & Stöber, B. (2010). Authenticity and place branding: The arts and culture in branding Berlin and Singapore. In B. T. Knudsen & A. M. Waade (Eds.), *Re-investing authenticity: Tourism, places and emotions* (pp. 66-79). Bristol: Channel View Publications.

Porter, M., & Kramer, M. (2011). The Big Idea: Creating shared value. *Harvard Business Review*, 89, 2-17. https://www.researchgate.net/publication/272576643

Schlenker, K., Foley, C., & Getz, D. (2010). *Encore festival and event evaluation kit: Review and redevelopment*. Retrieved from https://www.researchgate.net/publication/306400480

Stadler, R. (2021) Chapter 2: Knowledge Management Challenges in Event Organisations, In: Stadler, R. (ed). Oxford: Goodfellow Publishers http://dx.doi.org/10.23912/9781911635444-4902

Sustain SU (2010) University of Alberta Office of Sustainability. Working Definition. http://www.sustainability.ualberta.ca/.

Van Niekerk, M., & Getz, D. (2019). *Event Stakeholders*, Oxford: Goodfellow Publishers.

11

Wee, H., Mustapha, N. A., & Anas, M. S. (2021). Characteristic of green event practices in MICE tourism: A systematic literature review. *Social Sciences*, 11(16), 271-291.

Websites

www.betterevaluation.org/

www.edinburghfestivalcity.com/about/environmental-policy

www.edinburghfestivalcity.com/about/case-studies/187-green-arts-initiative

www.edinburghfestivalcity.com/
news/513-8-green-things-about-the-edinburgh-festivals

www.eif.co.uk/sustainability

www.eventscouncil.org/Sustainability/Sustainability-Pledge

www.geelongaustralia.com.au/events/planning

www.imexexhibitions.com/the-regenerative-revolution

www.ipcc.ch/

www.ise.world

www.iso.org

pjse.com.au/

Videos

youtu.be/xY99Q2noQ44 (Home studio for online teaching)

michaelduignan.uk/2020/06/18/events-a-new-international-podcast/

I **Index**

Printed by Printforce, United Kingdom